SECRETS

SECRETS

Swinging and Espionage Tales of the '80s

Zillary Zahn

SECRETS: Swinging and Espionage Tales of the '80s

Published by Ronasaurus Publishing
Walnut Creek, California

Library of Congress Control Number: 2017962775
Zahn, Zillary, Author
SECRETS: Swinging and Espionage Tales of the '80s

ZILLARY ZAHN
ISBN: 978-0-692-95624-3

SOC065000 SOCIAL SCIENCE / Human Sexuality
POL036000 POLITICAL SCIENCE / Intelligence & Espionage

QUANTITY PURCHASES: Schools, companies, professional groups, clubs, and other organizations may qualify for special terms when ordering quantities of this title. For information, email Info@ RonasaurusPublishing.com or visit www.RonasaurusPublishing.com.

Dedicated to the central participants who experienced the events described in this book, although their names have been changed to protect their identities. I had promised them that when the time was right, I would publish this book revealing everything that was not still classified.

Table of Contents

Introduction

WRAPPED IN SECRECY since the 1980s, the following story of international swing parties and Cold War espionage has remained untold to this day.

Officially, the government of the United States does not condone the sexual conduct and sexual practices described in this book. It will usually deny that there were government programs in which participants used "enhanced sexual activities" to advance their cause.

Now that the time is right and many files of this era are no longer classified, I have used our files and writings of that time to reconstruct our story. I and four others are the only fully knowledgeable participants of this story. They requested that I tell it.

The following is a fictionalized account of real events in which I participated. All names of the participants have been changed, including my own. Personal characteristics of each participant have been altered, so as not to reveal our true identities. Exactly who we are is not important; the important aspect is what we did and the exact manner in which our activities produced the resulting outcomes.

As much as realistically feasible, the following story follows the true one. In particular, great care has been taken to express the principles, practices, and logistics of swing parties.

Here now is our story.

List of Recurring Participants

(In Order of Appearance)

Chapter 1

Zillary Zahn (ZZ)	Author
Barbara	Party-goer
Don	Barbara's boyfriend
Roger	Swing party tour guide
Marc	New swinger

Chapter 2

Bill	Publisher
Naomi	ZZ's friend
Ed and Dianne	Gala host couple; Hesten friends; business people
Lorraine Hesten	Gala grand hostess; Mitchell's business partner
Mitchell Hesten	High-tech entrepreneur; Lorraine's husband
Renee	Gala guest; swinger

Chapter 3

Jasmine	Lorraine's older daughter
Kathleen	Lorraine's younger daughter
Nancy	Sexologist
Alice and Denny	Swing party hosts
Larry	Sexologist

Chapter 4

Bert and Marge	Hesten friends; artists
Jeffery and Vivian	Hesten friends; lawyers
"The six"	Ed and Dianne; Bert and Marge; Jeffery and Vivian
"The eight"	Lorraine and Mitch plus "the six"
Taylor	Swinger

Chapter 6

Sidney Colsome	CEO of video and film company
Monique	Renee's sister
Antoine	Maître d' at Chaillot Gardens
M. and Mme Lepic	French business couple

Chapter 7

Philippe and Marisse Chaubert	French business couple
Lou and Bob Swain	Brothers who developed FASTEC high tech company
Anna and Lou Swain	Renee's aunt and uncle
Stuart Swain	Renee's boyfriend; Bob Swain's son
Sondra	Lorraine's friend

Kate Atali   Young actress
Jacques Penard   Chemist

Chapter 8
Alan   Renee's boss
Kathy and Mary Jo   Alan's co-workers

Chapter 10
Marcel & Yvonne Auric   Parisian business couple

Chapter 13
Dr. Papalexopoulos   Lorraine's doctor in Athens
Dr. Laplace   Lorraine's doctor in Paris
Boss   Soviet bloc conference organizer

Chapter 15
Dr. Mann   Lorraine's doctor in West Berlin
Hans Schiller   East German lead scientist

Chapter 17
Philip Keslyn   U.S. government official

ONE

The Swing Party

Barbara's account of events that took place at
Circle S Ranch, Pleasant Hill, CA
Saturday, March 24, 1979

"Barbara, are you ready for your interview?"
"Yes, ZZ, I'm ready."
"OK, we are recording. Today is April 29, 1979."

YES, I REMEMBER that party! How could I ever forget an experience like that? I was a bit scared, somewhat surprised, and yes, quite shocked. I thought about that party for weeks afterward, and some images are still very sharp in my mind. Sitting here, talking to you, I have to remind myself that these parties actually do go on week after week at the same secluded ranch house. It's like being in another world.

What prompted me to go? Well, some months prior, my ex-boyfriend, Don, who had now become a very good friend, confided in me over coffee that he had recently attended several *swing* parties.

"What's a swing party?" I naively asked him.

Don told me that these parties are held every Saturday night at Circle S Ranch, not too far from here. Usually there are about 20 to 30 couples attending. "In the beginning," Don told me, "the party appears to be a dressy, couples-only, cocktail-type party, with guests flirting and socializing over a buffet dinner. But after an hour or so, the party becomes nude and just about everyone there is available for sex. Right there! At the party!"

"Really?" I questioned. "Fifty, sixty people! All there to have sex with each other over the course of a few hours?" I had a hard time believing that so many people from around here really get together every weekend and do that.

But Don assured me that they do.

Now I wanted to hear more. Much more. But Don wasn't too forthcoming. It fascinated me: just what goes on anyway? Just what do men and women do sexually if they are completely uninhibited? I envisioned these parties to be utterly outrageous, extremely erotic, the ultimate in free sexual expression. Wild orgies where one could truly be abandoned.

At my insistence at subsequent coffee dates with Don, he revealed more about these parties. Noticing my growing curiosity and fascination, Don made me an offer: If I wanted to attend a party, just to observe, he would take me.

"Great!" I told him, but I didn't want to interact with anyone. I just wanted to watch, preferably from behind a secure glass panel!

Then Don told me about party etiquette and discussed the rather gentle manner in which everyone behaves. Don emphasized that everyone has veto power. A negative reply to a sexual advance was not to be argued with, but rather accepted immediately and graciously under threat of possible expulsion from the party, and even possible banishment from future parties. Don further reassured me by promising not to leave my side the whole evening and that we would leave the party anytime I wanted to.

There seemed to be little reason for me not to go. I knew I had to experience a party for myself, so I said yes. I didn't want to be an active participant, mind you, just an active observer. I definitely wasn't going to do anything sexual. I didn't even know if I could manage to go around naked or not, but I figured I would leave that up to spontaneity.

We set a date for the party: Saturday, March 24th; destination: Circle S Ranch in Pleasant Hill, a San Francisco suburb about 25 miles east of the city.

As the eventful day drew near, I became intrigued by the clandestine nature of what I was about to do. No one knew of my plans except for Don. I didn't dare mention a single word to any of my friends, lest they think me a complete pervert, a sex maniac, or someone totally unbalanced. I guess I felt that there was something not quite right about these parties, that there was something perverted about them and all those who attend them. But still, I did want to go.

When party day arrived, I had my hair done, got a manicure and picked out one of my favorite outfits, since Don had emphasized that the parties were quite social and somewhat dressy. In the early evening, as I bathed and primped, I wondered: Why does everyone wear good clothes only to strip down and have them hanging about? Well, keeping in mind that I might be one of those to shed her clothes if the mood was right, I decided on an outfit that flattered me, but nonetheless was not too precious to my heart, just in case anything happened to it. I didn't know what Don was going to wear, but regardless, I always felt we made a strange-looking couple. Don is over six feet tall, lanky, good-looking, with big hands, big feet, straight dark hair and big brown eyes. Then there is me. A petite, five-foot-three, blue-eyed blonde.

Don arrived looking quite handsome in his dressy shirt and slacks and brand-new shoes. It certainly seemed as if we were about to go out on a date, just like old times. To San Francisco perhaps. But no, instead this was to be quite a strange date. Throughout the drive to Pleasant Hill, I could hardly believe I was actually doing this! I was on my way to a swing party! I was both excited and apprehensive. What have I gotten myself into?

It was a gorgeous evening as we drove east away from the setting sun. We were on schedule to arrive an hour early. As a newcomer, I was slated to take a tour of the facilities and learn all about what to expect come party time. This in itself, I thought, should be quite interesting.

Soon we had arrived. Up ahead was a driveway with a large white sign arched over it. In bold black letters, it read "CIRCLE S RANCH." We drove though the arch, up the driveway and parked. And there before us, plunked down in the midst of nowhere, it seemed, sat a splendid sprawling ranch house domed with the velvety-blue early night sky. These sensual sights, the sound of the crickets, and the feel of the fresh country air acutely activated my senses. I was so excited to be there! And, yes, a little scared too. I knew this evening was going to be a major event in my life. I was on the verge of experiencing things I never could have imagined.

We briskly walked up to the house and rang the bell. The host, a rather well-dressed gentleman, greeted us graciously, inviting us into the hallway. I cringed as he began talking to us about registration, whatever that was, noting that I had to fill out a membership card! Don, sensing my sudden paralysis, quickly took charge, filling out my card. Here I am thinking "I don't do this sort of thing," and suddenly, I am a member!

After completing the registration procedures in the hallway, Don and I entered the house proper. I was immediately struck by the homeyness of the place. I don't know why that surprised me. I guess I just didn't expect such a cozy atmosphere. And although there were not many members here yet, those present certainly did not look like perverts. Far from it. I was quite struck by the fashionableness of the women and the dapperness of the men. I had anticipated that I would have little in common with the people here. But now I realized that might not be the case at all.

At first glance, they seemed very much like people I knew. Gads! What if I actually met someone here I knew? What would I say? "Hi! I don't really do this sort of thing." Yeah, right.

Well, fortunately, my tour group was forming, helping me take my mind off my concerns. Our tour guide, Roger, was ruggedly handsome: very tall, good looking, good build, curly light brown hair, a charming smile, and, oh yes, dimples—loved those dimples. Since I thought of him as very sexually appealing, I couldn't help but think that his sexual prowess was used to stimulate us uninitiated females. I know I was stimulated. My nervousness and concerns disappeared entirely; he was the perfect tour guide.

Our group consisted of Don and me, three other couples, and a rather tall, thin, good-looking, dark-haired guy named Marc, who, despite all his attractiveness, seemed to be alone, nervous, and agitated. My heart went out to him. Apparently, his date took an earlier tour.

I felt an immediate attraction to Marc; he seemed to be as troubled and concerned as I was. I talked with him while we were all getting assembled; like me, he seemed vulnerable and in need of companionship. And the more I talked with him, the more attractive he became. Under ordinary circumstances, I would have been even friendlier, but I didn't want to lead him on; I realized I had better be careful around here.

Roger now took over. "Well, I'm glad you are getting acquainted. That's the purpose of our club: people getting to know each other, only we are a little unconventional about how we do it. We're now sitting in a socializing and relaxing area, the living room, so to speak. We request that you refrain from any overt sexual activity in this room. If you are starting to get it on with someone, please move on to one of the private areas I'm going to show you. Or, if you want to be an exhibitionist, just move on to our large group room, where just about anything can happen. I'll also be showing you that room soon.

"One thing you should keep in mind from the onset: no one is under any pressure to do anything he or she doesn't want to do. That's one of the main principles of what we call 'party etiquette.' If you want to stay fully dressed as you are for the whole evening, that's definitely okay. It's completely up to you. You can have a good time here just socializing, eating and dancing. Now, if everyone is ready, we will move on to other parts of the tour."

I was very impressed. According to Roger, this party was going to be much calmer and more organized than I imagined. I felt safer already.

Next, Roger showed us the way to some of the many rooms made up as bedrooms, each of which contained several beds and extra mattresses on the floor. "These are some of the private areas you may use. One rule of party etiquette: if a door is closed, leave it closed; if it's open somewhat and there are already people using the room, don't join them or bother them unless you are invited to do so."

Roger then showed us the bathrooms, which were complete with showers and a linen closet full of towels for use at the outdoor hot tub, swimming pool, or for just maintaining our modesty. And, he said, should we be naked, for sanitary reasons, it is always best to lie or sit on our own towel.

During this tour, as more and more members arrived, I seemed to have completely lost my concern of meeting someone I knew. Somehow it just didn't seem to matter any longer. Did my lack of concern signal that I now accepted my status as "pervert," or was I beginning to think that all this party stuff was okay? I hadn't yet decided the answer. I hadn't met many members personally, but I did find the group rather physically appealing. That's not to say they were all handsome and beautiful; just that they seemed to have style and were animated and energetic.

Throughout the tour, I noticed that the furniture was rather simple, mainly utilitarian, well-suited for a party such as this. The rooms were well spread out, not particularly large or impressive in themselves, just that there were many of them, creating much in the way of privacy. In all, this was quite a party house. I wondered if any regular-type parties were ever held here.

But it was the outdoor grounds, with a swimming pool and hot tub in the patio and tents in the vast grassy area, that really made the place for me. As our tour group moved outside, all my senses became aroused by the cool night air, the sensual evening breezes, and the magnificent cloudless night sky. I felt shudders of delight throughout my body. I could easily envision how a sexual encounter out here on these premises could be a very erotic experience. Well, perhaps...one of these days.

Standing on the outdoor patio, I marveled at the huge, magnificent redwood hot tub and the long rectangular swimming pool. Chairs with a crisscrossed pattern of white plastic and deck tables with umbrella stands in their centers completed the patio area. Floodlights rimmed the bottom perimeter of the pool, casting light on the bottom's center and illuminating the club's logo, a big letter "S" with a circle around it. A sensual glow was cast over the whole patio from various colored floodlights; appropriate soothing music oozed out from the house stereo.

Beyond the patio, into the grounds, tents had been staked in the vast grassy region. Roger began addressing the group. "These tents, which zip up, are equipped with mattresses and mood lights. So if you want to be private, just zip up your tent and nobody will bother you. If anyone is ever persistent in joining you after you have indicated in some manner that you do not want their company, that person is acting out of line and against party etiquette. Just report such people to the management. Those not adhering to party etiquette will be asked to leave the party and will be unwelcome at future parties, and possibly even events at other swing clubs.

"We are one of the many clubs across the country that belong to the National Swing Club Association, most of whom have adapted this style of party etiquette. So, in the future, should you wish to attend a party at another Association Club anywhere in the country, you would be welcome and should feel right at home."

After our outdoor tour was completed, Roger motioned for us

to follow him back into the house, and then into the group room, a room set aside where everyone could mix freely. As we walked, I chatted some more with Marc. I decided I really liked him and started giving more of myself in conversation. He was interested in me, too, I could tell.

As we approached the house, we regrouped near the French doors of the living room. One by one, we re-entered the house, now very busy with arriving guests. We proceeded to the group room entryway. When Roger arrived, he motioned for us to follow him through the curtain, consisting of many full-length strands of beads, all dangling and reflecting in different directions as we walked through.

The contrast with the well-lit, now noisy living room, was startling. This room was very quiet, dark, large, and empty. Red lights provided the only illumination. Mattresses blanketed the floor from one side of the wall to the other and from the far end of the room to the red velvet bench along the entrance wall.

Roger motioned for us to sit on the bench. He remained standing. At first I thought no one else was in the room except for our group, but as my eyes adjusted to the dim light, I could see a nude couple lying on the mattress in the far corner. I could feel myself blushing: my face was hot! Gads! A couple screwing! Well, they weren't exactly doing it, as far as I could tell, but I rather imagined that they were or going to. They were naked together, rolling around on the mattress-covered floor. The details weren't important; the intent was there. I had very mixed feelings about observing. Naturally, I was very curious to watch, but I was too self-conscious, mainly because I felt the others were watching me watch.

Since the room was dark and empty (sort of), Roger knew he

had our full attention. He had some important items to discuss. Standing over us, he began.

I think it's appropriate at this point to discuss what sort of language you will hear at a swing party. Vulgarities are definitely out. People here are basically very gentle and have put themselves in an extremely vulnerable situation. We see our activities as beautiful and loving; vulgarities debase these activities and are therefore out of place. So, you will hear couples talk about getting together, getting it on, going to play, or other such euphemisms.

Now, a word about sexually-transmitted diseases. The two main diseases most people seem concerned about now are syphilis and gonorrhea. Generally speaking, these diseases seem to be very much under control. But if ever anyone here has reason to believe they have been exposed to a sexually-transmitted disease, the protocol is to notify the club, and we will notify all the partners you can recall having sex with while you were here. You should definitely see your personal physician or go to your city or county health department.

For syphilis, you will most likely receive an injection in your butt; that should take care of it. For gonorrhea, you will probably receive a prescription or supply of antibiotic pills; you should take them according to instructions. In the last two years, the information from all the swing clubs nationwide is that syphilis and gonorrhea have not been a problem.

Now this brings up the subject of condom use. We have a supply here, if you want to use them. Generally, guys would

rather not. So, women, if you want your guy to use a condom, and some women here do, you just have to tell him up
front; something like 'I would like you to use a condom. Is
that alright with you?' He will either say, 'Hell, no,' in which
case the deal is off, or he might say, 'Yeah, fine,' and you
proceed from there.

Okay, I'm going to leave you with that. It's now about
8 o'clock; officially, party time. This is your virgin party, so
enjoy yourself however you desire. If you have questions or
concerns at any time during the party, see me or others in
charge. You have been a fun group. Thank you.

With the naked couple on the floor in the far corner panting and
moaning even louder now than before, Roger concluded the tour
and ushered us out of the group room, though he insisted we could
stay and watch the couple if we wanted. But I wasn't about to do
that. Instead, we joined the crowd in the living room, now alive with
social interaction. I couldn't remember a gathering in which I got to
know so many people so fast.

It all began over dinner. Having filled our plates from the buffet,
Don and I began our social whirlwind, eating while as we talked to
couples here and there, the conversations changing continuously
as people drifted into one group, then over to another nearby. In
several conversations, I could tell that the guys were interested in
me. I was fine with that as long as we were all together.

As Don and I strolled about, observing and conversing, I had to
admit I was very impressed with the people I met. I kept thinking:
too bad this is a swing party; this was one of the most fun groups of
people I've been with in a long time. Why couldn't everyone just get

together for fun? But I guess swinging is their fun! Too bad. . .

Don and I became very friendly with two couples who asked us to join them sometime for a San Francisco outing. And I, myself, became friendly with a couple of women who asked me to join them sometime for a game of bridge. And then, after about an hour of eating and socializing, dancing began. During this time I met several guys that interested me, and vice versa. That was fine, but I wasn't about to have sex with them here at the party! In all, I was having such a good time, I could easily dismiss that this was a swing party.

But now, at about ten o'clock, people began to scatter throughout the house. So did their clothes: tops and bottoms, pants and panties. Slowly but surely, the party was becoming nude. I had never socialized in the nude before and it seemed to be a strange way to talk to someone. How can you concentrate on conversation, pretending everything is normal, when everybody has all kinds of parts dangling about? It has to be distracting to sense everyone looking you over, eyeing you up and down.

For a while, I resisted undressing. But eventually, as the party-goers got almost completely naked, I figured what the hell. I'd be less conspicuous loosely wrapped in a towel like some others than walking around fully dressed. So I stripped and wrapped myself in one of the large towels supplied by the ranch. At my insistence, Don wrapped himself similarly. I wanted us to look like a couple.

Now, dressed only in a towel, I needed a little time to adjust to this new level of vulnerability. If a guy walked anywhere near what I considered to be my space, I avoided eye contact. It's hard for a guy to come on if you don't even recognize his presence. Eventually, though, I relaxed considerably, as everyone was extremely friendly and very non-threatening. But my friendliness was very guarded.

I certainly did not want to give out any false impressions, which is probably why I made a point of telling everyone that this was my virgin party.

At first, I was too preoccupied with my own partial nudity to notice others. I would have felt much better about strutting around nude like some of the women, if I wasn't so self-conscious. As I adjusted to my state of undress and began eyeing others, I realized that the nude women certainly didn't look any better than I; they just had more moxie. It was wonderful they could feel so at ease with their bodies. I wished I could.

As I eyed all the nudity, what struck me most was that there was no fashion! No different styles and color combinations of tops and bottoms. Everyone was the same shade from head to toe!

Well, I made it clear to all I met that since this was my first party, I was going to take it slow. Everyone was very supportive, and as time went on I began to feel much more at ease. I realized that no one was going to pressure me to do anything. So, eventually, I told Don that it was okay for me to be on my own for a while. I felt Don needed a little time for himself, and I felt I was up for the challenge of handling myself. We made an agreement: we would meet in about an hour by the buffet table. That way, whoever got there first could snack while waiting for the other. And, Don reminded me, if I needed him before that time, I could just look around and find him.

So off I went, feeling very adventurous. For a while I just walked about the house, constantly checking my towel to make sure it was securely around me and covering me properly. And as I strolled about, lost in my own thoughts, I kept thinking this was certainly a strange thing for me to be doing on a Saturday night. And oddly enough, I had this bizarre ambivalence about being approached by guys. I certainly avoided eye contact, but at the same time, I wanted some affirmation that men regarded me as interesting and pretty enough to approach. Somehow, I was beginning to feel like an ugly duckling or a wallflower.

Well, I kept slithering from one room to another, hoping no one would notice me while I spied on them. Suddenly, I passed a bedroom with the door wide open. A couple was in bed, doing it! Wow! I wanted to see this. But I didn't feel I could just stand in the doorway and watch. I paced back and forth for a while, passing the open doorway from time to time. It was really interesting to see.

And shortly thereafter, walking along, I came across two couples in bed together. I was so surprised! It was a fascinating site, but again, I felt I had to keep walking. Soon, just about everywhere I went there were couples screwing. Fascinating. And as long as I kept walking, no one ever got a chance to talk to me.

Then I went outdoors. The hot tub was the interesting place to be: crowded, noisy, playful. After standing around watching for a while, feeling quite apart from things, I contemplated getting in. I would, of course, have to be naked. Once in the tub, though, I could keep my body submerged and be bodiless in a way. As it was, I was constantly checking my towel, which was getting to be annoying. And I did want to be part of a sensual experience in some way while I was here! So, what the hell.

Checking to see that no one was particularly watching me, I rather bashfully unwrapped my towel and placed it on a white plastic-covered deck chair near the tub. Suddenly, I got a tremendous thrill. I fully realized I was standing there naked for all to see, but feeling the evening breeze swish over my body, I didn't mind one bit. I was beginning to feel much more at ease and part of the party.

The tub was relaxing and quite social. There must have been about twenty of us in it. Some were telling jokes, some were making out with their partners, others were just lying back. Me? I mainly listened and watched and enjoyed the moment. The water, the mood music, the night sky, the people—everything was arousing my senses. I felt just great.

As time went on, more people came in as others went out. I just stayed on, enjoying every minute. And while I found it amusing to watch couples getting it on, I never expected that they might become sexual in the hot tub. One woman, however, who was standing in the water on the bench along the inside rim of the tub, sat down on the rim, dangling her legs in the water in front of the guy she was with. Then she cradled the guy's head between her legs, instructing him on just how she wanted to be licked.

I was caught off guard, but quickly began to focus on what was going on. I had never before seen another woman in orgasm. It was fascinating! I watched the contortions of her face and listened to the rhythm of her voice. Do I look and sound like that?

I found the woman's behavior rather shocking, but I was glad to be there to see it. I was amazed that she could be so casually exhibitionist and so oblivious to the complete lack of privacy; that she could utter ecstatic moans, impervious to our observation and could loudly instruct her partner in just what she wanted.

My initial shock turned to curiosity as another couple became involved in oral sex, only this time, at the woman's request, the man was sitting on the rim as she fondled his erection in a variety of ways that intrigued me: licking it up and down, popping it in and out of her mouth, rubbing it against her breasts. I don't think I had ever been that versatile. I felt, if nothing else, that I was getting a sex education. One could almost look at it as lessons—see how the pros do it. It's not that I necessarily wanted to emulate them, but I was fascinated to see their sexual behavior and marveled how involved they could be, completely unconcerned about those around them.

As couples became sexually involved, they left the tub for drier areas. Now there were only seven of us. Then I gasped. Marc was coming into the tub. I don't think he saw me yet, as he stumbled in, almost falling.

"That's how you can tell the newcomers," everyone told him as he eventually sat on the rim on the other side of the tub from me. Then he recognized my presence. I began to get nervous as the tub occupancy dwindled. And shortly thereafter, when the last couple had departed, there were just Marc and me!

Hey! Where did everybody go? I couldn't have imagined the tub so empty. I so much wanted to get to know Marc, but not like this! I didn't want to have a social interaction in the nude! I didn't move a muscle as he got up from the tub bench, waded through the water toward me, and sat down flush beside me, the side of his bare body pressing against mine, his thigh against my thigh. Oh shit! There we were, two people who had just met sitting alone, naked, side-by-side in a hot tub. This was absurd!

And then, as I sat there, nervous, my heart racing away, he goes and puts his arm around my shoulder. Boy, this was really crazy! I could feel my body stiffen under his arm as he began talking to me in a very attentive and seductive way. I think I made polite replies at all the appropriate places; I don't really know. I was too nervous to listen to what he was saying and I was beginning to get quite upset. I wanted to give him some encouragement, but I just didn't know what to do.

He must have sensed my great discomfort, for after a while he moved his arm off my shoulder, creating an immediate sense of relief, as I certainly didn't want to be put in the position of having to refuse his sexual advances. But my relief soon turned to dismay. Now that I succeeded in discouraging him, how do I let him know that I would like to get to know him better? This whole thing was getting more absurd. Was this crazy, or what?

I was beginning to feel very adolescent. I was accustomed to being able to handle myself, but suddenly, in this liberated atmosphere of being more direct in social interactions, I realized how dependent I had become on the usual game-playing process. Why couldn't I just tell Marc how I felt, what I wanted and what I didn't want, as Roger had suggested we do? But I hadn't yet learned to do that.

So instead, I behaved as if I were still in high school. I muttered something about having to meet Don and climbed hurriedly out of the hot tub. I crept as close to my towel as I could manage, leaving Marc rather open-mouthed as I quickly wrapped my towel around me, checking to see I was properly covered in all the appropriate places.

Now, feeling considerably less vulnerable and more secure as I stood covered on firm ground, I tried to mitigate the rebuff by muttering something encouraging, and then ran quickly into the house. Feeling like a complete fool, I headed for the group room.

With my towel securely around me, I passed through the beaded curtains into the red glow. Finding some bench space, I sat down, and watched the performance in front of me in amazement. I wasn't quite prepared for what I saw. Never before had I seen naked men and women together sexually. Around the perimeter of the room, there were a few couples and some small groups indulging in sexual pleasure. But in the room's center, several groups were coming together and beginning to act as one, all intertwined, crisscrossed in a beautiful erotic array of caressing limbs and pulsing, interlocking torsos.

The gold color of their bodies sensuously contrasted with the red glow of the room, creating a visually stimulating display. And as the carnal network vibrated with sexual energy, it was as if an artistic kinetic sculpture had come to life, emitting sighs of delight and expressions of pleasure. It was a beautiful sight, a loving sight, not at all like the male-chauvinist orgy scenes I had seen in porno flicks. This scene was truly erotic. I was very aroused. I was transfixed. I could almost picture myself among them. To be part of the group, part of the loving oneness with a larger entity, seemed so natural.

Part of me kept saying, "Go ahead, Barb, join them," but then I would talk myself out of it. "Do it, do it," my body cried out. What was I being so virginal about? Would I? Dare I? I watched some more, several times flexing my muscles in an attempt to jump up, throw down my towel, and intertwine myself with the others. The appeal was compelling. But I didn't do it!

Instead, I watched and watched and was mad at myself for being just a spectator. Again it was the women who completely surprised me—indeed, shocked me. Most sounds of ecstasy came from women, each crying out a different tune, creating an orgasmic symphony.

Just then, Marc walked through the beaded curtain. Instinctively, it seemed, I jumped up, leaving my towel behind, and steadily walked over to him.

Stark naked, I confidently stood there before him. "I want to apologize for my behavior in the hot tub," I told him matter-of-factly.

"Oh, that's okay," he replied.

Then, I couldn't believe the words that came out of my mouth. "I just wasn't ready then...but I'm ready now. Do you want to play?"

* * * * *

"ZZ, I would like to stop here, if that's OK. I feel the rest is too personal."

"That's fine, Barbara. Thank you very much for your story."

TWO

Z.Z.

The Author's Story
Silicon Valley, CA
March 1980

I AM YOUR AUTHOR, Zillary Zahn. Having endured numerous jokes about my first name as a kid, and having to repeat it many times for clarity as an adult, I decided to just use my initials. People call me "Zee Zee." My family and old friends, however, still call me "Zill."

One fine, beautiful day a few weeks ago, I received a phone call from Bill, my publisher, asking when I was going to write "that" book.

"Hey," Bill continued, "Let's get together later this week when you get a chance. Come on down to the office; but early enough so we can talk over lunch," he remarked, noting the fact that he rarely sees me before noon, for the writing profession is not a nine-to-five endeavor. I feel I do my best writing in the late hours, preferring to sleep away the morning.

Indicating that I would certainly set aside one of my "precious" afternoons to meet with him, I wrapped up the conversation and started to think seriously about doing "the" book.

With my swing stories of Barbara and others in circulation, receiving good reviews and some acclaim, my publisher wanted more, much more—hopefully an entire book!

When I met with Bill later that week, he was quite intrigued as he handed over a very fancy-looking invitation addressed to me in care of the publishing company. Upon opening it, I was rather puzzled by the contents, which announced a private couples-only dinner, swing party, and sleepover at a Silicon Valley estate. The gold-and-crimson engraved invitation had my name and that of my anticipated date as the invitees. It read in part, "Only invitees will be admitted; no substitutions without prior approval; formal attire; swing party etiquette in effect; swingers are encouraged to stay overnight. This is a confidential invitation."

I shared the contents of the invitation with Bill. The name of my anticipated date was Naomi, one of the young artists working at the art and sketching department at the publishing office.

Bill noted, "Your popularity does seem to be increasing with your exposure. I guess they want a favorable writer at their snazzy Silicon Valley society party. They've seen how discrete you can be. Why don't you and Naomi go and give it a fancy write-up? Perhaps we can put it in your book."

This invitation was fascinating, perplexing, and also a little bit troubling. This wasn't an invitation to a party club, but to a private party; not to a party of the membership, but to a party of the invited. So who were the people invited? Who sent me this invitation, and why? And who knew to put Naomi's name on it, appropriate though it may be?

About eight months back, after reading some of my published swing stories with great interest and enthusiasm, Naomi excitedly expressed her desire to attend a swing party with me. And so we did. She had no reservations about going and didn't seem the least bit fazed or nervous about it. Upon arriving, she blended in inconspicuously, mixing with the masses for the next several hours, emerging only occasionally to assure me she was in fact enjoying herself. On the way home, she said nothing whatsoever about what transpired or what she had experienced.

I prompted her to relate her story so that I could add it to the others that were accumulating in exponential fashion. I had assured Naomi, as I had assured Barbara and all the others, that her true name and character would be fictionalized, while retaining accuracy in the description of events and her responses to them. She said she knew and understood this; she just wasn't ready to share.

"Don't wait too long," I cautioned, "because I try to verify your story as much as possible and this becomes more and more difficult as time goes by." Then I related what my nine-year-old nephew had to say upon enthusiastically returning to camp the following summer, only to discover that memories can be deceiving; another reason for timely sharing.

Since Naomi's initial party about eight months ago, she and I have developed a very special relationship, based on friendship primarily with a little bit of sex thrown in once in a while for good fun. The "special" part of the friendship began soon after her initial party when, while we were attending a ballgame, she leaned over to me and whispered, in that very sexy voice of hers, "You want to make love?"

Well of course I did, and so began the special part.

"What are friends for?" she would say. And that was just fine with me.

In that spirit, when party day arrived, Naomi and I dressed our best and drove the fifty-some miles to the Silicon Valley dinner and swing party. With the sun already set and darkness taking hold, we arrived at a sprawling, magnificent mansion. At the entrance, two gorgeous women in long flowing gowns were there greeting guests and checking invitations. We gave the greeters our invitation, they checked our names on their list, and in we went.

We were immediately met by two of the hosts, Ed and Dianne. He, handsomely clad in a stylish tuxedo with red and white trimmings, was enjoying smoking his pipe as he greeted his guests. He was the CEO of one of the new tech companies that have been springing up here lately.

Dianne, beautifully styled for the occasion in a long black gown with white lace trim and long sleeves, owned and operated several real estate offices, I was told. I learned they were typical of the couples here: wealthy businessmen and women well-connected in the worlds of finance and fashion.

After Naomi and I were greeted in the foyer, Dianne introduced us to one of her "very best friends," Lorraine Hesten, an exceedingly beautiful, elegant woman, gracefully adorned in diamonds and gold. With Naomi at one arm and myself at the other, Lorraine escorted us into the Gala hall, a breathtakingly elegant grand ballroom with hardwood floors and a twenty-foot high ceiling. A majestic arched stairway lead to the upper floors and a large loft-balcony dining room. We were dazzled by the sight of high-fashion women and tuxedoed men milling about, drinking champagne and eating appetizers of shrimp, crab, and other delicacies. Inching our way through the densely-packed crowd of haute couture gowns and superbly coiffed hair, we were awed by the grandeur of it all.

This was certainly a very elegant gathering in a stunning, luxurious setting. Someone or some group is paying big money to sponsor this event, which could probably be crowned as the area's fashion show of the year: so many beautiful people!

Were these hundred or so beautiful people going to strip off their expensive clothing and swing? Upon subtly approaching the subject with a couple of attendees, I was told, "Heavens no! What on earth are you talking about?"

Given the setting of all these very rich and well-connected guests dressed to the nines, the possibility of this gathering becoming a swing party was next to nil.

Maybe I received a special invitation to entice me to come here, with the host thinking the party would be too boring otherwise to attract my attendance.

Well, the only thing to do, I decided, is take the party as it comes, enjoy everyone and everything, and see what develops.

At this point, knowing that Naomi would prefer to wander off and do her own thing, I told her to just go on and I would see her at the party's end, if not before.

Then, ambling through the crowd, introducing myself, I was somewhat surprised that no one really seemed to know anything about me. One woman asked me my name and I said, "ZZ."

She said, "How do you spell that?"

I said, "Z dot Z dot."

She said, "Oh...well, yes...hmmm."

Here I thought I was invited to be the famous author in the crowd. But obviously, that was not the case. I suppose someone invited me to observe, possibly take notes, and write up the party in the next few days: "The Elegant Ball," "The Fashion Show of the Year," or something like that.

Oh, there is Lorraine again, standing a few feet away, talking to a few couples. I was thinking to myself, my God, she's gorgeous, probably the best-looking woman here, a delectable bundle of alluring sex. What a beauty!

Dressed in a long flowing black gown highlighting her ample breasts, slim waist, and long legs, she was absolutely stunning. Her hair, a soft blond, was swept up in the back and clasped with a jeweled hair ornament, enhancing her large hazel eyes, flawless complexion, and generous lips. Enchanted, I walked over to greet her again.

"Oh, ZZ, how are you?" she inquired as I stepped up beside her and the others. "ZZ, I'd like you to meet my husband, Mitch."

"Greetings," was his crisp reply, accompanied with a very strong handshake. "And this is Renee," he continued, referring to the shapely young redhead standing at his side, holding his hand. "Renee is one of the many interesting women I've met here tonight."

He turned to her and continued, "Renee, this is my wife Lorraine, and you are?"

"ZZ," I replied.

Mitch looked my way and asked, "And what kind of work do you do, ZZ?"

"I'm a writer," I replied.

Lorraine chimed in, "He wrote those articles you liked about swinging."

"Oh yes," Mitch acknowledged, "great stuff, great stuff, very glad to meet you. We must talk together some time. I'll have lots of stories for you!"

Mitch was a man who exuded enormous confidence. Though only of medium height, there was an aura of greatness about him. He was robust, with a full head of graying dark-brown hair spilling over to a full, well-kempt beard and mustache. Dressed immaculately in a black tux with all the accouterments, and aided by a gait that suggested that he was a no nonsense "I'm in charge" kind of guy, he was a man of very imposing presence.

Addressing Mitch, I continued, "I assume you are in the financial world—"

Lorraine interjected, "Mitch is in the jeans business, especially splicing them!"

"Well, yes," Mitch clarified, "but we're talking genetic genes, not blue jeans. Lorraine likes to joke, you know."

Lorraine continued, "Mitch heads one of the new international high-tech companies here in Silicon Valley. It's very exciting, actually!"

"Indeed," Mitch replied as he turned away from us, "we will see you two later."

At first glance, Renee, a very young beauty with long flowing red hair, appeared much too tall for Mitch; until, of course, he began to talk or you noticed his walk. Then he seemed to loom large over her. Oddly, Renee never said a word. She even avoided eye contact with me, which seemed strange, considering I was one of the few guys here who appeared to be even close to her age.

As Lorraine watched lovingly and, apparently, very approvingly, Mitch and Renee walked on, hand in hand.

"Well, if you'll excuse me now," said Lorraine, breaking the silent lull, "I have some things to do to help out my friend Dianne, one of the hostesses of this wonderful party. It's certainly a pleasure talking to you, ZZ, and I hope to see you later."

And with that, she strolled off and there I was, wondering what exactly was this evening all about.

I continued on mixing, eating, talking, drinking. I loaded up with a plate of freshly-grilled salmon and halibut; then later grilled filet mignon; and later still, slices of glazed ham, wild rice, salad with artichoke hearts, and fresh crab piled on top. Plenty to eat, no doubt about that.

The hours passed, and I didn't seem to be making a connection with any of the women here. Naomi wouldn't be around, I knew that. She gets involved fast and never tells me anything about anything. She is probably the one person I could trust to keep a secret.

More time passed, as I continued eating, drinking, talking, mixing...eating, drinking, talking, mixing. Finally, the party started winding down. Guests were drifting by, saying farewells and making their way to the exits. The jazz pianist had left, and soon the ballroom had just about emptied.

And then, the main lights in the great hall were dimmed to the point of near-darkness. Was I the only one left here? No, off to one side just a few feet away, keeping a watchful eye on me, were Mitch and Renee. They approached.

"We're finally getting to the fun part," Mitch said. "Stick around. You and Naomi have been invited to join us and four other couples for the rest of the night.

Get naked and find yourself a woman. There are five others here, not counting Renee."

And before my eyes in the very dark ballroom, Mitch and Renee began slowly peeling off their clothes, carefully laying out their fancy outer garments on the floor, then placing their inner garments and underwear on top, producing two huge bundles of clothes.

I fixed my eyes on Renee. I had to see what she really looked like under all those fancy garments...and wow, what a body! She must be a model, I conjectured. When I shifted over to Mitch, I was surprised to see a short, squat old man. In his case, the saying "clothes make the man" was definitely true.

Leaving their clothes behind, they headed up the arched staircase, waving me to follow them. Two other naked couples walked by me, clothes in hand, heading to the grand staircase. One guy I recognized as Ed, a host, and one woman was Naomi, who, laughing and giggling, beckoned to me eagerly.

Now, feeling overdressed for the occasion, my thought was to strip down too, but suddenly my attention became riveted on one naked couple still in the main ballroom. They seemed so intriguing that I pulled up a chair just to watch them. In the dark, I could see a few bar stools, she sitting naked on one of them, he sitting in front of her in an easy chair, her legs dangling in his lap. I'm looking at the two of them thinking how this scene just cries out for oral sex. I can almost imagine her exquisiteness, just sitting here in my chair, watching.

Yes, she is parting her legs.

Yes, he is saddling up between them.

Yes, he has each arm extending up a thigh as he closes in on her.

I can almost imagine her exquisite aroma as his head approaches her pubic area.

I can almost feel those smooth fleshy thighs along my face as he saddles his face between them.

I can almost taste those velvety vaginal lips and her warm juicy delicacy as he buries his mouth between her legs.

I can almost sense their ecstasy as I stare away into space...into space.

I was just dreaming away when my eye caught the figure of a woman descending from the upper floors and onto the balcony at the top of the landing.

In the darkness, it was as if there was a spotlight shining on her: a goddess at the top of the stairs. It was Lorraine, still fully dressed as I was, still looking as elegant as ever. She hadn't seen me.

"Lorraine," I called out, then pausing. "...I want you!"

"Well," she shot back with a charming giggle, "Come get me!"

And so I did, rushing across the floor, running through the corridor, racing up the staircase, reaching for her ankles, and then using them to glide my hands up her legs, under her skirt, past her knees, up her thighs to her panty-covered tush.

"I've got you, Miss Lorraine!" I laughed triumphantly.

"And so you do, Mr. Zahn!" she laughed as we rolled over and over on the balcony floor, squealing like a couple of teenagers.

"Come on," she whispered to me, taking me by the hand. She led me up another flight of stairs, down the corridor, and into a very large bedroom.

The room was dark, very dark, but I could see I was standing in an architecturally majestic room. I could barely discern the furniture, several large easy chairs and assorted other pieces that I could not see very well and a very large bed with mounds of decorative pillows and a fancy bedspread.

Lorraine whispered to me, "I have reserved this room for the whole night. This is one of the main bedrooms of the mansion. So now that you have me, I hope you still want me!"

"Yes, I do!" I affirmed emphatically, pulling her to me and

kissing her tenderly. Oh, those lips! So delicious. Holding her in my arms, I kissed her again, as I unzipped part of her dress.

"You will never be able to manage this," she whispered as she artfully undid her dress. Off came her gown, then all undergarments, everything, no preliminaries. I responded in kind, undressing as fast as I could.

Then, as we both stood naked, I took her in my arms and kissed her again. I reflected upon the fact that this was a very special moment. Rarely do you get to hold such an exceptional beauty in your arms!

"You are so beautiful, so absolutely gorgeous," I whispered as I eyed her shapely body, then felt her, moving my hands down her back to her waist, then down to her butt and, with one hand on each cheek, pulled her to me. Amidst the soft jingling of her bracelets and the gleam of her gold choker and sparkly rings, I kissed her again.

Slowly, walking hand-in-hand, we made our way to the bed, falling onto the spread, rolling over and over together several times, feeling the warmth of each other's bodies. We adjusted the pillows and covers, kissed softly and tenderly, making sweet, sweet love before drifting off into a dreamy, peaceful sleep.

* * * * *

That morning, while we were still in bed finishing off our breakfast, Lorraine excitedly exclaimed that she wanted me to record her story.

It was important, she said, that she tell me her story right away. So here it is.

THREE

Lorraine

Part 1: Lorraine's Story
Recorded post Gala by Zillary Zahn, Sunday, March 16, 1980
San Francisco, Berkeley and Oakland, CA
1968 - 1972

MY STORY IS about sex, love, money, and power. Sex first. Twelve years ago, in 1968, I suddenly found myself divorced with two teenage daughters. I had been married for over seventeen years and never once had an orgasm. Perhaps that led to my husband's apparent discontent with me. But I always did enjoy making love with him and I considered myself a very good sex partner. But he started having affairs, eventually leaving me for a woman much younger than I, which absolutely revolted my two daughters. After a few years of his new marriage, my ex-husband realized his big mistake, but by then my daughters wanted little to do with him, and I was very happy with my new single life.

Fortunately, my divorce had not been an economic hardship. Coming from a wealthy family, I had ample investments and a more than adequate trust fund. My older daughter, Jasmine, sixteen at the time, was a straight-A student. Kathleen, fourteen, was a teenage hippie, which of course troubled me deeply. Having married right out of high school, I never attended college (to my parents' horror), and had been a straightlaced stay-at-home mom for seventeen years. I loved raising my daughters and living in the beauty and sophistication of San Francisco, but other than that, there is not much I can say for those married years.

My divorce was my liberation. My first act had been to enroll in college; my second was to tackle my "sexual problem." Being a virgin when I got married—as a good girl was supposed to be in the 1950s—I had been completely faithful throughout my marriage. Now, I was going to need gargantuan assistance navigating the new sexual freedom of the 1970s. Women were on the Pill, liberating them to have sex any time, anywhere, without fear of pregnancy and—because of new antibiotics—fear of diseases such as syphilis and gonorrhea.

How was I going to re-emerge from the repressed sexual mores of the 50s to the exciting sexually-free mores of the 70s? I felt so out of touch. And in addition, I had a sexual problem.

Seeking professional help from a sexology clinic in Berkeley, I learned how to gently touch myself in just the right places and, using a vibrator, how to receive mild pleasure from time to time. But that was about the extent of my sexual satisfaction.

The female staffers who attended me were extremely sympathetic, understanding, and encouraging. I would need to be a more active sex partner, they advised, possibly directing my partners to satisfy me as much as possible through oral sex before intercourse. I didn't know if I possessed the courage to lead men to sexually do this or that; taking initiative and directing the sexual action was foreign to my upbringing and experience. I was now in a totally different era: one that seemed somewhat overwhelming, yet so exciting and so liberating. I yearned to be part of it.

I continued my association with the clinic, returning from time to time for advice. But during the first two years of my new singlehood, I hardly dated at all, recoiling from men who expected sex on a first or second date. I hadn't had sex with my husband until after I had known him for over two years, and that was on our honeymoon. Now, having two teenage daughters at home and being a student myself, I was much too preoccupied and much too busy to seriously date.

But two years later, with Kathleen in high school and Jasmine off to college, I did manage to sleep with a few guys. I had them lick me up rather well before they entered...I'm actually getting a little embarrassed talking about this, feeling a bit self-conscious. I don't know why; that was ten years ago! But I guess some of these old feelings stay with you. I'll try to continue. I did get pleasure from the licking experience, but no orgasm. I went back to the clinic.

Now in 1972, the clinic staff, consisting of both male and female therapists, facilitators, and psychologists, informed me of some Friday night sexual encounter groups and Saturday night sexual swing parties that were forming to help those like me enter into the sexually-free era in which we now found ourselves. "Was I interested?" they asked me.

"Well, of course!" Finally, something I could participate in.

Nancy, one of the staffers I had become friendly with over the years, thought I should seriously consider going to their very first swing party. "It's going to sound a bit strange at first, but I think this is an event you will find quite intriguing, fascinating, and hopefully, very beneficial. Have you heard of swinging before?"

"I've heard of it, yes. But I don't really know anything about it."

I learned that the concept of swinging arises when both members of a couple feel the need to experience new sexual partners. This is not a very common need. But it is very strong and powerful for those couples that feel it; powerful enough to break up their relationship.

To accommodate this need, like-minded couples find each other through ads in underground weeklies. If they can form a group of three or four couples, then they usually take turns hosting parties for each other. After a light dinner or snack, the idea is to pair up with someone other than your usual partner. Then each newly formed couple goes off to some private location in the house and enjoys a sexual encounter.

Based on this concept of swinging, two of Nancy's colleagues were going to begin hosting large, Saturday-night swing parties at their home. These would be nude, couples only, hot-tub parties at which all guests were open to the idea of engaging in sex. Alice, a sexologist on staff at the clinic, and Denny, her psychotherapist husband, planned to bring together various small swing groups from around the Bay Area to form a party of about twenty couples. At such a grand party, Alice and Denny could do what small groups generally couldn't: invite an equal number of desirable single men and women who could therapeutically benefit by participating at these parties and whose general demeanor meant that they could abide by the established rules of behavior.

"We think you perfectly fit the profile of a woman we would like to invite," Nancy told me. "What do you say?"

Wow! I was a little overwhelmed. But I was definitely interested. "Tell me more."

I learned that Alice and Denny view hosting swing parties as an extension of their professional duties and commitments. They feel that swinging fills a need that some couples have at some point in their relationship when each deeply feels the need to experience the stimulation and excitement a new sex partner presents. Hopefully, each gains insight and knowledge from the experience. Swing parties are designed to address that need in a way that presents minimal disruption to the commitment in their relationship. No affairs. No emotional entanglements. The sexual encounters, though physically very intimate, are usually rather impersonal. Each hopefully receives something of which they were looking for.

Sounded scintillating! I was excited.

A week before the inaugural party, all invitees were asked to attend an orientation meeting at Alice and Denny's home. I attended that meeting with Nancy. I was interested to hear more as to what swinging was all about.

Upon entering the party house, situated in a middle-class neighborhood in Oakland, we were greeted by a few of Nancy's fellow staffers, who quickly gave us a tour of the house. I mainly noted the dressing room, the adjoining hot-tub room, and the connecting floor dedicated to couples who wanted privacy or semi-privacy. There were additional rooms for those who wanted to be sexually involved with a group.

Nancy introduced me to her friends and co-workers. In particular, she reacquainted me with Larry, one of the young good-looking staffers who, like Nancy, was working in a degree program. At some of my past visits to the clinic, I had some fleeting fantasies about Larry—rather innocent really, since he is about ten years younger than I. But it was fun to fantasize.

Soon we were all taking seats around the fireplace, sitting on the sofa, in chairs, or on the floor on large pillows. Alice and Denny wanted to address us. Looking about the circle that was formed, I noticed it was a rather good-looking, well-dressed group. I particularly noticed Larry. Maybe it was the atmosphere, but at that moment he looked especially appealing.

Denny, a stocky, well-built man of medium height, began in his soft-spoken, stern manner.

He talked about swinging. He said most everyone goes to these parties for the same reason: to accumulate positive, quality experiences. "We come to gain insights. That is why we are here. We bare our bodies to enrich our minds. You come to form a better understanding of your sexual self and your sexual needs, and more broadly, of nature and society and your place in it. I don't think people usually look at it that way, but generally, that is what you are doing.

"To help rule out certain negative experiences, we have established rules of behavior that everyone must follow. Everyone has to respect the fact that all of us here have voluntarily placed ourselves in a very vulnerable situation. Everyone has to respect our vulnerability.

"Therefore, there are to be no crude remarks, crude language, or crude behavior of any kind. No one is to make any evaluating remarks regarding anyone else here. And everyone must recognize all forms of rejection and respect them immediately."

Alice, a very good-looking, small-framed woman with a booming voice, weighed in.

"I want to emphasize that everything you do at these parties that involves other people must be fully consensual at all times. At any time, you can voice or motion your rejection. That rejection must be recognized immediately. It is not to be argued or up for discussion. No one should ever feel that they have to do something they really do not want to do.

"And, if at some point in a party, you come to the realization that you don't want to sexually participate with anyone, you don't have to. No one is keeping score except you."

After that, a lot of logistical details were discussed. But I did not pay close attention. For me, the memorable moments of the evening were over, except for the conclusion.

When the formal meeting part ended and we were all milling about, Larry came over to Nancy and me to chat briefly. He concluded by asking me if I had any questions about next week's swing party.

"Yes I do," I replied. "Would you agree to being my very first swing partner?"

"Lorraine! Yes!" He replied quickly and assertively. He then gently hugged us each and departed, saying "See you next week at about nine o'clock!"

Nancy was shocked by my brazen behavior. "Well," I replied, "Many of the people here are already swingers. I feel much better going into this week knowing I can try out this swing concept with someone I know and trust. I feel he would be more in tune with what I want to achieve."

And so I felt very relaxed and comfortable about the upcoming swing party. Actually, I felt quite excited about it. What a great way to address my sexual problem!

Come party night, I again went with Nancy. She told me that she would devote the entire evening to me. She would be there to help insure I had a productive evening and she'd leave with me any time I wanted.

"Quite remarkable!" I thought. Rules stated that all guests had to arrive between eight and ten p.m. No one would be admitted after ten. Up to that point, guests could be fully dressed, naked, or any stage in between. But after ten, all guests must be naked. Otherwise, you would be a voyeur. "You don't have to physically touch anyone if you don't want to, but you must be 'participating' in the party." So, if for some reason, I felt uneasy about stripping, come ten o'clock, I would have to leave. I didn't think there would be much possibility of that, since my whole reason for going was to get that "positive quality experience."

Party night, Nancy and I arrived shortly after eight, well before Larry was expected. Nancy thought it would be a good idea to be among the first to arrive, getting to know people one by one, rather than meeting a mass of people all at once.

Like the previous week, we parked where we were supposed to— about a block away so as not to cause problems for the neighbors. Then we strolled past the middle-class homes packed close together until we reached the right one. I had to wonder if anyone one on the block had any idea of what was about to take place at their neighbor's house!

Entering the home, we became inundated with colors, sounds, and scents of a party house: balloons, flowers, music, greeters; quite a festive atmosphere. After we settled in, Nancy suggested we hang out by the food on the dining room buffet table.

"Everyone comes to eat something, so eventually you meet just about everybody by just hanging around here."

And that was good strategy. Just about everyone came over in the course of that first hour to eat and chat. Nice people. Outgoing and friendly. I chatted some with a few couples, particularly the women. And I received a few proposals from several of the men, which I very politely and truthfully deferred to "perhaps later in the evening". The guys were rather appealing, but for now, I was happy to have a date.

Then Larry arrived. My heart skipped a beat. I suddenly re-membered exactly why I was here. I had gotten somewhat lost in all the fun socializing.

After a light snack during which Larry and I conversed a bit, recalling times we had seen each other at the clinic, Larry took my hand and asked, "Are you ready to strip down and go hot-tubbing?"

"Yea, should be fun; let's do it!" The time had come to see how all this anticipation was going to play out. Wheels were now in mo-tion. Soon, I would be in bed with him! Handsome Larry. I was feel-ing a tingle of excitement all over!

Hand-in-hand, Larry guided me through the growing crowd to-ward the changing room, where there were a few naked couples and others who were about to be. Larry began removing his clothes, as did others around us. So it seemed perfectly natural for me to strip too; to do otherwise would be attention-getting.

Now naked, I noticed a concealing smile on Larry's face, after his sneak approving glance of my nakedness. He looked pretty good himself. Again hand-in-hand, we followed the naked people ahead of us, exiting the far side of the room into the steamy hot-tub room.

The tub was about half full, with five or six people already in it. So we plopped ourselves into the bubbly, foamy water. Not too hot and not too cold, the bubbly foam was a pure delight. This was quite an intimate, sensual situation, perfect for those looking for someone to hook up with. I will have to come back here, I noted, when I am alone on the prowl. All you have to do is physically move next to a person you are interested in and see what happens. That's probably why, once we were in the tub, Larry had his arm on my shoulder throughout, claiming "ownership". I was getting intrigued watching people coupling up and then leaving the tub. All this was arousing my sexual interest.

We chatted with each other and with some of the others in the tub. Then, at just the right moment, Larry asked, "Are you ready to play?"

"Oh, yes!" I answered with a seductive smile.

We climbed out of the tub, dripping all over as we helped ourselves to towels stacked up at several places around the hot, steamy room. We followed the couples in front of us to the couples' floor, a whole floor divided up into little decorative alcoves where couples could be somewhat private.

As we moved about, hearing moans and sighs of delight, we looked for an appealing vacant area. "How about here?" Larry asked, pointing to a cozy, decorative area with very fancy lace bedding.

Smiling, I nodded my approval. The place looked perfect; feminine. Alice must have done this, I thought. We embraced, pulled the curtain shut and, with arms around each other, lowered ourselves onto the bedding.

We chatted a bit and listened to the sighs and moans of delight emanating around us. Oddly, I thought at the time, those sounds were not distracting at all, not putting me off, but rather seemed to be moving me along the trail of sexual excitement. I was fascinated. I had become totally taken in, ready to do almost anything. I think I became the aggressive one. But Larry seemed to sense my mood completely, and moved with it perfectly, freely moving his hands all about me, kissing me all over my body, particularly my special spot.

It wasn't long before I became totally lost in the moment. I could tell this was going to be a defining experience. There was no way I was going to freeze up this time. I was too far along, way far. Soon, I could hear my own sounds of delight as I became totally absorbed and totally lost into an orgasmic swoon; it happened! What delight! What ecstasy! I couldn't believe I had gone all these years without it.

Well, I wasn't going to miss out any more. I was hooked. Totally hooked. I went to one swing party after another, week after week for months. It was very liberating to know that I could receive sexual pleasure anonymously. I enjoyed my various partners, but never attached any kind of romantic feeling to the experiences. It was just sex.

Today, I feel a very special connection to these parties, having experienced the initiation of my own sexuality at the birth of these ongoing Bay Area swing parties. Today, eight years later, Alice and Denny's parties are one of the oldest continuously-run swing parties in the United States, well known as one of the best swing clubs in the country.

I feel extremely privileged to have attended these swing parties. By observing people who became completely oblivious to privacy, I witnessed sexual activities rarely seen by anyone, especially women. I had seen couples in indescribable sexual variations, and watched threesomes, foursomes, and many-somes. Liberated from old habits and completely free to experiment, new variations of standard techniques were improvised at that very moment. These are magical connections that don't translate well into the written or spoken word. These are activities that have to be witnessed.

In retrospect, I understand why the Berkeley sex clinic was so eager to sponsor these parties and to provide personnel to keep them going. These parties are complete sexual laboratories! You can see there what you will probably never see anywhere else. If you want to study human sexuality, go to swing parties. The clinic staffers were provided with incredible data, while we swingers were very happily enjoying being their specimens. Many research papers and many Ph.D. thesis papers were written as a result of our activities. That's impressive! We swingers can always say we have made important contributions to science.

This concludes Part One of Lorraine's story.

FOUR

Swinging

Part 2: Lorraine's Story
Silicon Valley, CA
1973 - 1980

NOW IN 1973, after a year of swinging — five years into my singlehood — I met Mitchell Hesten, a non-swinger and the love of my life, during a late-afternoon tea dance at one of the classic downtown hotels in San Francisco. With an outstretched arm and a charming smile, Mitch approached me requesting a dance; and then another. After a festive evening of dancing followed by dinner at one of the classic nearby restaurants, we went for a stroll through some of the scenic historic streets of the city. It was a totally unexpected, romantic evening.

Feeling like we made a heartfelt connection, Mitch and I began dating. I immediately sensed that this man was different from anyone I had dated previously: very self-assured, confident, radiant, knowledgeable, intelligent, and adorable. Wow! I was smitten! I just loved his cuddly teddy bear appearance, his bushy beard, and his soft, gentle smile. He was the most dynamic, brilliant man I had ever known. I was in love! I felt so lucky that we just happened to meet. Every day thereafter, he told me how much he loved me, adored me, and appreciated me. I came to see my whole future with Mitch; I couldn't imagine life without him.

We were soon engaged and married shortly thereafter. There were about 30 people at our wedding party: both sets of our parents, my two daughters, some of my dear, longtime friends, Mitch's daughter and son-in-law, and some of Mitch's friends whom he had known for over 25 years, going back to his college days. Among the latter group were three high-powered, dynamic couples who captivated me with their inspiring, energetic approach to life. I was extremely eager to join them socially and, eventually, financially as well. All three couples were heavily invested in Mitch's scientific technology enterprises. Now, seven years later, these three couples are among my dearest, closest friends.

One couple, Ed and Dianne, have been our closest business associates since our marriage. Ed, a smart, savvy businessman, formed a powerhouse team with his wife Dianne, an up-and-coming business executive in the real estate industry. When Mitch needed their astute advice and business skills near the time of our marriage, they were there for him. Today, they are the two people in the world we most rely on for just about everything.

Bert and Marge were struggling artists when Mitch met them in his college days. Mitch said they married so they could be struggling artists together. But today, they have made it big in the advertising world and in the fashion industry with their clever and flamboyant artistic design work. They are dramatic in their personal appearance as well: she with her ever-present black, wide-rimmed hat and ruby red lipstick, and he with his large flops of dark hair that bounce continuously when he moves or speaks.

And then there were Jeffrey and Vivian, very outgoing husband-and-wife lawyers who met in law school and went on to become prominent attorneys, though in separate practices. Vivian is very vivacious (we refer to her as "Vi-Viv") and Jeffrey is handsomely clean-cut.

We usually refer to these three couples as the "six," or sometimes as the "others."

At the time of our marriage in 1973, my younger daughter Kathleen was preparing to go to art college, my older daughter Jasmine was beginning her senior year at the university, and I was entering graduate school in pursuit of a master's degree in business administration with a major in finance. And all the while, Mitch was busy becoming very successful, having just transformed his local science laboratory into a thriving national technology company.

Both a scientist and businessman — and genius at both — Mitch had developed several key patents, becoming a rising star in the high-tech industry, based on the use of silicon-based computer chips. This new industry, now dominating the area just south of San Francisco, is giving this entire region an unofficial new name: Silicon Valley.

Feeling enormously confident in Mitch's scientific and business abilities, I decided to invest as much of my own personal wealth as Mitch did his, making us the two largest investors in our newly-emerging international company. Two years into our marriage, in 1975, we had become a financial powerhouse to be reckoned with.

That year, 1975, marked an important year for us in several areas. After I proudly received my master's degree in finance, we moved to the Silicon Valley community of Los Gatos, where the "others" — lawyers Vivian and Jeffrey, artists Marge and Bert, and the business duo Dianne and Ed — had lived for many years.

Los Gatos was a sleepy yet upcoming little community: a mix of old-time, lifelong residents and young, high-income "techies." To outsiders, the community was mainly known by its business area consisting of two parallel streets, each about a mile long, lined with old-time mom-and-pop stores and newly-flourishing, cutesy little shops and good restaurants.

The community was much closer to Mitch's work than San Francisco, and also much more convenient for what had become one of our favorite relaxation activities: a day in the sunshine, reading, hiking, playing tennis or volleyball, swimming, hot-tubbing, dining, dancing, and prancing — all in the nude at the Hilltop Naturist Club, a sprawling nudist facility in the heart of the Santa Cruz mountains. The word "naturist" in the club's title speaks to its very essence: to be naked outdoors and feel oneness with nature; to experience the sensation that we are all creatures of the earth, just children playing in the sunshine. Having become accustomed to walking around naked at swing parties, I welcomed the opportunity to do so in the sunshine and open air with Mitch and the "others."

Catering to families, the club fostered a sense of community and fellowship with two large swimming pools and hot tubs, tennis and volleyball courts, picnic lawns and picnic tables, snack stands, a clubhouse, a restaurant, and a large wilderness area for hiking. On a beautiful day, over 100 families can be seen mingling with one another; you see many little kids running around, but you can't readily tell who goes with whom, for they wear no identifying patches of colored cloth (cloth-es). Here we are all family. For me, social nudity is a very freeing, very beautiful, and very spiritual experience.

Away from this playful world, back to the professional one, our international travels began in earnest. In 1975, Mitch and I traveled about a third of the year, setting up offices and labs in various European cities and meeting with businesspeople everywhere in an effort to expand our enterprise to key foreign areas.

Mitch was becoming a dominant international figure. His innovative style and ways of doing business as well as his breakthrough patented inventions had skyrocketed our little company into a competitive world leader. It was an exceptionally exciting time.

But staying competitive in this growing technological world is a constant endeavor; there is never any time for complacency. Realizing this, we soon decided to enlist the assistance of our very close friends and business associates, Ed and Dianne, who relished the idea of international business operations. Joining us in early 1976, they lightened our load considerably, also providing much-needed companionship for our relaxation time and business-related recreation.

Ed and Dianne became our advance team. They arranged our conferences, meetings, and dinners; they determined the participants, created the agendas, and invited the guests. The infusion of Ed and Dianne into our international business affairs was a boon to the entire company.

But almost two years later in 1977, with our total business operation spiraling into complexity, we realized we might soon need Ed and Dianne back home to head up the two new subsidiary companies we were forming.

Fortunately, my daughter Jasmine, now 25, had just completed her MBA and was ready to join the work force. She traveled with us that year, receiving on-the-job training from Ed and Dianne in all aspects of their work.

Meanwhile, back at home, the other two couples — Vivian and Jeffrey, Bert and Marge — had discovered swinging! Still going strong after five years, Alice and Denny's weekly swing parties had now become well known 50 miles south in Los Gatos.

Very early in our relationship, I had, of course, told Mitch about my participation at these parties, and over the years the "others" had come to know about them, too. Now, with Jeff and Viv, Bert and Marge going to swing parties, and with Ed and Dianne interested too, the foregone conclusion was that Mitch and I would soon be joining them.

However, I felt some apprehension about doing so. Suddenly, I was faced with the specter of sexually sharing my adoring husband of four years with other women, mainly younger women. Was this something I was prepared to do, having lost my first husband to a woman much younger than I?

Absolutely not!

When I attended these parties five years prior, I was a single mom in need of assistance in many aspects of my troubled life. But now Mitch and I had only been married for four years. We were newlyweds, unlike "the six," whose marriages had all passed the 20-year mark. Why would I now want to go swinging?

I told Mitch about my reservations and apprehensions. He felt we should absolutely feel no pressure to join "the six"; that we could decide for ourselves by going to a party together, agreeing to stay only about an hour or so to get the vibes, as they say.

So, with that plan in mind, we called in our reservations and set out one rainy evening in 1977 to visit Alice and Denny's weekly Saturday night swing party. Denny was very pleased to see me and to finally meet Mitch, having heard so much from me at the end of my swinging year about this "extremely fine person."

Alice was not present the night we attended, but as usual, her mom had prepared the home-cooked evening dinner, which included some of her specialties: homemade matzo ball soup, potato latkes, and gefilte fish.

The house looked much the same except for a few additions and improvements, but the parties themselves, I could see, had changed dramatically. The small Friday night "sexual encounter groups" of that initial year had now merged with the Saturday night swing parties. Instead of 30 to 40 participants, now there were about 80! Gone was all the psychoanalytic encounter stuff left over from the 60s.

Now, in the heart of the 70s, these were just parties — enormously fun parties where you could meet many new people and socialize, listen to good music and dance, eat tasty food, walk around in sexy evening wear, get a massage, and yes, of course, have sex.

What Mitch and I witnessed that night was a new type of swing party called soft swing, which places a strong emphasis on social interactions, not sexual ones. At the core of the party are 30 to 40 good-looking, physically fit, well-dressed couples. Then, with the lure of sex added to the mix, everyone generates their part of the collective atmosphere by their desire to meet each other, socialize, and perhaps participate in some sexual activity before the party is over. The result is a very high-energy, vibrant party.

The sexual element of the party is a necessary ingredient to serve notice that this is a party like no other. This is a party where sexual fantasies and desires can be played out and where people can feel free to explore their latent sexual desires. This is a party where plenty of sex is available, but much of the fun and excitement is just the thought that "sex is there!"

What Mitch and I noticed so compellingly is that when you are at the party, you definitely feel the excitement, and when you leave the party, you take some of that excitement with you. It stays with you for the next day or two, or perhaps the whole week. You can't help but think of the next party.

Part of the attraction of these parties is the knowledge that every Saturday night there is a special place where you can go and there is always a big, fun, exciting party taking place — just waiting for you! If you are not there when the time comes, you just might start to wonder, "What am I missing out on?"

In discussing these parties that night in 1977, Denny spoke of the quickly rising popularity of soft-swing parties and the rapid expansion of soft-swing party clubs throughout the country. Having witnessed the appeal of the soft-swing party for myself and having recalled the significant, positive impact that swinging played in my life, I had to rethink my rejection of Mitch and me swinging.

Recalling my swinging days, not once had I ever thought romantically about any of my sexual partners. To me, swing party sex is like being at a good concert; you get swept up by the music that rises to a crescendo, then you have an orgasm. The experience doesn't really depend that much on exactly who is playing the music. The sex is very physical.

And there is definitely something exciting about a sexual experience with someone new. But a swing partner is just a much more sophisticated version of a dance partner; you enjoy your time with your partner, but when the dance is over, you move on. Swinging is for sex play, not romance.

Sex with love is entirely different. It is a feeling of closeness and oneness; a feeling of loving and being loved. The sex is very spiritual as well as physical. So, upon reflection, my concerns about the possible negative effects of swinging on our marriage were essentially gone.

For me, swinging had been a life-changing experience. It helped transform me from the passive, accepting, dutiful wife of my first marriage into an assertive, energetic, and passionate partner for Mitch. I know Mitch loves me for the way I am now; I don't know that he even would have liked me very much had he known me years earlier.

As I see it, life presents certain opportunities that you choose to partake in or abstain from. And often, if you don't choose to participate in an opportunity at that crucial time, it is gone, lost forever. In business, Mitch is an expert at recognizing those opportunities, and he makes the most of them. In personal life, swinging can be one of those types of opportunities, as it was for me five years prior in 1972. I am a very changed person, much the better, I'm sure, for having chosen to participate in swinging when the opportunity presented itself to me.

Now opportunity was knocking again, this time for Mitch and me as a couple. As with all opportunities, there are risks; you can never foresee exactly where any opportunity may lead. The choice is always to partake or abstain. Having personally reviewed the festivities for ourselves, and having given the question ample thought, we decided to partake.

The "six" (Ed and Dianne, Bert and Marge, Jeff and Viv) had declared they would swing with outsiders only, never among themselves, agreeing that to do otherwise would be too incestuous, not to mention laughable! It's difficult to have any sexual fantasies about people you know so well that you sit around naked with them year-in and year-out, as we did at the naturist club.

So Mitch and I also agreed: swinging would be with outsiders only, never within our group of "eight." And, we both readily agreed, we would never allow swinging relationships to enter into our private lives. We would not give out our phone numbers, nor would we accept phone numbers from others. We do not date! We would tell any interested partners that we swing at parties only.

Across Europe as in the US, the phenomenon of the soft-swing party was spreading rapidly. On a quiet weekend in a small town in Europe, where would you expect to find international business couples? At the local swing club, of course! Many important business deals were taking place at these offbeat venues. Like the local tavern, but better, couples parties had become an important meeting place for doing business. Many locals and travelers would come early for the good food and good company, do some business, some drinking, and then leave before any of the late-night sexual activities had even begun. The non-sexual aspect of these parties had itself become an attraction.

That upcoming year, 1978, Dianne, Ed, Mitch and I attended party after party at the end of a hard week's work. In addition to the local and business people, many international couples like us were in attendance. They provided us with an ongoing international social network, a necessity for people who are away from home as much as we were. And these parties had become an important avenue for international business activities, as well as providing much-needed recreation. Our decision to partake in swing parties had already paid huge dividends, both socially and financially.

But now, in late 1978, the time had come for Ed and Dianne to return to our headquarters in Silicon Valley. Mitch had become so adept at putting together major business deals that our original company had now spawned off the two new subsidiaries, as we had hoped. And, as anticipated, we would now need Ed and Dianne to direct them. This left Jasmine, now 26, and her assistants taking care of all the daytime appointments and meetings, speaking to various groups on our behalf, smoothing out any diplomatic problems, security-checking all participants, and then arranging all our business-social evening activities, reciprocity dinners, and banquets. We had to get Jasmine top-level help; this was an overwhelming job.

The best of all possible worlds would be if we could find a swinger couple like Ed and Dianne with great business and communication skills who could completely take over and manage the evening activities, especially assisting us in the social-business aspects of the swing parties. To our knowledge, Jasmine did not know about our swing-party activities, and we certainly did not want her involved with them.

We noticed how much easier it was to do business at these parties when we presented ourselves as a foursome, rather than just the two of us. I think this phenomenon is akin to attending a dance with a date, rather than alone; it is much easier to join in with a date at your side. With the four of us, we were already a party in itself; couples wanted to join us; we didn't have to try to join them. Without Ed and Dianne, Mitch felt at times that we did not obtain the maximum benefits available from our business opportunities. We just needed that other couple to sway the dynamics more in our favor.

So finding a swinger couple to replace Ed and Dianne was an important priority. Our preference would be to find the right people for the job from within the company and then get them interested in swinging. Ed, Dianne, Mitch, and I scrutinized our lists of company executives for those who could possibly do the job. The majority still had kids living at home, which of course eliminated them from extensive traveling. That left us with a small yet promising list of candidates.

But after eliminating those who were wedded to the Silicon Valley area for some reason, those who did not have the required social or communication skills, those who were too nerdy or quite unsociable, and those who were just too sexually unattractive, that left nobody...nobody at all!

We were aghast. How could that be? With a little analysis, it became clear why we found ourselves in this quandary. We were looking for responsible people who were amiable and sexually attractive, had good communication skills, valued friendships, and were also loyal and trustworthy. People with these characteristics tend to make commitments to others, become good husbands, wives, and parents, and form ties to the localities in which they live.

As Mitch put it, there is a negative correlation between the type of people we are looking for and the type of people who are free to travel the world.

It was becoming clear we would probably have to hire a swinger couple from outside the company. But this idea was fraught with anxiety: loyalty risks, conflicts of interest, and other such issues that would make this hiring difficult. We would be looking for a swinger couple who were amiable and attractive; had good social and communication skills; had no conflicts of interest with regard to the tech industry; could travel extensively; were loyal, discrete, and extremely trustworthy; and finally, a couple with whom we could develop the rapport necessary to withstand the rigors of traveling and swinging. Finding such a couple was going to be a formidable task!

I know I have talked much about my older daughter Jasmine: smart, savvy, driven, hard-working, straight-A student in high school; Phi Beta Kappa student in college; an MBA graduate from U.C. Berkeley, and now the hard-working, dedicated Director of International Operations at our company.

My younger daughter, Kathleen, two years younger than Jasmine, was always an entirely different sort of kid. My ex-husband and I thought we were such wonderful parents with our one "ideal" child. But when our second child came along, we were completely bewildered. She was so different from Jasmine.

Contrary to the popular 50s concept that babies were born a "tabula rasa" (clean slate) and that upbringing was everything, we could see that so much depended on genetic factors beyond our control. Kathleen was not a problem child, just a much more artistic, non-academic type. As a teenager, she was very attracted to the psychedelic culture gaining popularity in the streets of San Francisco, and especially in the now famous Haight-Ashbury district.

Unfortunately, my divorce proceedings began when Kathleen was only 13, coinciding with the 1967 "Summer of Love" in San Francisco, which saw many of the nation's youth coming to San Francisco "with flowers in their hair."

Kathleen, a native of San Francisco, became a flower child, a teenage hippie, hanging out in Golden Gate Park with hundreds of others like her, dancing to free concerts performed by up-and-coming rock groups and rock stars. She even changed her name to Jade.

At the time, I thought all of this was a terrible influence. You know, "sex, drugs and rock 'n' roll"; only now rock 'n' roll had been replaced by fully-electric, ultra-high-volume, blaring rock music. Being a single mom those five years until Kathleen entered art college — and being a college student myself — I constantly wrestled to forge the balance of responsibilities toward myself as a student and toward Kathleen as a parent.

Jasmine had always been easy for me to understand because she was very much like me. Kathleen, on the other hand, was much more like her father; I had to struggle hard to understand her and help her become the person she wanted to be.

I thought I had failed. Though she never developed a drug habit and was never arrested during those five years, she was very much a child of the streets with wild pink or green hair and hippie clothes that included full, bright flowery dresses, heavy dangling beads, and very dirty sandals. She always looked like she needed a bath; I thought she was a mess.

But as I said before, opportunities present themselves, and often you need to take advantage of them at that crucial moment or else they are lost forever. Well, Kathleen, following her instincts against mine, lived in the flower-child culture, which became a unique opportunity.

Now, gone forever are the flower children, the ubiquitous psychedelic artists, and the great free rock concerts in the park. Kathleen lived that life to the fullest, through what we now realize was a golden age of its type. Today, she is a very happy, successful artist, having developed a unique psychedelic art style, capitalizing extensively on her teenage hippie experiences. It is amazing how two children raised in the same family can be so different, yet so wonderful in their individual ways.

Back at home, we only went to a few of Alice and Denny's parties that first year we started swinging. Driving 50 miles to a party is not something you do very often. That, of course, led Mitch and me to launch the "Los Gatos Parties," our own private swing parties the eight of us took turns hosting about once a month. We started with three other local couples, growing to where today, two years later, we usually have five or six additional couples.

Our private parties are quite extravagant: loads of great food and champagne and outrageous decorations, music, and lighting effects from our own artists, Bert and Marge. We have been giving these parties for two years now, and they are always extraordinarily fun. We are, of course, always looking for that perfect swinger couple who could also travel with us. But all those who have attended our parties are tied to the Los Gatos area because of family or because of a dedication to a committed profession. No luck yet.

Now it is early 1980, and we still have found no swinger couple to replace Ed and Dianne. We have continued to go to Alice and Denny's on occasion, usually when we are in the area anyway for some daytime activity. And sometimes we go with Jeffrey and Vivian, who of the "six," are the most interested in swinging; they say it has added a lot of spice to their marriage.

"Jeffrey really enjoys the women," Viv confided in her still-present Southern accent, "but I don't mind as long as I can have my gentlemen." Viv loves to chat, which is one reason we are so close. I hear a lot about her legal cases; some would be hilariously funny, were they not so tragic.

About five weeks ago we went with Jeff and Viv to a swing party at Alice and Denny's house. Upon entering, we were warmly greeted by Denny, paid our $25 per couple "donation," and made our way through the crowd to the dining area. It was packed with well-dressed couples drinking an assorted variety of provided beverages and snacking on an exquisite buffet, home-cooked as usual by Alice's mom.

We chatted with many guests, some of whom we had met at previous parties, as upbeat, sensual music emanated from variously located speakers. The party, exuberant as usual, provided Mitch and me with a thoroughly enjoyable experience. But for us, what distinguished this particular party from others we had attended there, were two events occurring late in the evening, well into the sexual time of the party, which later proved to be of great importance.

The first event involved a swinger couple, Renee and Taylor, whom Jeff and Viv had gotten to know through several previous parties. Interestingly, Viv recently re-met Renee under entirely different circumstances; she was an outside attorney called in by Viv's company to assist in a recent court case. Realizing that they were both swinging attorneys, Viv told us that she and Renee have since become quite chummy.

Well, at the party that night, I saw Renee, a tall, beautiful young redhead, hold out her hand to Mitch and ask him, "Do you want to play?" In swinging, an invitation to "play" is an invitation for sex. Mitch, appearing rather pleasantly surprised, gave me a quick reassuring glance, and replied, "Yeah, sure!" and off they went.

The other incident of note occurred at the very end of the party. As Mitch and I were dressing in preparation to leave, Jeff and Viv told us about a "fantastically fun couple" they had just finished "playing" with.

"They are gung-ho interested in attending our Los Gatos parties," Viv beamed, showing us their business card. It read "Zillary Zahn (ZZ)." Beside his name he had penciled in "Naomi." The address and telephone number were that of a publishing company.

Because the four of us had this discussion in Denny's presence as we were about to leave the party, Denny joined in and told us that ZZ was the author of all those swing stories that were recently published. Too bad Mitch and I didn't get a chance to meet him!

The very next morning over breakfast, as Mitch and I were reading the Sunday newspaper, Mitch had a breakout idea.

FIVE

Seduction!

Part 3: Lorraine's Story
Los Gatos, CA
March 1980

"**H**EY LORI," Mitch addressed me excitedly that morning over breakfast.

"Yeah, hon," I replied.

"You know that swinger guy who writes all those stories? He can travel! A writer can write anywhere! And he will probably want to travel with us and learn about those swing parties all over the world so he can write about them. He can become the international authority on swinging!"

"Well, hon," I replied rather casually, "let's just invite him and his girlfriend to join us on our upcoming trip and see how it works out."

"We could do that, sure. But most likely they won't be able to afford the expenses of a four-month European trip in the style we travel. But if this is the couple we want to hire, then we should go ahead with our usual background checks and hiring procedures so that everything will be in place when the time comes. I say let's move forward with the process. If the results turn out negative, then there is no point in even inviting them as guests."

"Great, hon!" I said, getting a little excited myself. "Let's do it!"

Now, over coffee, we began reviewing our criteria for our ideal swinger couple. The first is a swinger couple who can travel. ZZ and Naomi seem to be good candidates for traveling, which is why we got so excited about them in the first place. But we have to verify that neither has a spouse, committed partner, or kids they can't readily leave. Also, we need to confirm that ZZ and Naomi are truly interested in traveling. Our background check should clarify these issues.

Our second set of criteria is that our couple be fun and attractive; that they present the proper image at our social gatherings; that they be of value in putting together business deals at international swing parties. Jeff and Viv have already given us some positive feedback on these issues.

The next set of criteria has to do with their social and communication skills. Do they enjoy socializing in groups both large and small? Do they mix well with others? Are they gracious and sensitive to others in a social situation? Once we see the couple in action in social settings, we should be able to answer questions such as these.

And then there are the security issues. Do either ZZ or Naomi have a history or involvement with any other tech company or affiliates, any history of working in a data-gathering capacity (spying concerns), any financial holdings that would present a conflict of interest? Our background check should soon provide these answers.

(At this point in our discussion, it was time for more coffee and Danish.)

We next came to the all-important criteria of character issues; these are very difficult to assess in a short period of time. Are ZZ and Naomi loyal, dependable, and trustworthy? Can we count on them to keep secrets about sensitive matters that they will see, experience, and learn? Do they have integrity, or will they tell all, given the right inducements? These character issues were always at the heart of our concerns whenever we looked to hire someone from the outside. Some assessment of these issues, as difficult as it may be, is absolutely essential before proceeding to employ anyone for such a sensitive position.

Lastly, there could be an issue of rapport. If, for some reason, we felt a lack of comfort with a candidate, it would probably be a signal that something was wrong. All may not be what it seems. There are many intangibles that are difficult to measure or assess. So, we have to pay attention to our feelings of the gut, as well as to our decisions of the mind.

By now, we had completely stuffed ourselves with Danish and finished up all the morning coffee. But I could tell by Mitch's intensity that our meeting would probably continue for a while.

"So, hon," I began, "how are we going to proceed?"

"Well," Mitch began, "first thing tomorrow, let's get all those background checks going. Then, we need to invite ZZ and Naomi to some social functions and swing parties. What do we have coming up?"

"Well, that's part of our problem," I replied. "We're leaving in six weeks and there are no Los Gatos parties between now and then. All we have coming up is our formal Gala Ball. We should invite them, of course, and hope they come. But even if they do, I doubt we will get to know them very well at such a huge, formal gathering as that. But, of course," I reflected, "the Gala will give us a chance to see them in action at a large social event."

"Yes!" Mitch exclaimed, rising excitedly out of his chair. "And we could have a swing party after the Gala! We 'eight' are going to be sleeping over, anyway, and some of our Los Gatos swinger friends will be attending, I'm sure! From the way Jeff and Vivian were talking, ZZ and Naomi would definitely come to a big, fancy swing party. Let's send them a special Gala-swing party invitation with a fancy RSVP card."

The rest of my Sunday was devoted to designing that special invitation with ZZ and Naomi's names engraved in gold. To entice them to come to the Gala, I referred to the party as a formal dinner gathering and swing party, stating that they should plan to stay the night.

Personally, I wasn't feeling too excited about the idea of swinging after such a big, dressy event as the Gala. But, given the importance of getting to know ZZ and Naomi rather intimately, it seemed to be the perfect activity.

Our annual Gala Ball is our company's one big extravaganza of the year. It is a formal gathering we sponsor for our executives, key employees, many business associates, and, of course, our numerous friends. Over the years, as our event has become more elegant and fashionable, we have added more and more guests to our invitation list. Attendance has swelled to where this year we are expecting over 150 guests!

For the event we obtained one of the most elegant mansions in the area for a full weekend. The stately residence is an imposing structure, part of what used to be a splendid estate. The mansion is noted for its majestic grand ballroom, ideal for our large, sprawling crowd. A graceful arched stairway leads up to an expansive balcony, which is a perfect setting with tables and chairs for those who prefer to have a full view of the party as they dine. The crowning glory is two upper floors that includes bedrooms, guest rooms, a library, and a billiard room.

Since we had reserved the mansion for the whole weekend, we "eight" planned to stay the night, making good use of the four splendid bedrooms. We each chose bedrooms in advance, with Mitch and me reserving one of the charming, beautifully-furnished main bedrooms.

RSVP cards had started coming in from the Gala Ball invitations. It was too soon to expect ZZ's RSVP, but with all the background information now in hand, Mitch and I sat down for another one of our weekend breakfast meetings.

"So, hon," I began, "how does it look?"

"Well, Lori, so far, so good." Reading mainly from the background report, Mitch continued. "He's 37, she's 30. ZZ was married for three years, divorced six years ago, no kids. His ex-wife has remarried and is out of the picture. Naomi has never married, no children. Neither seems to be seriously involved with anyone else. They see a lot of each other, but it seems to be a close friendship, not a romance. It says here he would probably jump at the chance to travel abroad."

Mitch went on, "Naomi has a job at the publishing company, but does not appear to be devoted to it. Given the very large salary we're prepared to offer her, I see no problem. Neither of them has high-tech involvements or conflicting investments of any kind, so they are as clean as can be."

"Oh, wonderful!" I sighed. "It sounds like they should be coming to the Gala unless they have other commitments on that day. In that case, I thought we might need to get Alice and Denny involved somehow."

"Great backup, Lori, good idea. But first, let's see how it goes."

That whole week went by with me checking each day for that "special" RSVP; on Friday, there it was. They're coming! That day, February 29, 1980, was a very special day, of course; it was Leap Day. Mitch and I celebrated by going into "the City" (as the city limits of San Francisco are referred to), enjoying its offerings like a couple of tourists.

We started with the late afternoon tea dance at the hotel where we had met seven years prior, then we strolled over to one of the City's great seafood restaurants for one of their famous dinners. Not to be outdone by tourists, we took a couple of cable cars, hopping off at the wharf to indulge in Irish coffees at the café where history has it that Irish coffee was first introduced to the United States.

We had a great night out in the City, the kind you need every once in a while to remind yourself why you work so hard. And after the drive home, we continued the romantic evening in our own home in our own bed. It was marvelous!

Of course, that Sunday morning over breakfast, we had our usual weekend meeting. The Gala was now less than two weeks away. I began our discussion.

"Hey, hon, that swing-party idea was just perfect for enticing ZZ and Naomi to the Gala." Mitch was nodding in agreement. "But now that we know they're coming, I think we should revise the plan to just sleepovers."

"Really! Why's that?" Mitch jumped in.

I continued, "A swing party is not going to tell us anything we don't know already. We had our swing party, only we ourselves didn't participate. Viv and Jeff did at Alice and Denny's, and they gave us a full report. Now, we need to go beyond the swing party. We are going to need to assess ZZ and Naomi's character: their loyalty, dependability, and trustworthiness. I think you and I are going to have to spend the whole night with them."

"Exactly what I was thinking," Mitch chimed in. "We can all sit around the table and talk till all hours of the morning — really get inside their heads."

"Well, what I was thinking, really, is that we need to get inside their hearts; we need to get a sense of their emotions, their feelings. I'm suggesting I sleep with ZZ, you sleep with Naomi."

"Really!" Mitch exclaimed in utter surprise and disbelief. But he only needed a quick second before he was nodding his head in agreement. Of course that had to be the way.

So that was our plan. But that evening, when I discussed it with Viv, she didn't think Mitch should plan on sleeping with Naomi, whom he hadn't met yet.

"Why not, Viv?" I inquired.

Viv replied, "How do we know Naomi is going to want to spend the night with Mitch? We know ZZ is not going to kick you out of bed, but we don't know about Naomi and Mitch. And aren't you going to offer her a huge financial incentive to leave her present job?"

"Yes, we will," I agreed, "About a $100,000 annual contract; the same for ZZ."

Viv continued. "Well, usually a woman would not want to feel that she landed a big job right after she slept with the boss. And even though in this situation that would not be the case, she would probably always believe that it was."

"You're right, Viv, I never thought of that. Any suggestions?" I asked.

Viv continued, "Why don't we invite Renee and Taylor as a sixth couple to sleep over? We do have two guest bedrooms. We'll just tell them we're having a sleepover swing party. Then you sleep with ZZ as planned. Mitch can sleep with Renee; they hit it off so well at Alice and Denny's party a couple of weeks back, we know that's a 'go.' Then, I'll sleep with Taylor," she chuckled. (I knew she liked the idea of sleeping with Taylor.) "And then," she went on, "Jeff can rendezvous again with Naomi and really get to know her. He can give you a full report in the morning."

"Viv, I like it!" I replied enthusiastically.

That night, listening to my account of Viv's proposal, Mitch nodded in agreement.

"Oh, I think it's great!" he exclaimed excitedly. So with less than two weeks left before the March 15th Gala, everything seemed to be in place.

Those two weeks passed quickly. Suddenly the day arrived and by mid-afternoon, we "eight" are all at our rented weekend mansion. The grounds are simply breathtaking, a sweeping panorama of various shapes, colors, and hues; a visual symphony for us to leisurely enjoy in tomorrow's sunshine. But for today, there is much on our minds. In a few hours, as darkness approaches, the first guests will be arriving.

Ed and Dianne, one of the four host couples for the Gala, look elegantly handsome. I know they are happy not to be participating in any of our nighttime fun and games. They have been working hard and are looking forward to just luxuriating in their special bedroom together. (I believe they are probably there right now, enjoying it to the fullest.) Likewise for Bert and Marge. But Mitch and I and Jeff and Viv have our two new couples to entertain. We are enjoying all the intrigue.

The idea of all these sexy sleeping arrangements has certainly added a lot of spice to this event, which is usually more dutiful than fun. I, of course, am anxious to see my chosen bedroom again, not having seen it since we rented this mansion months ago. So through the ballroom I go, up the stairs to the upper floors.

The bedroom is even more breathtaking than I remembered it. But all this beauty will go unappreciated in the dark hours; ZZ and I will just have to have a long, lazy morning after to take it all in.

The arrangement is for Mitch to call me in the morning after talking with Jeff, who will be with Naomi. If Mitch says it's a go, and I say it's a go, then ZZ and I will have plenty to talk about as we watch the sunlight filtering through the windows while nature's clock ticks the hours away. I'm getting goosebumps just thinking about it.

Now, standing here, reflecting that I will be returning to this bedroom in a few hours to "freshen it up," I give the room quick admiring glances in all directions before exiting and descending the stairs to the main ballroom.

Soon the light of the late afternoon begins to darken. The "six" look very special. I don't think I have ever seen all of them together looking so beautiful. Ed and Dianne are especially glamorous in their roles as host and hostess. Life has been good to us "eight;" it is a very special time when we can all get together and have so much fun.

The ballroom has now come alive with waiters and waitresses scurrying about, plates clanging, champagne corks popping, and delicacies sizzling. And soon the first guests are arriving; it's time to take up my position at the front door, assisting Dianne and Ed in greeting people, hoping that in the process I will be meeting ZZ and Naomi.

After a half hour of handshakes, kisses, chatter, and smiles, Ed and Dianne check off ZZ and Naomi's names. Now, standing before me is the couple over which so much discussion has taken place and so many plans have been made; the couple whose presence we hope will be of great assistance in the transaction of future business negotiations.

The first thing I notice about ZZ is his attentive, sparkly eyes and broad ingratiating smile. I am attracted to him immediately before he says a word, because he is already engaging me. And Naomi is just darling: fluffy dark blond hair, a heart-shaped face with creamy complexion, and such a soft, sexy voice, I could melt.

As Dianne introduces me to them, I can't help drifting into daydreams about traveling with them, city to city, hotel to hotel, party to party. After all, they will be our traveling partners, dinner partners, party partners. Yes, I can see it. And it looks very good. I am truly dazzled. But is it them or just hopeful imagination about them for the past four weeks? This evening will tell.

I take each by the arm and lead them into the ballroom. It is a beautiful gathering. Food and beverages are being served, the jazz pianist is playing, the quartet is setting up, a few couples are dancing and others are just milling about, engaged in one party conversation after another.

Catching a glimpse of Mitch in the crowd, I can't help but notice a tall red-headed woman approaching him, making eyes, acting sexy, all smiles. Wow! It's Renee, Viv's attorney-swinger friend whom we invited along with Taylor for our special nighttime activities. She is giving Mitch a quick reminder of who she is, having only met him five weeks ago at Alice and Denny's. Those two should be seeing a lot of each other this evening.

Now, glancing in another direction, there is ZZ. He seems to be alone at the moment as he charts his way through the noisy crowd. Holding a drink in one hand and shaking hands with his other, he is smiling, laughing, chatting with people he's most likely never met before. I am impressed to see how he artfully speaks to each group for the appropriate amount of time before moving on. I'm wondering if Mitch happens to be watching this impressive display.

Looking over in Mitch's direction, there is Renee, still with him, now with her arms draped all over him. What is with this woman? Oh, she's making a catch, that one! Why all this possessiveness? Perhaps she is making a statement right now as to the man she wants to be with for the night. Good thing we planned it that way!

Time for Mitch and the others to meet ZZ and Naomi. Not having any success in spotting Naomi in the crowd, we meet with ZZ alone. We all chat, mainly about ZZ's writings and his recently-published swing stories. Then, of course, we bring up Mitch's "jeans" business and the tech industry. ZZ is very animated and engaging, in contrast to Renee, that "tall glass of tomato juice" at Mitch's side, who never says a word.

Mitch puts on a subtle, yet important, display at the introductions. He, in essence, signals to ZZ that "my wife is available; I'm busy with this other woman!" Sensitive guys, Mitch says, are usually reluctant to show much interest in a married woman attending a party with her husband, unless they know directly from him that it's okay. By his actions with Renee, Mitch gives ZZ that essential okay.

After we disperse, I resume my greeting responsibilities, feeling that it is of great importance to personally welcome every guest to the party. This, of course, prevents me from much conversation with ZZ during the Gala hours. I will have to wait for our post-Gala activities before I can devote my full attention to him.

I now realize my prior error in misleading ZZ and Naomi that this large gathering would become a swing party. I inadvertently led them to believe that guests would be open to meeting others in a much more personal way than just polite social conversation. That would account for ZZ and Naomi going off in different directions. Flirting here could be fun, but nearly everyone here is associated with Mitch and me and our companies in some capacity. Furthermore, since this gathering is more of a professional one than a social one, ZZ and Naomi could start to feel out of place.

So far, ZZ seems to be handling all the social aspects beautifully. And now, having just spotted Naomi, I see she, too, is doing just fine, holding court with a slew of film and video executives, five other couples standing in a semicircle around her. I think she has them hypnotized with those big blue eyes, soft sensuous smile, and of course that sweet, sexy voice. As Mitch and I and the "others" approach her, we can abundantly appreciate how her radiant charm and captivating warmth have the film people so entranced.

We interrupt her "audition" so that we can meet with her and chat. (Mitch, as impressed with her as he is with ZZ, whispers to me that he hopes all this is not just some kind of one-act show they put on for parties, that their attitude is genuine and enduring.) They both seem so absolutely perfect, so ideally cast for the parts we have in mind for them; all the more reason why our sleepovers are so vital in our decision to hire them.

Now that we "eight" have chatted with each of them, we feel all is in place for the afterparty activities. For the next hour or so, I am able to just relax and get completely caught up in our Gala party, dancing to the music of our jazz band, meeting and chatting with guests, and appreciating the wonderful party we "eight" have put together. Everyone seems to be having such a great time, I am feeling immensely satisfied!

Eventually, the splendid party starts to unwind. I am hoping now to say farewell to each and every guest, just as I greeted them upon arriving. As the party dwindles to a very few guests, I am satisfied that I have finished my responsibilities as far as the Gala is concerned. My thoughts shift to our plans for the afterparty. I realize the time has come to revisit my special bedroom and prepare for our nighttime activities.

Without much notice by the few remaining guests, I depart the ballroom, ascending the stairway to the balcony and the upper floors. Slowly strolling down the hallway to my bedroom, I say to myself, "The next time will be with ZZ!"

Upon entering my bedroom, I am at first taken aback because the room has become so dark, its beauty is completely hidden. The room lights restore much of its radiance, but its magnificence certainly will not be evident again until morning.

The time to reflect is over; the time to act is now. I close the drapes, fluff the pillows, turn down the bedspread and sheets, turn on the stereo, and go about the room freshening everything. Satisfied that all is in order, I go to the door and turn off the lights. In the dark I pause: I have a look, a listen, and a sniff. All seems perfect.

I leave the room and step out into the hallway, closing the door behind me, I tell myself again: "Next time with ZZ!" I am very excited; this is definitely fun!

Now the time has come for our post-Gala plans to unfold. Comforted that all is going well, I walk down the upper staircase onto the balcony. There are still a few guests remaining.

Upon seeing me on the balcony, Mitch gives me a nod and then lowers the house lights, encouraging the last guests to depart. When they are gone, Mitch lowers the lights still further until we are in near darkness. Safety lights glow on the balcony, in the grand arched stairway, and in key spots around the main ballroom. I count all present: eleven on the ballroom floor and, of course, me on the balcony. Now what? ZZ is walking around looking very confused.

Mitch gets the ball rolling. He starts stripping off his clothes, encouraging everyone else to do likewise; after all, this is to be a swing party! Viv gives me a quick look as she strips, grabbing Taylor by the hand as he stumbles all over his clothes. Viv gathers up her garments in a big ball, quickly helping Taylor to do the same, and up the arched stairway they go, a comical looking nude pair with humongous bundles of clothes.

Viv wants to capture Taylor, of course, for (unknowingly) he is her partner for the night. Equally important is preventing him from any possible hookup with Naomi. She must be free to choose Jeff. Now Mitch takes charge again. He motions to ZZ to strip down. "We're finally getting to the fun part! Get naked and find yourself a woman," he says, with Renee tightly affixed to his arm. Again the message: "My wife is available!"

Next, Mitch ushers everyone up the grand arched stairway: he with Renee, Jeff now with Naomi, and Dianne with Ed, happily heading for "heaven in their bedroom suite." That leaves all accounted for except for ZZ, who is still completely dressed in the main ballroom. Bert and Marge, completely naked in the main ballroom, keep a watchful eye on ZZ, who hasn't yet acted in any way that commits him to our grand scheme. He's not thinking of leaving, is he? No, he can't leave Naomi 50 miles from home!

Bert and Marge now swing into action as only they can, apparently preparing to put on some kind of show for ZZ. There is Marge, sitting on a bar stool in a spotlight, her legs parted; there is Bert sitting in a chair facing her. They are such exhibitionists, and ZZ is fully cooperating as the voyeur. Bert now begins to nestle his head between Marge's legs, with his big flops of hair shaking about as he buries his head deep between her thighs.

Now all is in place. When the "peep show" is over, when the moment is right, before ZZ even has a chance to think about it, I will have to "capture" him. I will make my grand entrance by stepping right into the balcony spotlight.

The show is still going on. I am ready and waiting. Marge is beginning to go into orgasm! What an extravaganza!

The moment is approaching. The exhibition is ending; ZZ is just staring into space.

Now! The time is right. I step into the spotlight. He has to see me!

I rustle my dress. I hear ZZ shout, "Lorraine!"

I pretend not to notice.

"I want you!" he shouts.

He is captured! He's mine! I turn to recognize him. I smile and I giggle. "Well," I say, "Come get me!"

And he does just that. He comes swooping up the staircase and literally sweeps me off my feet, gliding his hands up my legs, under my skirt, up my thighs to my butt, which is tingling with pleasure.

"I've got you, Miss Lorraine!" he laughs triumphantly.

"And so you do, Mr. Zahn!" I reply with glee.

Oh, he is very romantic. This is definitely fun. He knows how to make the most of the moment. There isn't anything awkward about him. He is very, very appealing.

"Come on," I whisper, as I take him by the hand and lead him up another staircase and down the hall. We enter the dark palatial bedroom. I close the door. He takes me into his arms and kisses me. I sigh. . . the exciting, romantic night has begun.

SIX

International Parties

Part 4: Lorraine's Story (as taken from her diary)
Los Angeles and Paris
April 1980

ZZ's Comment: And so, in March 1980, Naomi and I were hired to travel with Mitch and Lorraine. Now, six months later, I asked Lorraine to give me an account for my book of what had transpired during this time, as she saw it.

IN THE SPRING of 1980, after two years of searching for the ideal swinger couple to replace Ed and Dianne on our international business ventures, Mitch and I hired ZZ, a charming, engaging writer, and his friend Naomi, an alluring, sensual artist.

Not being well-versed in either business or finance, ZZ and Naomi were clearly surprised to be offered lucrative contracts with us.

"To do what?" they asked.

"To just be yourselves," we replied. Mitch continued, "Over the course of the next few months in Paris, we four will be meeting bankers, real estate developers, venture capitalists, and the like. We will need to establish good working relationships with them so we can buy or lease land for our new scientific laboratories and obtain the requisite financing for our huge, innovative projects. You will see how it all works out as the various dinners, banquets and swing parties unfold. In the fall, we will be attending scientific conferences. For business and social purposes, your attendance and participation in them will be vitally important."

For Mitch and me, the prospect of traveling with such a young dynamic couple, more of our children's generation than ours, seemed fresh and exciting. ZZ, of course, was a major find: a swinger and writer, who, by traveling with us and attending many international swing parties, could amass enough data, interviews and anecdotes to write a book establishing himself as the international authority on swinging.

But Naomi was the big surprise, an absolutely fascinating person. She had such effervescence and was completely devoid of the pretentiousness and trappings that often plague such appealing personalities. And there was something intriguing about the way she spoke — full, rich voice, lips contorting in all kinds of sexual ways when she formed her words, dimples deepening on her cheeks, and eyes sparkling.

The plan was for the four of us to begin our travels in Los Angeles, where Mitch and I had some meetings to attend, key people to see, and a mound of business details to take care of before embarking on our four-month trip abroad. From L.A., our plan was to fly to New York and board one of the new transatlantic cruise ships to Paris. On the cruise we four could leisurely — and in splendid comfort — discuss the nature of ZZ's and Naomi's contributions to establishing our new Parisian office as a key European center of high-technology enterprise.

As per our arrangements and instructions, Naomi and ZZ arrived in Los Angeles on Thursday, April 3, and checked into the luxury suite adjoining ours. At our request, they joined us and three other couples for a business dinner that night, in part so our foursome could develop the rapport we hoped would flow into easy repartee at our business parties abroad, which would begin in just three weeks' time.

We introduced ZZ as a writer traveling with us to begin his work on an international travel book. Naomi was introduced as a sketch artist, hoping to capture the essence of magnificent, romantic old-style European structures, walkways and gardens.

Everything went quite well on this "practice" dinner, except by the evening's end it was plain to see that the three businessmen at our table were all gaga over Naomi. I socialized with the wives somewhat, hoping to distract them from their husbands' obtrusive behavior. At future events, Naomi might have to tone down her natural exuberance.

The next evening at another practice dinner party, our new companions did very well; their charming presence and lively discussion added a tangy spice to the occasion. At the dinner's end after our guest couples had left, Naomi boldly announced, "I am already hired, but I haven't had my overnight interview with Mitch!" Looking directly at ZZ, she quipped, "You already slept with your boss, but I haven't slept with mine yet!"

I rather think that ZZ had prearranged this proposition with Naomi, knowing now that Mitch and I do not date and we do not do overnights — unless, of course, we are doing interviews! While I don't generally want to do overnights, on this particular occasion, I felt immensely gratified, nourished by ZZ's desire for me.

And so, while Naomi got her wish — a whole night with my husband — I enjoyed another splendid night with ZZ, this time with no ulterior motive in mind. It was a night of tenderness, dreaminess, a new beginning.

As we parted the next morning, ZZ said he understood he could not expect future overnights with me, but hoped that he could establish the same kind of sexual friendship he enjoyed with Naomi.

I assured him of that.

I had come to realize that these overnights with ZZ were expanding experiences, connecting me more personally with the younger generation. I did not really consider ZZ my peer, lacking 10 years' existence in this world, as well as knowledge and experience in finance and technology. But I did enjoy him very much as a somewhat romantic figure. He had been quite amorous in fact, and I am not sure why. Perhaps he did not think of me as a peer either, realizing his inexperience in the things that drive me. Or maybe he was just enjoying the fun of being taken along on this ride. After all, if nothing else, he was going to have the opportunity to become the international authority on swinging.

In any case, I developed a certain security with ZZ, an affirmation, perhaps, that I am still sexually attractive to younger men. I felt deep within me that ZZ was sincere and completely trustworthy, a true friend. And I valued that. Likewise, Mitch developed very positive feelings toward Naomi; he felt she was an unpretentious, genuine person with a sparkle and glow.

Everything seemed to be going so well.

But the next morning, Mitch and I heard, "Wake up, wake up!" Naomi's unmistakable voice came booming into our sleeping ears. "Wake up! Wake up! I have been offered $1 million! — $1 million!"

And there standing before us at our bedside were Naomi and ZZ. "I could make as much as million dollars!" Naomi screamed with excitement.

Apparently, Naomi had just met with two men in the lobby she had recognized as part of the group of video executives who had attended our Gala three weeks prior. The executives had just flown down from San Francisco, Naomi reported, specifically to present her with a big contract. Depending on sales, rentals, and other specific criteria, Naomi could earn as much as $1 million for modeling, performing and doing voiceovers in their video and film productions; $100,000 was guaranteed.

"They want me to start working for them right away!" Naomi boomed.

They requested, she said, that we meet with them over Sunday brunch here at the hotel, whereupon they could formally present their offer.

This all seems rather silly, I thought to myself. Why are Naomi and ZZ dragging us down to the lobby so early in the day? This must be some kind of hoax. But to accommodate Naomi's request, Mitch and I dressed and proceeded downstairs for Sunday brunch. Meeting ZZ and Naomi in the lobby, we entered the hotel restaurant.

And there they were, the two video executives who had attended the Gala, just as Naomi had described.

Mitch was incensed. "Victor! Charles! What are you guys doing here?" he demanded.

"Excuse us," one of the men began very humbly, "but our company needs to hire Naomi. We understand you have her under contract. That's why we've come here today to discuss the whole matter with you and Lorraine. We would like you to release Naomi from her contract so she can be free to sign with us. We desperately need her to begin shooting film for us starting next week."

Why did they specifically need Naomi? I wondered. But there we were, the six of us, now seated in the restaurant to discuss all these details over brunch. As Naomi had proclaimed, the video execs had a $1 million contract for her plus a cashier's check for $100,000 that she would receive upon signing her contract. Thus, with the stroke of her pen, Naomi could earn instantly what Mitch and I were going to pay her for the entire year.

I kept thinking this had to be some kind of ploy, but the executives assured us that the contract was legitimate. They suggested our legal department examine their document for authenticity and a clear understanding of the terms. Mitch assured them that we would. The execs requested that we six meet here again the next day, Monday, over a late lunch to discuss any questions about Naomi's contract. They asked that Naomi give them a definitive answer at that time, and expressed their hope that she would begin her new job the following week. And with that, the executives excused themselves and departed.

Naomi was in a state of delirious pleasure. "Three weeks ago I was just a sketch artist. Now, everyone is throwing money at me!"

Mitch believed in the probable legitimacy of the contract, knowing the two executives who brought it. He suggested that Naomi and ZZ take this offer seriously and meet with us at our suite later in the afternoon. Then, as top priority, Mitch arranged to have a photocopy of the contract flown up to our San Francisco legal office that very afternoon so that our attorneys could look at it first thing in the morning.

By the way, at our office we can send (almost instantaneously) a copy of a document to another office far away. This is called sending a facsimile ("looks alike"). You put the original document in a large machine that looks like a copy machine, and out comes a copy at a designated machine anywhere in the world! Facsimile is usually abbreviated *facs* or *fax*. Mitch says that 20 or 30 years from now, everyone will be able to fax each other without all these big office machines. But for now, at a hotel on a Sunday, the best we could do was to airmail the document.

Later in the day, Mitch and I assured ZZ that we still wanted him to travel with us, but we were prepared to release them both in case they wanted to stay together if Naomi accepted the offer.

First thing the next morning, Mitch called our lawyers in San Francisco. Sure enough, the contract seemed perfectly legitimate and could offer Naomi a very good performing opportunity. When Mitch called the film and video office in San Francisco to speak to the authorization officer, he was told that the contract offer had come directly from Sidney Colsome, the CEO of the parent company in New York. Realizing that this was probably the same Sidney Colsome whom he had worked with and highly regarded some years ago in Silicon Valley, Mitch phoned him and talked with him at great length.

"Why was Naomi offered such a huge contract?" Mitch asked Colsome.

"To finish projects that had been started and needed that special person to model, act and perform," he replied.

"And why is Naomi that special person when there are so many well-trained and highly-qualified actresses out there?"

Colsome went on, "Let's just say that we recognize in Naomi some exceptional qualities, and everyone, including Naomi, is going to cash in."

"And why so much money?" Mitch inquired, to which Colsome replied, "This $1 million is in lieu of any other financial considerations. Naomi will receive no royalties for her work during this one-year period, no bonuses, and no renegotiation of her contract. This offer is a very fair amount. We expect to make big, big money on these film productions. If things go the way we anticipate, we will probably have to pay her much more the following year just to keep her."

He paused and went on, "Look, we need Naomi right away. We don't have time to negotiate the specific terms of her contract, or the amount of her annual compensation. You are offering her travel, parties, companionship and excitement. We are offering her a career opportunity and the possibility of making as much $1 million. We need her right away, so we want her to make a clear, decisive choice."

As a result of this conversation, Mitch suggested that Naomi accept the offer. Having developed a more complete understanding of her interests and passions in the last few days, he felt her heart was in modeling and performing. He assured her; "I talked with Colsome for some time. I know him and think he's trustworthy. He assured me you would benefit professionally as well as financially. He has big plans for you!"

As for ZZ, Mitch advised him that traveling with us was going to be in his best professional interest. He stood to write a definitive book and become an authority on international swinging. In agreement with Mitch's assessments, ZZ declared he would travel with us, and Naomi declared she would take the film and modeling position.

As agreed, that Monday afternoon we all met again at the hotel restaurant for the contract signing. And, sure enough, Naomi was presented with a cashier's check for $100,000, which she promptly deposited into her bank account at a nearby branch.

Within hours she was packed, picked up by an airport limo, and was gone.

Gone was that sparkly personality that was so engaging; gone was the sound of that sexy voice that was uniquely Naomi; and gone, too, was the pervasive festive atmosphere of our first few days together. Now all was somber. It was as if she died; we felt a terrible loss. Perhaps the people at the video firm really knew what they were doing in pursuing Naomi. When we sought out ZZ, we fortuitously obtained Naomi as well. How would we ever replace her now, we wondered?

The three of us moped around the rest of the day and into the evening.

We discussed how, hopefully, once settled in Paris, ZZ might meet desirable English-speaking swingers at the Paris parties, and that eventually, one of them might ease into Naomi's position. However, we doubted that anyone would be so well-suited to take her place. But until that time, we would have to operate as a trio with ZZ's swing party date arranged from week to week.

That evening I decided to do what I normally do when I feel down and need some ideas: I phoned Vivian in Los Gatos.

Vivian was her usual vivacious self, telling me about a dance and a few swing parties she and Jeff had attended. And I, of course, discussed our days in L.A., all the fun stuff with ZZ and Naomi, and her contract offer and departure.

As usual, Vivian had some very constructive ideas. She mentioned that her attorney friend, the tall red-headed Renee who had spent the night with Mitch at the Gala, was going to be in Paris for the next few months. Apparently, Renee was on leave from her job and, as a result, had agreed to switch apartments with her sister Monique in Paris. Monique, it turns out, had obtained this Parisian apartment in her divorce settlement from a French doctor. So, while Monique visited San Francisco, Renee was going to be in Paris. Viv gave me Renee's phone number in San Francisco and suggested we call her right away. "You might even be able to catch her in time for her to join you on your cruise!" Viv exclaimed.

I was grateful for the information but thought to myself, *I don't want to go on a cruise with that woman who was draped all over Mitch at the Gala and then slept with him while I slept with ZZ. I have never even had a conversation with her.* Neither had ZZ, as he later revealed to me.

And Mitch was reluctant to accept Renee without a full background check. He also thought it curious that after two years of an unsuccessful search for an acceptable couple, one woman was readily available to replace another. But he was willing to consider her now for swing parties. After all, she had passed her "overnight interview"!

Mitch was soon on the phone to Renee in San Francisco, telling her personally how delighted we were to hear that she would be in Paris while we were there. He extended an invitation for her to join us for upcoming Parisian social and swing parties, beginning with a very upscale dinner-dance-swing party at Chaillot Gardens just outside Paris, on the last Saturday of the month. Renee accepted the invitation, giving Mitch her travel plans, her Parisian address, and her telephone number there.

So, we felt we had a plan. We would have to find a fourth person soon, because swing parties are always couples-only to maintain gender balance. But until then, hopefully, Renee could fill in and possibly even assist us in finding that fourth.

Without Naomi, we decided to cancel our cruise and chose instead to enjoy a few extra days in New York before flying to Paris. Then, after experiencing some of the delights of the city and catching up with my daughter, Jasmine, we called Renee at her Paris number, and moved our dinner-dance date at Chaillot Gardens up by a week. We told her all about the setting, what to wear, and what to expect. She responded graciously, telling us how excited she was to be invited; as a swinger, she had heard so much about it.

Chaillot (pronounced "shy-yo") Gardens, a large private estate about 15 miles outside of Paris, is one of the most exceptional sites in the world for elegant dinner-dance-swing parties. The sprawling, two-story grand villa, enhanced now to a magnificence and beauty exceeding the original, holds weekly, couples-only, dinner-dance-swing parties for its all-male membership along with their wives or companions.

Some years back, the governing board created the exclusive businessman's club that exists today, and subsequently decided to allocate resources to bring their vision of these elegant parties to fruition. Rather than try to duplicate the facilities and functions readily available at other gentlemen's clubs, the directors and members dedicated much of their resources to the creation of fantasy parties, with swinging and overnights as possible optional features near the end of the dinner-dances. The Villa was designed to encourage the progression of drinking to eating to dancing to swinging.

The Villa is able to host these extravagant, lavish parties because it has the facilities to do so. The main entrance opens into a large yet cozy Art Deco cocktail lounge; an exquisitely designed, well-appointed, spacious dining room; an intimate, romantic dance floor beckoning couples to the swing area; and the swing area itself on the entire upper floor. This floor consists of plush, decorative bedrooms, numerous bathrooms and showers, a hospitality room for swinging couples, and an eye-dazzling group room highlighted by wall-to-wall mirrors, ceiling mirrors, and a mattressed floor.

I was not interested in participating in group activities in those days, as I preferred my sexual interactions to be more personal. But I very much enjoyed watching all those sensuous bodies writhing in motion. Mitch was just the opposite. He viewed swinging as pure sexual fun, and didn't particularly care who he was with. For him, the group room was perfect for anonymous sex.

One of the most important features of the Villa — the one that distinguishes Chaillot Gardens from most other fancy swing facilities — are the state-of-the-art lockers and dressing rooms where swingers can securely lock up their fine clothes and valuables. In addition, the Villa provides fluffy robes to wear in the swing area, full-length zip-up bags in which clothes and valuables can be placed, and sweats to wear for the drive home, so people do not need to redress. The Villa strives to provide "all that you can imagine" for a fantasy experience.

Oddly enough, the feature that has most enhanced the dinner-dance attendance over the years is not swinging, but the opportunities presented by assembling business-oriented individuals from so many different parts of the world in a friendly, relaxed atmosphere. Many local businessmen attend as well — in fact, quite regularly. It is what they do on a Saturday night: take their wives or companions to dinner at the club, where they know they will get excellent service, fine cuisine, and colleagues to mingle with.

When Mitch and I began our international travels back in 1975, often with our business companions Ed and Dianne, we were thrilled to be introduced to Chaillot Gardens. Mitch was so impressed by the Villa operation and the quality of output per dollar input that he joined the club immediately, becoming quite active in the recruitment of international businessmen. In appreciation of his hard work, last year Mitch was elected to a directorship of the Gardens.

It was to this site, on Saturday, April 19, 1980, that Mitch and I brought ZZ and Renee, beginning our evening at the entrance of the large Art Deco cocktail lounge. We arrived early in order to be conspicuously displayed at a desirable table. We were dressed fashionably, yet sexually bold, advertising to the oncoming crowd that we four were ready to do business and ready to swing. Antoine, the maître d', greeted us gracefully, "Good evening, Mr. and Mrs. Hesten. Welcome back to Chaillot Gardens. It is our pleasure to be of service."

"Thank you, Antoine," Mitch replied as he gestured toward ZZ and Renee, introducing them as his guests.

"Very pleased to meet you both," Antoine acknowledged, handing Mitch what appeared to be the wine list, but which was actually the evening's dinner reservation list.

"Thank you, Antoine. Any recommendations?"

"Well, sir," Antoine continued, now in very low voice, "I would highly recommend Monsieur Alvin Lepic. He is relatively new to the club; he and his wife have been here on several occasions during your absence. He is a local landowner and real estate developer. I think the two of you could do business together. He and his wife are dining alone tonight and could be inclined to join you."

"Yes, I know of him. That sounds perfect. Could you ask the

gentleman and his wife if they would like to join the four of us for dinner?"

"Indeed I will, sir."

The maître d' walked across the lounge floor past many tables before arriving at a suave, very handsomely-dressed couple, perhaps slightly older than us. We could see the maître d' discretely locating us for the Lepics. I'm sure we presented an inviting visual image: I, looking very elegant, Mitch and ZZ very dapper, and Renee very sexual, bursting out of her tight, sheer white blouse, her breasts perfectly accented by a fashionable dangling pendent. The vision presented to the Lepics was apparently stimulating enough and, looking our way, they nodded in the affirmative.

Shortly thereafter, the large, decorative doors at the far end of the lounge swung open, revealing the well-lit, ornate, beautifully-appointed dining room. The staff began seating guests according to the advance seating plan, which was devised and continually modified by the maître d'. After the four of us had been seated rather quickly, Renee asked Mitch if she might approach Monsieur and Madame Lepic, who were waiting in the lounge, to personally escort them to our table.

"Yes, splendid," Mitch replied, approvingly eyeing Renee's sexy appearance and deep cleavage.

So off she slinked, wriggling her way in her tight skirt, her bra-less boobs bouncing along in her nearly see-through blouse. Having arrived at the Lepics' table, she confidently displayed herself and then cunningly leaned forward just enough to give M. Lepic a quick glance down her blouse to admire her voluptuous breasts. Renee said something to the Lepics, probably in French, that had them both nodding and laughing. And then with the monsieur on one arm and the madame on the other, Renee led them back through the lounge into the dining room and to our table.

The Lepics seemed very pleased to be escorted by the beautiful young redhead. After introductions and exchanges of pleasantries, we six sat relaxing with a few selected wines. I had to admire Renee's initiative and foxy behavior. She was winning me over.

During dinner, Mitch briefly discussed our technology companies, mentioning that we were in the market for a possible suburban site for a state-of-the-art scientific laboratory to supplement the fine but aging laboratory we already had in Paris. Then, having concluded company business, Mitch shifted topics, expecting that Lepic would subsequently contact us with several offers to consider; then negotiations could begin. Renee did not contribute much to the conversation, but she was visually spectacular. M. Lepic could hardly take his eyes off Renee's nipples protruding through her sheer white blouse. And all the while, Madame Lepic sat quietly smiling, looking adoringly at ZZ.

Dancing had soon begun the next room and the Lepics were rather insistent that we join them. And so the six of us made our way through the restaurant and onto the dance floor — Mitch with me, ZZ with Renee, and the Lepics with one another.

It was not long before M. Lepic wanted to dance with Renee, and the madame with ZZ. And so they did for quite some time. Once again, Renee took the initiative, boldly asking M. Lepic if he wanted to go "play" in the adjacent swing area.

"In there?" inquired a totally surprised Lepic, pointing to the couples-only swing entrance.

"Uh huh," replied Renee, seductively smiling, nodding in the affirmative as she held out her hand to him.

Lepic, apparently startled by the invitation, jumped at the opportunity. "Ah, bien sur!" (of course), shouted Lepic, momentarily forgetting his English.

Off they went across the dance floor into the vast swing part of the villa. That left Madame Lepic looking expectantly at ZZ, who, taking his cue, took her by the hand and escorted her to the swing entrance.

Having learned during the course of dinner conversation that the Lepics would not be staying the night as we were, I was now wondering just how we four might pair up for the night. Was Renee finally going to give ZZ some attention, possibly spending the night with him? Or was Renee going to once again cling to Mitch like she did at the Gala?

As for me, I was receptive to the possibility of having another night with ZZ. But where was he? He was off screwing Madame Lepic!

In point of fact, I did feel somewhat annoyed. Mme Lepic was a woman in my age range and ZZ was interested in her! I would not have cared if ZZ went off with Renee or some other young woman. That I could understand. But this woman was probably older than I was!

I felt sure ZZ was making the madame very happy, and that was the important point to keep in mind. It was probably the first time that either Lepic had been in the swing area.

Now it was time for Mitch and me to join the others. Having changed our clothes into the Villa robes, we entered the hospitality suite, where swingers generally congregate after a sexual encounter, eyeing one another, drinking coffee, eating pastries, making small talk, and seeking that magical mutual attraction that could possibly lead to another sexual experience. And it is here that Mitch and I ate and drank, chatted and watched, awaiting the return of the Lepics.

And soon they did: first Renee and a wheezing Lepic, then ZZ and a smiling madame. The Lepics thanked us profusely for their memorable evening, departing to the dressing rooms in preparation for their drive home.

Quickly, Renee grabbed Mitch's hand, coaxing, "C'mon, play now and talk later," she declared, leading him to an area where swingers were coming and going, leaving me alone with ZZ, apparently for the night. I was happy with the circumstances, but I didn't want this pattern to continue. For seven years I had Mitch at my side at night, and that's the way I wanted it. It was cozy and reassuring. Spending the night with a certified romantic stranger was fun at the Gala, but ZZ was no longer a stranger, although he remained thoroughly romantic. I think that's just his nature.

Now, reminiscent of Gala night, I took ZZ by the hand and led him up a stairway towards one of my favorite bedrooms.

"Are you leading me on again?" ZZ asked.

"Uh huh," I replied in my best Renee imitation.

And so ZZ and I enjoyed another overnight together, this one full of playfulness and coziness. ZZ and I had now formed a close sexual friendship. But it was not in any way a threat to my marriage, and Mitch understood that. Of course, there was no way that ZZ would be interested in me, either, other than as a sexual friend.

But what about Renee and Mitch? Were they developing any kind of special friendship? I didn't think so. Why did Renee feel it was necessary to capture Mitch for another night? Didn't she think that her first overnight interview at the Gala was sufficient? Just why did this young, beautiful woman want to spend so much time with Mitch, a married man 20 years her senior? I felt Mitch must be wondering the same thing.

That next evening when Mitch and I were alone together, we discussed Renee's viability as our fourth. I had mixed feelings about her; my gut reaction was that I just didn't trust her. But her performance at the party was outstanding.

Mitch agreed. "The way she dressed, her attitude, her initiatives were all perfect. And did you notice how she charmed the Lepics from the very first moment she walked over to their table? I would say her French is even better than fluent; she is obviously at ease with French ways and customs and very attuned to cultural nuances. Did you notice how she introduced us? Very French. She had them in her pocket from the very moment she met them and got them laughing. All that sex stuff afterward was really unnecessary, as far as business was concerned. But she sure made their evening memorable!"

Then I mentioned what ZZ had told me last night at the party: that Renee was not available for dating and only swings with married men or those in committed relationships. "I think she must be involved with someone," I told Mitch. That would certainly explain her lack of flirtatious behavior or physical interaction with ZZ. Perhaps that also explained her strange behavior at the Gala: when she was introduced to ZZ, she said not a word, and didn't even look him over. We presented to her a charming, available guy, a potential swing partner who was closer to her age than others at the Gala, and she didn't even glance at him. However, I noticed ZZ gave her quite a once-over.

"No, her attention, except for Lepic, has been entirely focused on you, Mitchy. Why is that?"

"She probably doesn't want any emotional complications; I'm safe," Mitch replied.

"She's a spy!" I blurted out in disgust.

"What?" queried Mitch.

SEVEN

She

Part 5: Conclusion of Lorraine's Story
Paris
May - August, 1980

I WAS CONCERNED that Renee was a corporate spy. "She's a spy," I repeated. "A high-tech corporate spy, trying to make a quick strike, trying to find out as much as possible in a short period of time before we know all about her."

I was referring to the corporate spying that had continually plagued us over the years. Most people don't realize that corporate espionage is a major concern for companies like ours. What is there to spy on?, you might ask. Well, Mitch is a key scientist in the field of genetics, holding more than 20 patents. For Mitch, owning a patent on a process means that other companies have to go through him, which earns profits for us — big profits. Most everyone in the field of genetics knows what we work on. But it's like the space race: who can get there first? Owning patents is key. Our style of work and the patents we already own have made our company an international high–tech leader. Companies like ours that keep producing results are rewarded with generous funds from government contracts and private grants.

Mitch's interests are what authors like ZZ like to write about: genetic engineering, redesigning the human body, greatly expanding the human lifespan, artificial intelligence, and the like. Mitch and ZZ spent hours taking about these things in the last few weeks.

Whenever Mitch is in one of these conversations, he likes to ask, "Did you ever stop to think that we have 20th-century minds trapped inside caveman bodies? Our bodies are essentially the same as the caveman days when people were not expected to live beyond the age of 30." Mitch sees a process whereby we genetically redesign the body so that it rejuvenates itself, and keeps itself new and strong. Surgical transplants and replacement of body parts will become unnecessary. The body will rejuvenate defective parts just like it now grows new fingernails.

Another of Mitch's passions is finding cures for genetic diseases: birth defects, multiple sclerosis, rheumatoid arthritis, ALS, and so on.

And then there is one of Mitch's favorite topics: Artificial intelligence. Will robotic supercomputers one day be so smart that they can think and do everything people can do, only faster and more efficiently? If so, there might be no jobs left for humans! The machines could do everything and rule the world.

Then what would be the fate of mankind? Everything will be automated, even restaurants, coffee houses, fast food: you just go in and press buttons for what you want. And everything comes to you, nicely served by the restaurant robot all decked out in the restaurant colors with logos all over the place. And if you need to go to the doctor, well of course all health issues will be automated. Who better to investigate your health problems than a health service robot?

But the hot topic right now, the one all companies in the field are feverishly working on, is slowing down the aging process, extending life expectancy by 50 percent or more! A 60-year old will look and feel like 40, and a 40-year old will look and feel like 30, or maybe even 25.

Think of the business that is now generated by the population of fertile women who take birth control pills. Now think of the possible business that can be generated by an entire population taking age-control pills. It's mind-boggling!

I thought, if you wanted to hire a spy, who better than Renee? A very intelligent, beautiful woman who is fluent in the French language and knowledgeable about the culture. She would know just how to proceed and what to look for as she moved along. She would make the perfect spy. And with the huge amount of money she could be making as a tech spy, she would certainly be prepared to kiss her civil-service attorney job goodbye.

Against that grim assessment, we had to consider the alternative: we were being completely paranoid and Renee was not a spy at all, but just here in Paris enjoying herself.

In either case, we still needed Renee to accompany ZZ to swing parties. It was possible that once ZZ started dating local women, he would find one available for swinging. But that scenario was highly unlikely. You can't just ask a woman, "Hey, you want to go to a swing party tonight?" No, that doesn't usually work. ZZ would have to meet possible partners at swing parties and then find one who is available to escort to other parties. But that, too, is fraught with difficulties, because a female participant is nearly always accompanied by the same man: her husband, lover or friend. That's why we were hoping Renee would work out as our fourth. When Naomi left Los Angeles, we knew we would have a huge problem replacing her.

Mitch reiterated that Renee was not to attend any of our business luncheons, dinners or banquets — only swing parties until we received a background check on her. If she really were here as a spy, Mitch reasoned, she would hardly learn much useful information by just accompanying us to parties.

Well, that whole evening with the Lepics was a huge success. Lepic called our office on Monday to set up a meeting to review various properties we might be interested in for a scientific laboratory. He also expressed how much he and his wife both enjoyed our evening together, wanting to know when we might be returning to Chaillot Gardens. They extended an invitation for us to have dinner with them again soon.

"Tell them we will get back to them on that," Mitch said. "Let's give them a few weeks to look forward to it. In the meantime, let's attend a few other party places around town. Saturday, let's go to that trendy place in the 7th arrondissement."

So, on Saturday night the four of us attended a city swing club. This party place had a young business clientele; nearly everyone was in their 30s. Mitch and I felt like chaperones. It was a mob scene of young people milling about, talking and laughing.

As we four settled into at a large corner table, Renee said she would scout around. Off she went into the crowd, stopping to speak to various couples as she moved along. Was she screening couples for us, looking for the right one? I believe she was.

After talking at some length with an interesting-looking couple buried in the crowd, Renee escorted them back to our table so we might meet them: young venture capitalists Philippe and Marisse

Chaubert; he, tall and extremely handsome; she, petite and quite attractive.

Over drinks and a light dinner, we talked at length about finances, Mitch making a point that he and I were looking for investors. By dinner's end, Philippe expressed great interest in our proposals. He also seemed very taken by the beautiful Renee, occasionally whispering in her ear, obviously annoying his wife Marisse.

ZZ was seated beside Marisse and, realizing what was happening, took charge and spoke to her in his very best French. ZZ knew he had to charm Marisse sufficiently so she would not care about her husband and Renee. ZZ began completely occupying her time at the table, then dancing with her in sexy fashion. Finally, she could not stand it any longer and she, not ZZ, took the initiative, leading him by the hand to a more private area where they could continue in reckless abandon.

Now, of course, Philippe was free to pursue Renee, which he did lustfully. And again, as in the first party, after our business couple had been thoroughly entertained sexually, ZZ and I paired up, as did Mitch and Renee.

"This is getting to be a pattern," I whispered to ZZ. After about an hour, we took taxis home, Mitch and I in one and ZZ and Renee in another. But I doubt that ZZ was able to get any further than Renee's front door. And so went our second party with Renee and ZZ. Renee was obviously making herself indispensable for future swing parties.

On Thursday, May 1, Mitch and I received a Mayday alarm: the background check on Renee had arrived. It was troubling; more than that, it confirmed my greatest fears. Renee was worse than a paid spy; she worked for a rival company! Renee's uncle was Lou

Swain, who along with his brother Bob had founded and developed FASTEC (FAScination TEChnology), one of our major competitors.

These were the facts from the report: Renee was born on February 13, 1950, which means she was just 30 when we first met her two months ago. Renee's mother Eva and father Arturo emigrated from France shortly after World War II. They settled in Santa Clara, California, where Eva's sister Anna lived with her husband, Lou Swain. In the early 1950s, Lou and Bob formed the engineering company that later developed into FASTEC.

Renee and her younger sister Monique attended school in Santa Clara. The family name, Clare, had become Americanized from "Clare-RAY." The girls spoke French at home and English in school, thus becoming not only bilingual, but native bilingual.

And, of course, there were many cousins. Lou and Anna Swain had two boys. Bob Swain and his wife had a daughter and a son, Stuart, who was born only 11 days before Renee.

Renee and Stuart, being the same age and attending the same schools, were always sort of boyfriend and girlfriend. They were high-school sweethearts and continuously rumored to be engaged. Renee and Stuart were not blood relations. They had the same Uncle Louie, but Renee was related to Lou through the marriage of her Aunt Anna. During summers in high school, both Renee and Stuart worked at FASTEC.

After high-school graduation, Renee and Stuart did not marry, but remained close. Renee entered the University of California at Berkeley, about 50 miles from Santa Clara. Stuart stayed closer to home, attending Orchard Valley College and working for FASTEC, moving up into managerial positions after graduation.

At Berkeley, Renee majored in science and technology. She

continued to work at FASTEC her first two summers at the university, as did her sister, Monique, before she moved to Paris to marry a French doctor.

After four years at Berkeley, Renee graduated with honors at age 22, and then moved east to attend Harvard Law School, where she graduated three years later near the top of her class. At age 25, she passed the bar.

She was hired right out of law school by the federal government. For the next five years, Renee had been a rising star in the Department of Justice. She worked at the San Francisco Federal Building representing the government position in civil-rights cases, illegal-immigration issues, and other cases involving U.S. law enforcement. Six weeks ago, she was placed on unpaid leave.

Those, then, were the facts given to us by our security team.

Mitch and I thought back to when we first met Renee at that eventful February swing party at Alice and Denny's about ten weeks ago. A tall, completely naked redhead had strolled across the crowded floor, boobs bobbing, hips swaying, and then randomly, it seemed, selected Mitch from a group of toweled swingers, asking him if he wanted to "play." But was it really by chance that she chose Mitch? Or did Renee, in fact, know exactly who Mitch was, and made it appear that her actions were random?

What if Renee had deliberately befriended Vivian knowing full well she was a good friend of ours, then coaxed an invitation to the Gala from her, taking full advantage of Vivian's gracious nature?

No wonder then, on Gala night, Renee made sure Mitch was always at her side, not even bothering to look over other prospective swing partners, not giving ZZ a glance.

No, Renee had her man: Mitchell Hesten.

But now she had to get Naomi out of the picture. Renee would not have been able to join our circle in Paris with Naomi there.

Now it made sense to us that Naomi, a sketch artist of dubious modeling and acting talent, was offered $1 million to go play with Sidney Colsome and his friends.

That money wasn't from Colsome; it was from FASTEC! They had to get Naomi out of the way so Renee could step in! It would be nothing for a company like FASTEC to back a $100,000 signing bonus. The development of anti-aging pills alone would be worth the investment of millions of dollars for the possible return of billions.

Now, with Naomi gone, Renee just happened to be in Paris at the same time we were. But she bided her time. She wasn't pushy and she waited for us to call her. She knew we would need her for swing parties.

And when we did, she had to perform, had to produce. She dressed the part and worked her charm, whispering sweet pleasantries in native Parisian French to the Lepics and Philippe Chaubert, seducing them so completely they could not wait to reciprocate, hoping to meet up with us again soon for another rendezvous.

But Renee had to know the day would come when we had all the details of her life before us, as we did that May Day. Time was running out. So she had to act fast, snatching Mitch for two overnights, hoping to learn some useful information, hoping to hear names of key people to see. Hoping, perhaps, to learn something about our personal lives that could be of future use to her.

"And so, now what?" I asked Mitch on that gloomy May Day afternoon. How appropriate, I thought morosely, that "mayday" came from the French word *m'aider,* meaning "come help me!"

"We keep on going," Mitch replied. "These next three months

are a key time; we need to keep things rolling. We don't need to say anything to Renee or to ZZ either. She is not going to learn anything technical by just attending swing parties. My bet is she is looking to connect to lab personnel to learn specifics about our basic research. So we do need to replace her as soon as possible. She's a clever gal; we better watch out! We need to put a tail on her, find out exactly where she goes, who she sees, what she mails, and who she calls."

In the weeks that followed, Mitch was exceptionally busy at our Parisian laboratory, working on several of his pet scientific projects. And every so often, he would fly back to Silicon Valley to take care of important matters. I stayed in Paris, weighed down by numerous financial reports, analyses and projections in preparation for upcoming meetings. And all the while, we were both busy attending frequent meetings and social functions with our committee heads, science project leaders, local business leaders, financiers, European businessmen and scientists. All of these functions had been well-timed and smartly arranged by my daughter Jasmine and her capable staff.

But for me the pivotal moment was a day in early May, the point at which ZZ first met Jasmine: the moment of first sight. I had anticipated this moment for weeks, wondering how each would see the other and what their initial gut feelings would be. I had anticipated many possible variations, but mainly I wanted to observe ZZ.

To dampen ZZ's natural appeal in Jasmine's eyes, I had informed her weeks before that he was engaged to Naomi and was therefore unavailable as a single man. I later had to modify it by saying that Naomi is now traveling and fulfilling contract obligations, but the engagement was still on.

Over the course of these many weeks, I had debated with myself whether I should say anything to ZZ in regards to meeting Jasmine. I had decided not to. Now I had to wonder if ZZ would initially experience any sexual interest in Jasmine. After all, she is only two years younger than Naomi and, I have to admit, is exquisitely beautiful. She looks just like me, only 20 years younger.

If ZZ doesn't show even two seconds of sexual interest, should I feel relieved or insulted? To have some instinctive, reflexive interest would of course be natural, I suppose. But in ZZ's eyes, Jasmine is the daughter of his sex partner. In my eyes, for ZZ to engage in any flirtation with my daughter, however slight or insignificant it may seem, would be a treacherous act of betrayal and an incestuous act of infidelity!

Now it had arrived, the moment I had been anxiously anticipating: the initial contact was here.

And what happened? ZZ's eyes did light up upon meeting Jasmine. He was stunned, I believe, by her remarkable resemblance to me. His eyes glanced down momentarily to observe her slim, feminine frame, but he was all business from the onset and totally professional in his demeanor.

I was relieved that ZZ had passed this crucial test of his loyalty to me and I knew I could trust him with my daughter. From that moment on, I could let go of any doubts about ZZ; I now had complete faith in him.

The weeks passed quickly. ZZ was comfortable working in the adjoining, private office we had set up for him. He had use of his own copy machine, an IBM Selectric typewriter, pens, pencils and stationery supplies, all in a spacious well-lit room with an extra-large desk, a reclining swivel chair, and a beautiful city view. Here, he could write if he chose, relax if he wanted, and also assist Jasmine overseeing the arrangements for our evening business dinners and social events.

As the weeks passed, ZZ had also begun dating a variety of local Frenchwomen he had met at various cafes, bars, restaurants, clubs and parties. All of them spoke some English, of course, but as far as ZZ knew, they were not swingers, and therefore not to be considered for a Saturday night swing party.

And so we kept taking Renee to swing party after swing party, fully cognizant of her possible spying activities, while benefiting greatly from her specialty of reining in prospective business associates with her overtly-flirtatious behavior. Two years prior, we had set out to find a swing couple to replace Ed and Dianne with the intention that they would facilitate getting together with other business couples. However, we did not necessarily expect the couple to engage our prospects sexually. Renee had taken the concept of engaging to a whole new level!

Now in late June, Mitch and I were comfortable with ZZ taking on a more expansive role in the company, relieving Jasmine and her staff of planning and arranging most of the evening activities. In appreciation, we offered ZZ an extended contract with a substantial raise in salary. Our plan was for ZZ to continue in this role when in Paris, then join us as we travel around Europe. Mitch and I would be attending scientific conferences, setting up local offices, buying out small laboratories that we could retool, and hiring bright local scientists to help us intensify our efforts in key areas of research. ZZ enthusiastically endorsed our plan. After all, if he were to become the international authority on swinging, he had before him many more swing parties to attend, many international cities to visit, and many more stories to acquire.

ZZ's quest to find a Parisian swinger as his escort to a party had not yielded any immediate results. He made vague plans with several women after repeated interactions with them at July parties at the Gardens, but whether they would be available when we returned in a couple of months was questionable. There was also the possibility that upon his return to California, ZZ might renew past relationships with swinger friends, one of whom might be available to travel part of the year in Europe. Mitch and I felt it was crucial for ZZ to have one or more women available as a swing partner, not only for Paris parties, but also for parties wherever we went in Europe and beyond. ZZ assured us he had someone in mind; someone he was romantically attracted to.

Now, in early August, we were concluding our personal operations at our Paris office and Jasmine was wrapping up our meeting and activity schedule. Since virtually all of Paris closes down in August, we planned some of our last meetings of this trip in Brussels, Stockholm and Amsterdam.

Before leaving Paris we bade farewell to Renee, thanking her for her assistance throughout the spring and summer. We never mentioned anything about FASTEC and, of course, neither did she.

Matters went well in all three cities we visited. In Amsterdam we met up with Sondra, an old swinger friend of mine who had been living there temporarily. As expected, she took us to a very intriguing swing party. I'll let ZZ tell you about it later — that's his department. The occasion reminded me of how enjoyable it was to attend a party with an old friend.

During the evening, Sondra gave us four VIP tickets she had acquired for the following night; *An Evening with Kate Atali*, a special film screening and reception to meet the young lead actress.

Sondra said that she herself would not be able to attend that night, but we three should definitely go and meet Kate Atali, who was generating much interest with her new film.

But that next day, we received devastating news from our security team. Mitch and I felt that we had been successful at keeping Renee at a secure distance from company affairs while reaping huge benefits from her sexual performance on our behalf at the weekly swing parties. However, this evaluation was shattered as a result of monitoring her daily activities.

Renee, we were told, had been having a serious affair with one of our head lab chemists, Jacques Penard, who was married with two children. Mitch phoned Jacques immediately and talked with him for some time. Mitch wanted to make sure that Jacques understood Renee's connection to FASTEC and remind him of his confidentiality agreement not to disclose or even discuss work matters with anyone outside the company. Jacques told Mitch that he had abided by his agreement. But knowing just how sexy and alluring Renee could be, we were not feeling too confident about her not having learned anything significant. We had no idea where and how Renee had met Jacques.

Next came the clincher, a news item from Santa Clara, California. "Stuart Swain of FASTEC announced his engagement to his high-school sweetheart, Miss Renee Clare. The marriage is to take place on New Year's Day in Santa Clara, followed by a honeymoon in Paris, where Miss Clare has numerous relatives."

So Miss Renee was going to become Mrs. Swain and married to FASTEC. With her intellect and ambition, we felt confident that we would be meeting her again soon, maybe someday as FASTEC's CEO.

Mitch and I were stunned by the news of Renee's marriage; ZZ seemed to take it all in stride. That evening, in a completely somber mood, perhaps feeling that Renee had gotten the better of us after all, we entered the famous Art Movie House. Previewing before a VIP packed house was the yet to be released film, *Queen of Erotica,* featuring Kate Atali.

The film was already being hailed as groundbreaking, destined to usher in a new era in erotic filmmaking, and on its way to becoming a classic. As we watched, we found ourselves transfixed, completely captivated by Atali's erotic, sensual style. The film was engrossing, somewhat sophisticated, and stylistically enchanting. Kate Atali, one of the scantily-dressed nymphs, so compelling to watch, was singled out to be crowned "Queen of Erotica."

As the crown was bestowed upon Atali's head, a radiant glow emanated across her face. Her eyes sparkled and dimples danced on her cheeks. When the radiant queen spoke, her lips pursed with rich sexuality. Her voice was throaty and alluring, distinctive and unmistakably unique.

In utter astonishment, the three of us exchanged glances and then exclaimed in unison for all the audience to hear, "It's Naomi!"

EIGHT
_____

Renee

*Renee Clare's First Report
Silicon Valley, CA
1978 - July 3, 1979*

MY NAME IS Renee Clare. You are already familiar with many of the facts and facets of my childhood. I grew up in a closely-knit family of aunts, uncles, and cousins in the booming locale of inventive geniuses and entrepreneurs that would eventually become known as Silicon Valley. I enjoyed a happy and secure childhood, sharing many of my experiences with my childhood friend and high school sweetheart, Stuart Swain. His father Bob Swain was one of the founders of the high-tech engineering firm that would eventually become the Fascination Technology Corporation, or FASTEC.

Nearly all of my initial sexual experiences — kissing, petting, and eventually screwing — were with Stuart. I have to admit that I often took the initiative in these sexual adventures. I have always had a daring nature, enhanced curiosity, and enthusiasm for experiencing the unknown. Interestingly, Stuart and I hardly ever spoke of marriage. We deeply loved each other, but we both knew we had college ahead of us, and probably advanced degrees as well. Our focus needed to be on education, not marriage and family.

Once we started college, we no longer saw each other daily as we had since childhood. I moved to the campus at the University of California at Berkeley, about 50 miles north of home, whereas Stuart elected to go to school locally at Orchard Valley College. At Berkeley, I majored in science and technology, courses that intellectually stimulated me. My Uncle Lou often derided me in those years, saying I had too many brains for my own good. "Technology courses are great, but take some finance and business courses like Stuart, so you can be of some real use to us at FASTEC."

But my ambition at the time was to become a chemist or biologist at the lab. It is hard to believe that only 20 years ago, back in the 60s, there were no female scientists employed at FASTEC. Actually, there were not very many female scientists in the U.S.

The summer after my freshman year at Berkeley, I was back home and working again at FASTEC, as was Stuart. Although we had resumed our lifelong friendship, something had changed. Stuart confided that he had a very serious problem, one that was making his life unbearable. He sought my advice and support, asking me to promise I would never tell a soul. No one else was ever to know. Then he told me. He had concluded, after various experiences at college, that he was a homosexual.

I was stunned. I just could not understand it. I really had no clue that Stuart could be gay. We talked about it but he refused to use the word "gay." He said there was nothing at all that was gay or happy about it at the moment, except that he felt relieved to have finally sorted out his confusing sexual feelings over the years. But Stuart was in a state of panic over the possibility that his family and others might find out. "Nobody else would be understanding," he said, "Nobody!" He felt sure that if people knew, he would be the object of ridicule and scorn and possibly even face beatings from local thugs. "It's not easy to be different," he said. "People hate you."

As we kept in touch over the course of semesters ahead, Stuart appeared to be coming to terms somewhat with his secret life and how to navigate it with his family and friends. He asked me if he could still refer to me as his girlfriend. "Of course," I replied. "And just tell them that we're planning on getting married after we have launched our careers."

Meanwhile, my college experiences at Berkeley were having a profound effect on me. I had many brief love affairs over the course of my four years there. In the 60s, everyone was beginning to experience a new wave of sexual freedom. I even started taking those new birth control pills for a while, which was so much easier than always having to think about putting in my diaphragm before sex.

But the main impact of those Berkeley years was the formulation of my political outlook. I was attending one of the most politically radical campuses in the country. From 1968 to 1972, I witnessed many passionate anti-war demonstrations, massive student protests, the "People's Park," and the teargassing of the campus. And forming nearby in adjacent Oakland were the Black Bears, a militant Black political organization.

Bobby Greere, one of the ministers of the Black Bears, would often speak on campus at the Sproul Hall steps. So would Georgia Rylan, wife of a jailed party minister. I was deeply moved by Georgia, a dark-skinned beauty, sporting one of those new Afro hairstyles symbolizing Black independence from white culture and white standards. She spoke eloquently about the plight of Blacks, their struggle for freedom, and for their need to exercise "Black Power." She was an inspiring speaker and a very independent, smart woman.

My exposure to the political events and movements of the times was shaping my passions and my future. At the end of my sophomore year, I had decided on a new career path: becoming a civil-rights attorney, fighting for justice for those whose rights were being denied. I was becoming an activist, but not anti-government or anti-American — quite the opposite. I became fiercely patriotic, realizing what my parents had endured in war-torn Europe, how fortunate they were to have immigrated to the United States to become American citizens, and how fortunate I was to be an American. With law school in mind, the focus of my junior and senior years was to earn excellent grades while participating in the student political activities that deeply moved me.

Upon graduating from the University of California at Berkeley in 1972, I entered Harvard Law School. I loved being at Harvard, a great place to be a student. But law school was hard work, very challenging; no more summers in California. Of course I came home during Christmas and short summer breaks to be with family and friends, and especially to be with Stuart. He seemed much happier now, accepting the fact that he was a gay man, and secure in the fact that he could manage the facade of being heterosexual. In the eyes of family and friends, Stuart and I were still boyfriend-girlfriend, waiting to launch our careers before the consideration of marriage. While at Harvard, I did have one serious love affair among all the fleeting ones. But I knew I was not ready for marriage; I felt I had a calling and couldn't consider marriage for many years to come.

Upon graduating and receiving my law degree in 1975, I returned to California, passed the bar exam, and entered the job market. There were relatively few female lawyers in 1975. To obtain better gender balance, corporations, institutions, and law firms were feeling the pressure to hire women attorneys. Consequently, I had many job offers, some quite lucrative. But I was most interested in an offer that came from the Department of Justice in San Francisco. There, I could work on cases I felt passionate about — the ones I went to law school for. I was determined to do something in life that would make a difference in this world.

With great excitement and enthusiasm, I accepted the Justice Department's offer and began work at the Federal Building located in downtown San Francisco. I was extremely pleased to be working there.

During my first years, because of my smarts and daring, along with my youth, good looks, and willingness to be trained for almost anything consistent with my goals and ambitions, I was able to obtain numerous interviews for more advanced positions within the department. I underwent physical tests, mental tests, psychological tests, background checks, and security checks. The Justice Department eventually knew all there was to know about me, including, I'm sure, my strong political views and my many sexual adventures. I was moving right along, getting promotion after promotion, and working on more complicated and intricate cases, many of which contained highly-classified information. I could see the department was demonstrating supreme confidence in my skills and abilities.

In late 1978, about three years into my tenure at the Federal Building, I had a rather special interview. My boss Alan and two very attractive, slightly older higher-ups, Mary Jo and Kathy, told me how impressed they were with my abilities; so much so that they felt I would make an exceptional candidate for a promotional position that each of them had held in prior years. They asked that I seriously consider entering into an extremely rigorous and grueling training program, leading to the position of undercover agent for the FBI.

Yes! The FBI. This, I could sense, was my calling!

I was told that the three main qualities a female agent should have in relation to a criminal suspect are: the beauty to attract him, the sexuality to engage him, and the intellect to outwit him. I, they said, could be such an agent.

"We have assignments in mind for you," they told me, "that we think only someone like you could handle. There are other agents out there who, like you, are young, attractive, and sexy. But for special cases that we have in mind for you, we will need more than that. We need someone who can go toe to toe, brain cell to brain cell, with the smartest guys out there. Besides youth and beauty, you have intellect. You are the most complete package we have ever seen.

"You would be one of the few agents selected to infiltrate smuggling operations, crime syndicates, and espionage rings. We think that you can do this with training. What do you think?"

"Yes! Definitely yes," I answered calmly and assertively.

I am one of those people who loves to live on the edge. I am never quite content unless I have that rush of adrenaline that comes with danger. So, yes, I was willing to put myself in danger in exchange for the possibility of making a positive contribution to my country. I knew I was attractive, youthful, and sexy. But these are temporary attributes. Youth ages, beauty fades, and sex appeal diminishes. I reasoned that while I was still young enough, pretty enough, and sexually appealing, I needed to utilize my qualities in a manner that would produce the greatest positive impact on society. For me. I could think of no more important use of my talents and skills than working as an undercover agent for the FBI. This, then, was what I had to do.

They informed me that FBI regulations required a minimum two-week period for me to consider their offer before they could officially accept an answer. In the meantime, they wanted me to seriously consider the risks and dangers involved.

Contrary to popular perception, they emphasized there is no glamour or glory to this position. In fact, I could not tell a soul about it. Disclosure to anyone — parents or siblings, boyfriend or girl-friend — could eventually lead to my exposure and possibly place my life in danger. No one was to know.

Furthermore, I had to realize that if my suspect is unmarried, I would have to be prepared to marry him. Should he be already married, I would need to do whatever seemed appropriate to be-come as close to him as possible. And all during this time, I might have to endure dismal conditions and debasing circumstances to gather information against a suspect who later could be freed for lack of sufficient evidence, on a technicality, or as a result of a "not guilty" trial verdict. This work could be extremely frustrating and life-threatening. If I were discovered as an agent, I could be gang-raped to death, severely mutilated, thrown in a river, or simply shot.

They were telling me the worst, they said, so that I would not have any illusions or misconceptions; they wanted me to understand the dangers involved. Of course, I would be trained and prepared for all conceivable situations. But I would have to be phys-ically and psychologically tough, totally motivated and dedicated.

"If your eventual answer to our conversation is yes," Mary Jo stated, "then you will need to begin a grueling after-hours physical training program spread out over a year. And you will have to overcome natural embarrassments and self-consciousness about sex to engage in a sexual training program consisting of participatory sessions of six to eight months. You have to ask yourself if you are seriously willing to undergo such a training."

Mary Jo continued, "You have a big advantage over most candidates for this position: beauty and brains; we can't teach that. We have to find a natural like you. We can teach you the sex stuff and self-defense skills if you are as teachable as we think you are, and if you are willing to put yourself through this rigorous training program."

I figured the FBI certainly knew I had been sexually loose enough over the last ten years to be trainable.

Mary Jo then concluded, "We never want to lose an agent because she was unprepared for the dangers that beset her. Hopefully, you will be well-trained. We want to make you as knowledgeable and effective as you can be. Then we will have to be extremely cautious and careful how we use you. You have rare qualities. Good luck in your decision-making process."

I now had two to six weeks to declare my decision. I had many questions to ask them, sure; but I never had any doubt that my answer was going to be yes.

Over the days ahead, I talked with each of the three, separately and together, about all sorts of details as I thought matters through. I asked why the FBI didn't have its own training facilities and why I had to train on my own time. I was told that the FBI does have its own training school for agents who will be doing investigative work and police-type activities, but I wasn't going to do that. I was to be an undercover agent. And as such, it could not appear that I used government time, at a government building to build a strong, super-fit body.

My after-hours training was mainly for self-defense; there were numerous classes throughout the city. Many men and women of my age group train at these local facilities for various competitions. Mary Jo thought I should consider entering and competing in some of them. I could expect, she said, that most criminal suspects I might be assigned to would aggressively investigate my background. Entering competitions would not only be a good measure of my training success, but would also serve to deflect possible suspicions about my being so well-trained.

Mary Jo also informed me that if my training went well and I became an agent, I would need to resign my position with the Department of Justice. With a wink and a smile, she said I might just have to live on the generous trust fund that a long-lost uncle just left me when he died.

When the minimal two-week waiting period expired, I declared myself ready to sign up and begin my training. I had many official papers to sign, documents to read, and oaths to take. Nothing drastic was to occur. I was to continue to work at my legal position just as before. Only now, I had to arrange for various evening and weekend training classes. For the sake of appearances and continuity, I would be assigned about the same number of new cases, but my involvement in them would be much less intense. My official pay would not change, but I would be receiving a huge bonus pay in a secret account. Work hours would be partly training activities and partly work as usual, with a little bit of relaxation time for the hard work after hours.

And so, my training began. Mary Jo gave me a list of approved, professional-level training facilities in San Francisco along with the name of the person to see at each site. It was up to me to schedule my training sessions in the evenings and weekends as I chose. I scheduled fitness and body-building sessions, martial arts, karate, and other self-defense techniques, as well as wrestling and hand-to-hand combat classes.

I even joined a local fitness club where I could swim laps for fitness and endurance. The club provided some sociability and an opportunity for me to dabble in various social sports: tennis, ping-pong, and squash (if I had any time left, of course). On weekends I enjoyed long jogs at the Marina or through Golden Gate Park.

Not having handled a gun before, I scheduled sessions to learn how to shoot a pistol and a rifle; target practice was available at various places in the City. I would not be carrying a weapon when on assignment; my job was not to apprehend anyone. But I should know how to use a gun in self-defense if necessary.

To monitor my progress, Kathy or Mary Jo would often join me at various activities. They were completely supportive and encouraging; Alan too. No one wanted me to fail or give up.

A couple of months into my training, I felt strong, very strong. But I still needed to be better at defending myself in various situations as if my life depended on it, because on the job, it very well could. I had to keep in mind that I was going to be the object of lust, not love. And as such, the guy I was assigned to might get rough. I had to learn how to physically defend myself and, if necessary, to escape the premises.

So now I began escape classes. My trainer, wearing a well-padded bodysuit, told me that in these sessions he was going to forcefully attack me without actually harming me. My job was to fight back with every skill I had ever learned and escape the training room. "If you manage to get out that door," the trainer said, pointing to the exit, "then you win. If I subdue you, I win. The object is for you to get better each time. We are going to videotape each battle and then watch the recording together. You will learn from your mistakes and from what I have to teach you."

My first battles were terrible, embarrassingly bad. But with all the techniques I was learning, I progressed considerably over the weeks and months to come. I still, however, could not escape the room; but, after all, I was battling the trainer! To make the battles fairer, I would sometimes take on Kathy or Mary Jo. Of course, I was younger and stronger than either of them, but they were more knowledgeable, cunning, and experienced. They were not going to pull any punches, they said; they were going to battle me! And they beat me every time — until months later, when I learned to be almost as smart as they were. Then, eventually, I escaped the room fighting each of them. What an exhilarating experience!

I was beginning to feel my power. Now as I walked down the street, rightly or wrongly, I feared no one. I was ready to do battle. I would say to myself: "Nobody better mess with me! I could flip him, sock him, wrestle him to the ground, karate chop him, slice him up with a knife, and shoot him to pieces. He had better watch out!"

Toward the end of June 1979, about six months into my training, I was ready to move on to the next phase. This included specialized classes in undercover and detective work, behavior training for various situations, more fitness sessions, more self-defense schooling, and most importantly, sex school.

The stated purpose of sex school was for me to learn how to

enhance my sexual appeal and master my sexual abilities so as to be the one in control in sexual interactions. I had to lose any natural inhibitions and embarrassments about sex. As an agent, I couldn't be squeamish about such things. Because sex is the usual avenue to becoming intimate with suspects, effective use of my sexuality was going to be of prime importance; it would play an essential part of my assignment. For my own protection and effectiveness, I would need to master it. Sex school, then, was of vital importance. I relished the thought of enhancing my sexual power!

Sex school took place in participatory sessions held at various locations; I would be escorted by Mr. Dash, a retired agent. I was not to worry or concern myself with the nature of the participatory part; everything that occurred would be with my full consent. I would have complete veto power over any and all actions initiated upon me, and I would not have to perform any actions I did not completely wish to do of my own free will. This would be a somewhat self-paced course.

I learned that on Saturday evenings I would be attending well-dressed, highly-social sex parties, generally referred to as swing parties. My handlers stressed that, aside from my escort, retired agent Dash, nobody else attending would have any connection whatsoever with the FBI or the Department of Justice. I was to participate, or not, in any activities that took place there. I was to sexually prepare myself for assignment by observation and participation in any way I chose.

I was told not to concern myself about unwanted sexual advances on the part of agent Dash, because, they said, "He prefers men to women; but he will satisfy a woman, if necessary, in the service of his country."

"In meeting people at parties," they said, "you are to refer to agent Dash as your boyfriend; you are in a relationship with him. In all other matters you are to present yourself as you are: a San Francisco civil-rights attorney working at the Federal Building. You should be friendly and open; just be yourself. Act as you would at any social gathering. And, for practice, try to learn people's names and remember the places you go. When on assignment, you will need to memorize everything. Nothing should ever be written down.

"We think you are going to enjoy these parties," they said.

NINE

Sex School

Renee Clare's Second Report
San Francisco Bay Area
July 4, 1979 – February 11, 1980

TO EASE INTO sex school, a nude afternoon swim party was chosen as my introduction to social nudity, an activity I had never before participated in. Never before had I pranced around naked in front of more than one man at a time. Now I was going to have that experience in front of about thirty other nude couples.

I was wondering what was it going to feel like, socializing in the nude with all those strangers? I would soon find out. I was invited to attend the afternoon segment of the Fourth of July swim and swing party at Circle S Ranch, a suburban swing club located about 30 miles east of San Francisco in the East Bay town of Pleasant Hill.

It was in the early afternoon of that Wednesday, July fourth, 1979, when retired agent Dash came knocking on the door of my San Francisco apartment to escort me to my first experience in social nudity. Because Mr. Dash had been repeatedly referred to as a retired agent, I was expecting a rather older-looking gentleman.

When I opened the door, I was pleasantly surprised.

"Hi, I am Taylor Dash."

Taylor Dash was young and gorgeous, a beautiful hunk of a man. I could see why the bureau sent a guy not quite straight. Otherwise, one of us was sure to attack the other before leaving my apartment. Taylor and I made an instant connection, engaging in continuous back-and-forth chatter and laughter as we leisurely drove along to our party destination.

During the drive, I asked Taylor how he could be retired and look so young. He revealed that he retired only last year at the age of 41, after twenty years of service. Now, he said, he takes on special assignments such as escorting me to parties.

At the pool party, we were warmly greeted at the ranch house door by several well-dressed couples who graciously escorted us around the house, giving us a quick tour before showing us the dressing room area, where Taylor and I stripped down, stashing our clothes in one of the empty lockers.

Then, hand in hand, we strolled into the summer sunshine, where we were cheerfully greeted by a nude gathering of about 30 couples. For the first few minutes, it certainly did seem strange that no one was wearing any clothes at all. But everyone appeared to be so at ease and so completely comfortable socializing in the nude that it wasn't long before I did too. Hell, I had grunted and sweated for months building this strong, beautiful body of mine. Now I was going to show it off!

So, show it off I did. Over the course of the next few hours, I felt very confident as we strolled about, introducing ourselves along the way, enjoying the cold drinks, excellent barbecued chicken and beef, good music, swimming, and volleyball games in the pool. How freeing it felt to swim naked! My afternoon had been a very positive experience, a confidence builder. But come five o'clock, well ahead of the evening's "sexual fireworks" and according to plan, Taylor and I said our goodbyes and departed the festivities.

So ended my initial adventure into the world of social nudity. My first experience in social sex, however, would have to wait for another ten days until Saturday evening, July 14th, when Taylor Dash again knocked on my door, ready to escort me to another party at Circle S Ranch. This time I would have the opportunity to observe and perhaps participate in the various sexual activities taking place there.

I was truly excited to have the opportunity to attend such an unusual party. I had no idea what to expect. But during the early evening drive, Taylor explained many aspects of swing parties, the most important of which is swing-party etiquette, the tenet that everyone has veto power at any time to any type of sexual invitation. A declining declaration, be it by verbal commands or physical gestures, must be respected. Anyone not in compliance with swing-party etiquette can expect to be escorted out of the party and very possibly banned from attending future parties.

Although it may seem contradictory, there is a dress code for these parties. Guests are to look their best. Women are to wear blouses or sweaters, skirts, and heels. Men are to wear collared shirts, slacks, and dressy shoes. Casual clothes such as T-shirts, jeans, or flip-flops are not allowed.

For my first party, I wore a white blouse with puffy sleeves, a bright full-length skirt, and three-inch heels. When Taylor and I arrived, I was impressed just how snappy and snazzy everyone looked. Embarrassingly, I had met many of these guests at the nude

Fourth of July party, but I didn't immediately recognize them with their clothes on!

As Taylor and I moved about, meeting one couple after another, I couldn't help but think that this social gathering had a certain spark to it because of the anticipation that after dinner, we would all be stripping down naked and likely available for sex. As the evening progressed, the intensity of the party kept elevating. I think everyone was sizing up possible partners for the swinging that would follow. I, myself, was getting enormously excited about all this. The party felt so daring, so adventurous, with no real dangers involved; something akin to teenage kissing parties.

After socializing over a delicious buffet dinner, the clothes started coming off! The excitement in the room heightened as couples began exchanging their clothes for large white ranch beach towels, used by some to protect their modesty, but mainly distributed for sanitary purposes; everyone is encouraged to use their towels when sitting or lying down.

With the very comforting knowledge of party etiquette fresh in mind, I stripped, too, but mindful that as a redhead, it would be difficult to walk around unnoticed. Then I began wandering about to see for myself just what went on here. What I witnessed over the next three hours truly astounded me.

Before that night, I had never before seen a couple making love; had never seen a couple involved in oral sex; and had never witnessed group sex. That night I had an opportunity to observe all these things.

I was in awe. I hadn't anticipated that sex school was going to be this fascinating! I had always thought that, by nature, sex was a private act. It was only natural, I believed, that a couple would prefer privacy when involved in any sort of sexual activity. But my observations at this party and others showed me that this wasn't necessarily the case. To my amazement, nude couples and groups performed sex acts in front of one another, seemingly oblivious to adjacent onlookers. Some couples sought privacy or semi-privacy, but surprisingly, there were many couples who just didn't seem to care if others watched or not. I imagined that knowing there were onlookers probably heightened the thrill of the sexual acts.

Having thought of myself as a very sexual person in the last dozen years or so, I was struck by the fact that I had never before witnessed another couple having sex. I had always wondered, what does it all look like? What positions do others favor? What do other women do, and what sounds do they make? What techniques do they use to arouse their men?

Tonight I found answers to all these questions as I watched couples in beds on the padded floor and in bedrooms, playrooms, and other rooms of the house. And I watched them outside, doing it in nature. It was so intriguing to observe the nuances of it all. Did I get physically involved with anyone at this party? No, nor at the next two parties. I was too busy watching! I didn't want to miss a thing! I was struck by how fortunate I was to witness these activities. I told Taylor that were it not for this training, I probably never would have seen, live before my very eyes, the variety of sex displayed at these parties.

At my next party the following Saturday, again at the Circle S Ranch, I resumed my voyeurism. At this party my observations were concentrated on the group room, a room specifically designed for those who want to get sexually involved with more than one partner at a time. The assumption was that if you are on the padded floor, you are receptive to engaging in group activity. Of course, everyone still had veto power over any unwanted actions by others.

The room itself was dimly lit and empty, devoid of any windows or furniture, save for a long red velvet bench along a wall adjacent to the beaded curtain entryway. Sitting on the bench, observers and potential participants could watch all those involved in the various sexual configurations.

As in my last party, I became enraptured by what I saw there. So many bodies intertwined, with others joining in from time to time; a spontaneous, sensual, kinetic sculpture. So fascinating! How would I ever have had the opportunity to witness something this extraordinary, had I not been required to be there?

Watching all this group activity, I asked myself, could I do that? Could I be one of the women in those groups? At that time I didn't think so. During sex, I wanted to be the total focus of my partner's attention. I wanted his interest to be totally on me. But, I felt I should keep an open mind about such things. After all, I enjoyed breaking boundaries...

At the next party, my voyeurism was devoted almost exclusively to oral sex, which at all of these parties had been quite prevalent and ubiquitous not only in the bedrooms and playrooms, but also outdoors on the patio, poolside, around the hot tub, and in the grass. Generally, oral sex was part of, or a prelude to, most other sexual activities. I wanted to closely watch, to observe details of the various techniques the women employed in arousing and satisfying men. I felt that as an agent, I would need to perform oral sex at the highest level. Although I had practiced oral sex on previous partners in my life, I felt a willingness to learn, through personal instruction over the weeks and months ahead, even greater skills of performance.

In all sexual activities, it had become increasingly apparent how much my sexual skills and my knowledge of sexual variety were going to be significant, contributing factors in determining my effectiveness as an agent.

At all three of these parties, I had been curious to see what particular actions the women initiated and how they reacted to those they received. What sounds did they make, especially during climax? To my surprise, throughout these parties, female orgasms did not necessarily sound that similar. There seemed to be variation in pitch and rhythm. After three parties, I could sometimes identify a woman in another room simply by the sound of her orgasm.

As I reflected on these parties, I realized how much I had enjoyed them. They have a very special appeal, a unique flavor: The intense socializing over dinner in anticipation of the sexual activity that would surely follow; the gradual smooth transition from dress-up to nudity; and then the exciting, high-energy atmosphere in which all this sex takes place.

There is something especially attractive about the party participants, a special quality that very much arouses me. They, like me, are risk takers, attending parties in secret, unbeknownst to most of the people they know: their friends, neighbors, family, and co-workers. Like me, swingers have a secret existence. They have a daring quality to them and they share a secret life. No wonder I feel such affection and affinity with them.

I understand now why swing parties have been continually studied by behavioral scientists. They are spontaneous and genuine; they are not rehearsed for a camera or scripted for a show; everyone is just performing for their own pleasure and the pleasure of their partners. You can observe spontaneous sex acts not observable anywhere else; here you can observe the universality and naturalness of sex.

At the following week's party, again at Circle S Ranch, I was ready to participate. I was ready to cross the line from the one-partner sex I had always done in private to engaging in sex acts in front of others at a party. After three parties of socializing and observing, I knew some of these guys better than many of the guys I had hopped into bed with at college.

I usually vividly remember my sexual experience with a new partner, and so it was with Gary, my very first swing partner. And about an hour later, along came Roger. For me, that was a unique experience — two different sex partners in one night!

As the weeks rolled on, Taylor took me to party after party at other swing clubs around the Bay Area. Previously, for learning purposes, Taylor had allowed me to roam around on my own. Now, for social purposes, he was usually at my side. And occasionally I would see Taylor get involved with a woman. He was clearly AC/DC, meaning he was bisexual. He could go either way.

With each successive party, I steadily climbed the ladder of sexual adventure. But aside from experiencing these new adventures in sex, I was now embarking upon other aspects of sex school: mastering abilities, enhancing my appeal, learning sexual variety, and acquiring "defensive sex" techniques. I was going to learn to be prepared for physical aggression during a sexual situation, a possibility that hopefully would never occur.

"We would be remiss in our training if we didn't prepare you to handle these situations," Taylor said. "Remember, you are going to be involved in an underworld situation: espionage agents, smugglers, and such. These men are known to get aggressive."

Taylor emphasized that I would not always find myself in safe, secure surroundings when I had sex with my assignee. I needed to be on guard for physical aggression against me by either the suspect or his wife, mistress, girlfriend, or buddies. This was a situation both Mary Jo and Kathy had experienced as agents.

In discussions at work, Kathy usually took the lead. "Ideally, you always want to be at your apartment, where you are in a known environment. But that will not always be possible. In any new environment, always know where the exits are: room, apartment, and building exits, and which ones are the closest and the easiest to use. During sex, never be totally passive or submissive. Be on guard. Be aware. If your suspect begins to doubt your loyalty or feels you have betrayed him in some way, he may seek revenge. What may begin as sex could soon become rape, even gang rape. You have to develop a keen sense of just when you are playing hostess and when it is developing into a rape situation. If you ever fear you are in severe danger, your job then is to fight your way out, whatever it takes. Escape and seek safety."

We discussed what constituted an ideal room environment during sex. The first aspects we considered were acoustics and lighting. "You don't want to be listening to loud music or in a noisy environment," Kathy pointed out. "That could drown out important audio signals. Suggest soft mood music. Tell him that it's what you like; what turns you on."

She continued, "Also, you don't want to be in a dark room. You need to see what is going on around you. Use lots of candles, mood lights, or even a well-lit room. Tell him you 'get off' on seeing his expressions, his smile, and so forth. Have a large mirror installed over your bed. Where it looks appropriate, set up other mirrors around your apartment. While all of this is not very important for safety at your apartment, he will learn that this is your style. Then it will seem very natural that this is your environmental preference elsewhere."

I learned that, if at all possible, I should make these modifications at other settings where I might be having sex regularly. I should try to arrange candles, lighting and mirrors such that I could get a good view of the doorways to each room. "You know guys like to watch themselves in mirrors during sex. That shouldn't be a tough sell," Kathy pointed out.

"Always have some small, slow-burning candles in your purse so that you can use them in a strange environment. Also, you want to use lots of pillows," Kathy continued. "Why? Because if you are in a position where you are flat on your back and he is over you, you don't have a chance of seeing much of anything unless your head is propped up on a bunch of pillows."

Over the next sessions, we began going over advantages and disadvantages of various sexual positions. Kathy began with the traditional man-on-top position. "Generally, he is going to prefer this position. And this is a good position for you to display yourself. As long as you psychologically feel comfortable in this position, go with it. But always be alert and aware, because this position, defensively, might not be very good for you. It could be hard to see and it could be difficult to hear. So when you are in it, prop yourself up with lots of pillows, if you can, and be alert. If you feel there is an urgency to the situation, you would need to flip him over fast. You have the strength to do that, especially if he is not expecting it. Or if you just feel a bit threatened or uncomfortable while on the bottom, ease him over to where you are on top, explaining that you want to switch positions for a while."

Kathy continued. "Now you are in the 'woman-on-top' position. With a big mirror over the bed, you are in a prime position to see everything in the room, and your arms and hands are free. He will learn to favor this position if you do your stuff. You want to make sure he can see you well. Let him admire the beauty of your body, face, and hair. Shimmy your breasts slightly or overtly, whatever seems appropriate. Make sure he can see your nipples jiggle about. With what you've got, you could just about hypnotize him. Let him feel them or lick them if he wants.

"This is the best position for you to exhibit your sexual appeal and for you to use your sexual skills. You control much of the movement. That means you have greater control over when you want him to climax and when you don't. Here is where knowing how to use your sexuality is important. Practice this position at upcoming swing parties. Enhance your appeal. Control the action. It is important that you learn how to be the one in control in most sexual situations.

"Overall, the woman-on-top position is going to be the best for you. It is a defensive position; you can see, hear, and act. It is a sexy position; you can display yourself; show him what you got. It is a control position; you can take charge. If you are trying to make a big impression on a guy, don't forget to be affectionate, flirt, kiss, and tease."

At swing parties, I was practicing everything I had learned thus far. The major swing party of those weeks was the annual costumed Halloween party at Circle S, attended that year by over 50 festive couples. A local physician, Ted Acula, captured first prize for best costume dressed as his name appears on his office door: "DR.ACULA."

Back at work, we continued our discussions about sexual positions. Kathy resumed, "What about control if your suspect enters
you from behind? The worst of these positions would be if you were
lying almost flat on your stomach with him hovering over you. You
can see very little and are almost totally captive.

"Should you find yourself in this position and you feel uneasy
about it, you can use your strength to ease him into a shadow or
spoon position, in which both of you are lying on your sides. Now
he would be completely behind you. You have a view of half the
room — with properly-placed mirrors, the whole room. Your arms
are free, your hands are free.

"Other types of rear-entry positions, such as doggie style are
good for sexual variety, but not for security, unless you can set up
an ideal mirror situation. Overall, probably the two best positions
for you are going to be woman-on-top and spooning. If you ever feel
uneasy about the sexual position you find yourself in, you can gently
glide into one of these two positions.

"Generally, let him be in charge when it doesn't seem to matter
much. But always be on guard and prepared to act. Take charge
when the situation seems more threatening. On balance, he won't
notice who seems to be in charge and who isn't."

Next, Kathy emphasized the danger of not having sex at my own
apartment. She related how on several occasions she was having sex
with her guy at his place when his wife or girlfriend would appear
and want to join them. "When that happens, you need to quickly
size up the situation. You may be in great danger. Decide on your
best escape strategy and how to execute it, if necessary. Be ready
to go into attack mode. Wives and girlfriends, past and present,
can be very jealous and want to attack you, maybe disfigure you,

possibly even want to kill you. Be extremely cautious and prepared for action."

So that I could observe differences between weekly swing club parties and those set up from time to time at someone's home, Taylor took me to several private holiday parties in November and December. Although party etiquette was the general model, how well it was enforced depended on who was hosting the party. I could see where these parties were much more loosely run, mainly because the hosts sometimes gave these parties so they could be chief beneficiaries of all that good sex.

One event I recall quite vividly was a fascinating party game called "Daisy Chain." The chain began when several women on the floor lay out in a line, head to toe, all lying on the same side facing the same way. Next, facing the women, a line of men did the same. Then the two lines inched closer together until they met up, not head-to-head, but rather head-to-genital. Both men and women bent their legs somewhat so that everyone could simultaneously engage in oral sex. A Daisy Circle was formed by bending the chain around until the two ends hooked up.

Afterwards, one of the women participants told me that there was something very psychologically pleasing about being part of the circle. "You can feel the sexual energy flowing around, circulating back to you." At that party, I realized how acutely aware and careful I had to be at a private swing party; I could quickly find myself in a very vulnerable situation.

Meanwhile, during the weeks at work with Mary Jo, Kathy, and Alan, we reviewed old case files, concentrating mainly on those with undercover activities. There were many different types of cases, with many different types of outcomes. I reviewed the detective work involved and the dangers the agents faced under various circumstances. I had to ask myself: What would I do in the same situation? There were hundreds of old files available for review. They were fun to read, and of course, for me, vitally important.

At parties I was now practicing everything I had learned in the previous six months. Although I had never before considered myself an extrovert, I always shone when the spotlight was upon me. Now I wasn't even waiting for the spotlight to come around. I was just out there struttin' my stuff.

It was strange for me to have so much self-confidence. I felt as if I had drunk a magic potion: I now had the power to make men want me, and I was enjoying that power. Taylor said that this newfound sensation was a very positive sign. He emphasized that swingers have often experienced so many partners that, over time, no one particularly stands out from the others. Therefore, if I wanted to make a lasting impression, I would have to give my partner a time he would long remember. To put it more bluntly, Taylor said I would have to give him a "fucking he would not soon forget!"

I laughed. I mentioned to Taylor how I especially liked the word "fuck." I told him how I had never heard it uttered in public until I started college. To this day, it is not part of my general vocabulary. But occasionally, using the word "fuck" enhances what you want to say. His use here, I told Taylor, perfectly expressed his intention.

I knew that I was so highly-trained that, if need be, I could give a guy a fucking he would never forget! I mused that if I didn't make it as an agent, I had the skills to be a very high-priced call girl; but, of course, my ambitions were much higher than that.

At the beginning of the New Year, the very first Saturday in January, we began to regularly attend parties at Alice and Denny's, one of the oldest and top-rated swing clubs in the country, located in the beautiful Lake Merritt district of Oakland. I could see why this club was so well run. Denny is a soft-spoken yet stern, no-nonsense type of guy, while Alice is rather vocal and somewhat saucy. She leads by example, getting involved in all sorts of activities. The two are a perfect pair, hosting about 50 couples on Saturdays, 30 on Fridays, and a cozy five-to-ten-couple party on Wednesdays.

I asked Taylor why we hadn't come here sooner. He said that I wasn't ready yet; there were people here I needed to meet and get to know and I had to be in top form before meeting any of them. At the very next party at Alice and Denny's, Taylor pointed out such a couple.

"Let's give them each an experience they will not soon forget," Taylor said.

Taylor and I approached them. "Hi," I said. "You look like a couple we would like to meet. I'm Renee and this is Taylor."

They introduced themselves as Jeff and Vivian, a very good-looking couple who I'd say were in their late 40s. He was extremely handsome, trim and clean-cut; she had a beautiful face, was slightly heavyset, and very talkative. Both were extremely friendly, very congenial. In fact, both were attorneys, as it turned out. Vivian was particularly excited to find out I was also an attorney.

I showed Jeff a time he will not soon forget. And I think Taylor knew just how to satisfy Vivian, because afterwards she was beaming, all smiles, talking up a storm.

That following week, the Justice Department notified Vivian of the government's interest in an upcoming court case on her calendar, and informed her a department attorney would be provided for her assistance. I was the attorney they assigned. The bureau, it turned out, had several such cases lined up for me, depending on timing.

Well, imagine how puzzled Vivian appeared that day in court. She kept looking me over, trying to figure out how she knew me. Who was Miss Clare? My last name meant nothing to her. And of course my clothes gave her no clue at all.

At the break she came up to me and asked, "How do I know you?" I looked her straight in the eye and smiled. When she flashed on my face, she suddenly realized. "Renee!" she screamed in delight. She threw her arms around me, hugging me. "Wait 'till I tell Jeffery about this!"

Vivian and I quickly became very good friends.

One day Vivian asked me, "Have you met the Hestens yet?"

"Not that I am aware of," I replied.

"Mitchell and Lorraine Hesten. Oh, you would know if you had met them. They are a very impressive couple, and she is absolutely gorgeous. Are you and Taylor interested in attending a big fancy ball the Hestens are giving in mid-March? Afterwards, we are having a small private swing party and sleepover at the site. I am going to be one of the four hostesses, so if you are interested, I will put in a word to make sure you get invited."

"Oh sure, we would love to go!" I told her.

Now into February, we attended a party of note again at Alice and Denny's. During the sexual segment of the party, Taylor and I were amused to hear a distinctive female orgasm, a musical medley of giggles, gasps, and spasms emanating from a bedroom across the hall. After waiting an appropriate period of time, curious to see who produced that sexy orgasm, we approached the open doorway and peeked in. "C'mon in," they said. They introduced themselves as Sid and Naomi.

"Everyone at the party knows when Naomi comes," volunteered Sid, a rather gregarious fellow of medium stocky build, older than most of the partygoers. He liked to talk a lot, laugh a lot.

"Hey, this gal is something!" Sid continued. "I keep telling her to come see me in L.A., but so far I've had to settle for just a few visits up here."

"He wants to put me in some of his video productions ," Naomi responded. "I asked him, do you do porn? He said no. So I said, too bad!"

"Do you want to do porn?" I asked Naomi.

"Oh, not really. What would my mother say? But still, I've had this fantasy of becoming 'Porn Queen of America.' That would be fun."

Naomi continued, "There is a writer guy who I go to parties with sometimes. He thinks he is so hot, he only goes by his two initials. Someday, he wants to become known as the 'Definitive Authority on Swinging.' Then, if I become the porn queen of America, we will both have titles!"

"I don't do porn," Sid told us, "but I sure would like to find something for her. She would be great!"

"Okay, make me an offer!" Naomi chimed in.

"I'm thinking about it, really I am. But you need to send me a video of yourself," Sid was explaining. "You can do porn in it, if you want, anything, but send me something for the others at the studio to see. And hear too! You need to have your sexy voice on that video."

"OK, I will. You'll see!"

After the enjoyable conversation, we helped tidy up the room. Sid gave us each his card.

Sidney Colsome
Film and Video Productions, Inc.
Culver City, CA, and New York, NY

The week after next, there was another party of note at Alice and Denny's. Naomi was there but not Sid. I guess he had to get back to L.A. Instead, Naomi was with a good-looking guy I had never met before. Perhaps he was the author who went by two initials. I wanted to go over and greet them, but Taylor had some other new guy he wanted me to meet. About halfway through the party, when it was mostly nude, Taylor pointed out a man across the room in the center of a crowd, with his hand on a post. "That guy is important to meet," Taylor told me. "Go over and pick him out accidental-like, and then give him an experience he will not soon forget!"

And so I threw off my towel and sashayed across the room, hips swinging slightly, one arm lifted high as I twirled my index finger about. Then I slowly lowered it, random-like, pointing my finger at a very surprised, handsome, older gentleman. "Do you want to play?" I asked him very seductively.

He hesitated slightly, glancing quickly to the woman beside him, and replied, "Yeah, sure." So off we went to a slightly private area where we wouldn't be disturbed, and I went about making sure he would not soon forget me. We had quite a time and I could see he was just loving it.

We must have been together for quite a while, after which we introduced ourselves. His name was Mitchell Hesten.

"C'mon, I want to introduce you to my wife, Lorraine," Mitchell insisted.

I rousted up Taylor, so that he could meet them both.

"Wow!" That was all I could utter upon meeting her. With her highlighted blonde hair beautifully coiffed in a stylish upsweep and wearing nothing at all except a distinctive wide gold choker and dangling gold bracelets, she was the most elegant woman I had ever seen, wearing no clothes whatsoever.

That next workweek was a short one, just Monday and Tuesday. The rest of the week was mine to celebrate my thirtieth birthday with family and friends in Santa Clara. On Monday morning, the civil rights office put on a big birthday bash for me, complete with balloons, cake, and candles. Afterwards, Alan, Mary Jo, and Kathy had a private present for me: an announcement awaiting in Alan's office that my training had been successfully completed. If I signed official papers the next day, I would become Undercover Agent Renee Clare.

TEN

The Assignment

Renee Clare's Third Report
Silicon Valley, CA
February 12 – April 11, 1980

O N TUESDAY, February 12, 1980, one day before my 30th birthday, I signed papers, took more oaths, and was declared: Agent Renee Clare. Before leaving for my long weekend in Santa Clara, I was presented with a possible assignment, an espionage case which required considerable technical knowledge. The trio hoped that I would embrace it, as I was one of the very few agents well-suited to handle the case. They wanted to give me the overall scope of the assignment so that I could read up on the technical features and think about it during the long weekend. They expressed the hope that, while in Santa Clara, I could meet with the Swains, the FASTEC founders, to discuss some of the technical aspects in the guise that it was a civil-rights case I was working on.

The overall case was this:

In 1977, our very reliable sources inside the Soviet bloc countries made us aware that the Soviets had copies of many top-secret documents, some as long as a hundred pages. For verification purposes, our sources have been able to make copies of a few of their pages.

At this point, we made a rather startling discovery. When we compared the Soviet pages with our own copies, they were not exactly the same! There were a few unimportant words here and there that were different. How was that possible?

This means that their copies could not have been photocopies! They must have been machine-copied, probably by computer. We wondered whether the Soviets realized this or if they were the ones doing the machine copying.

The lab guys think that the original photocopies, taken in the U.S., could have been "computer shrunk," meaning that they were reduced in size so as not to be detectable. Later, possibly halfway around the world, they were magnified back to their original size. In this process, word definition and clarity get lost. Re-emerging words may not be clear, requiring the use of computer enhancement, a process in which the computer searches for words that look somewhat like the original garbled word, and whose meaning makes sense in that context. When two words might fit, the computer chooses the most likely word. This occasionally leads to a very small number of errors, which appear like typos. For example, the letter "c" and the letter "e" look very similar. In this page, the word "check" was wrongly chosen over the word "cheek."

We don't know why this process was engaged. The difficult aspect in passing secrets is stealing them. Once photocopied at the original site, there are various ingenious methods of transporting them across to the Soviets. There seems to be no obvious purpose to have shrunk them to the point where computer enhancement would be required.

This is the gist of the case. We feel this case is perfect for you. You have the requisite technological background, plus experts in your family whom you can consult. We are not going to ask you to solve all the technical aspects of this case or do the detailed detective work. We just want you to understand the basics of what is involved and to be the human element. We will tell you more about this case after the weekend. For now, we would like to give you these unclassified pages to take with you to Santa Clara. See if you can get your uncles' expert advice on how these documents were computer-copied. Tell them you are one of the lawyers on this case and see what they think. Learn all you can technically about how these pages were copied.

"And so here you are," Alan declared, holding out some pages for me. "Happy birthday!"

That afternoon, as I drove down the San Francisco peninsula to my family and lifelong friends in Santa Clara, I felt exhilarated. Here I was on the eve of my thirtieth birthday, a time when many of my friends experienced foreboding and a feeling of sadness that their youth was over and their future uncertain. I felt much differently. Like them, my childish youth was behind me, but I felt my adult life was beginning in the most exciting of ways. I felt pride that I had already accomplished so much. I had earned a college degree and a law degree, had served as a civil- rights attorney for the

Department of Justice, and now, here I was, a highly-trained undercover FBI agent on the verge of immersing myself in my maiden assignment. I hereby pledge to all of you out there who had faith in me and assisted me along the way that I will not let you down! I will not. Thank you, world, for this wonderful thirtieth birthday!

That Tuesday evening, there was a big gathering in honor of my birthday. All my family and friends were there. It wasn't just my birthday; Stuart had turned 30 ten days prior. Of course, Stuart and I faced the usual questions: "So, are you getting married soon?" "When are you going to set a date?" "Time to be thinking of when you're going to have children."

Stuart, I could see, was quite happy rising in the ranks of FASTEC management. During the gathering, I told my uncles that I was working on an interesting case for the Justice Department. I asked them to help with the case by giving me a refresher course on FASTEC's technology and some technical advice.

Over the course of the weekend, my uncles Bob and Lou reviewed many things I had learned years ago regarding aspects of the technology their research in genetic engineering was based upon.

"Microtechnology," they reminded me, "is the scale of one-millionth of a meter. Researchers are now attempting to usher in the field of nanotechnology, based on the size of a nanometer, which is one-billionth of a meter".

Over the years there has been a constant quest to make smaller and smaller computer circuits. When I was a kid in the early 60s, the company computer occupied the whole bottom floor of the building. It was huge! Eventually, smaller electrical circuits could be built that utilized stronger and thinner circuit wiring and silicon-based semiconductors. By the 80s, the computer that used to occupy a whole floor and weigh tons was portable enough to sit on a desk. Not only are 80s computers much smaller and lighter, but they have much more circuitry with more memory, enabling them to do more complicated computations at a fraction of the speed. The thrust of the computer business has been to build smaller and more powerful machines that can do computations much faster.

In another discussion that weekend with my Uncle Lou, I showed him the pages from my "case" and asked how these copies could have been made. He agreed with the assessment that these pages could have been machine-copied, but he was surprised that there were any errors at all. He pointed out that if you had a 100-page document that was shrunk down to one-hundredth of its original size, it could all fit on one page. You could have one page with 100 little rectangular pages printed on it. If you magnified this one page back to original size, you should have 100 perfect pages with no mistakes.

If you had wanted to shrink the original information even more, say to one-thousandth of its original size, you could go back to that one page with 100 little rectangles on it and shrink that page to the size of an inch. It would now look like a postage stamp with 100 tiny rectangles printed on it. When magnified back to original size, every word should still appear correctly.

Uncle Lou explained, "The fact that these pages have typos suggests to me that, for some reason, these pages were shrunk down to perhaps one-millionth of their original size in order to be totally invisible to the human eye. At some point, this invisible dot containing the information of 100 pages was magnified back a million times so it looked the same as the original document. Now, there is no way you are going to get back 100 perfect pages. You would have a lot of blurred letters and lines. The page would look like total gibberish. To avoid this smearing-out process, you would have to use a computer. As magnification slowly occurs, the computer is constantly searching out the correct letters to put together to compose words that make the most sense.

"Now, you can see how this word, *check,* could have been *cheek,* in the original. The letters "e" and "c" look almost the same.

"This is how it *could* have happened. But I'm not aware of any process where you could shrink words to a microscopic dot one-millionth of its original size, magnify them back, and still have them be readable.

"Looks like a very interesting case. If you find out how it is done, let me know. FASTEC could really use this!"

During the drive back to San Francisco, I thought about all I had learned over the weekend about this case. Why weren't 100 pages shrunk down to just one page, I wondered? Then you could just fold it up and put it in a pocket or sew it into the lining of a piece of clothing, then walk across the border of a Soviet-bloc country. If one page seemed too big, just shrink down to the size of a postage stamp and just stick it on an envelope. Nobody would know what it was.

So why? Why was the document shrunk to such a microscopic size that not even a computer could restore it perfectly?

I was warmly greeted at work Tuesday morning. "Welcome back, Agent Clare," Alan exclaimed. I was thrilled to hear Alan refer to me as Agent Clare. After hugs from Mary Jo and Kathy, the trio began reviewing the case with me.

They emphasized that there was no direct evidence implicating an individual or group in perpetrating these activities against our country. However, computer analysis of the contents of the recovered documents together with the records of all the individuals who had access to the files pointed to several individuals — and one in particular — who could have masterminded these transfers.

"This individual has no obvious motive to be perpetrating these acts against our government: no relatives in Eastern Europe or Asia, no desperate need for cash, no known ideological alignment with the Soviet-bloc. But if we look at capability rather than motive, this individual stands out. Our suspect attended a scientific conference in Moscow three years ago. At that time, with the participation of the Soviet authorities, he could have set up a chain of events in which future documents were passed from one location to another, eventually landing in Moscow.

"We have had this suspect under surveillance for some time. But we need human analysis as well as computer analysis and electronic surveillance. We need to have someone on the inside; someone who can get to know him. We would like to attach you to this suspect.

"His name is Mitchell Hesten. You met him at your last swing party, and we understand you made a very positive, indelible impression on him. Excellent work! You successfully engaged him sexually and the prospects are excellent that you will be able to keep him interested in you for at least the next six months. You will be in a perfect position to spend significant time with him."

In a flash, I realized that my training had effectively ended six or seven weeks ago. All these parties at Alice and Denny's were for me to meet the right people for this assignment. I felt somewhat annoyed that I wasn't told. But I suppose the bureau wanted to see how I handled it before committing to me. They were trying me out! I guess I was auditioning for this assignment. Well, that's OK. I nailed it! I got the part!

"What we have for you," Alan continued, "is an initial six-month assignment from March first to September first. Then we will see from there. Your job will to spend as much time with Hesten as possible. Get to know him: how he thinks; how he feels about things; his tendencies; what sorts of things bother him. Get to know his friends, his business acquaintances, his contacts — anything you can possibly pick up.

"This is a relatively safe assignment. You probably will not be in mortal danger, but you can easily be found out and rendered useless. To be effective, you will have to be cunning and smart. Remember, you will be dealing with very intelligent people; never underestimate them. Always assume your suspect knows all your comings and goings. You always need to have a very plausible explanation for your actions and an alternative possible scenario for activities they may deem suspicious.

"The Hestens are sure to do a background check on you. That's good. They will know all about your FASTEC connection. Although that could be an alienating factor, FASTEC will give you perfect cover for any suspicions they may have about you.

"The Hestens plan to be working at their Paris office from April through August. We want you to be there. Stay with your sister Monique, if you can.

"We will not be able to have all our surveillance systems in place in Paris, so your connection with the Hestens will be of extreme importance. A Parisian couple, Marcel and Yvonne Auric, will be your contacts there and you will meet them soon. You will want to schedule lunch with Yvonne once or twice every week at an outdoor café or restaurant. From memory (no notes), tell her everything you have noticed during the week. She will be secretly recording you. Assume you are being watched at all times. And assume that Monique's apartment is bugged and your telephone is wiretapped.

"You have perfect cover. You have a sister and other relatives living in the Paris area. It makes perfect sense for you to be there and you are fluent in French. We think this case is an excellent fit for you.

"Put in for an unpaid leave of absence, effective March first. Now that you have reached the age of 30, you will start to receive your 'inheritance' checks every month.

"Congratulations, Agent Clare; and good luck on this assignment."

The very next evening when I looked over my mail, I found a formal invitation to the Hestens' Gala. Vivian must have made sure Taylor and I were invited and, of course, we responded in the affirmative. A little over three weeks later, March 15, 1980, Taylor and I attended the Gala, dressed to the hilt.

I had been briefed that this night might be the last opportunity I would have to make a grand impression on the Hestens before leaving for France; one significant enough that they would seek out my company once they were in Paris.

My job that night was to latch on to Mitchell Hesten early; to be sexy, even brazen if necessary, so that there would be no doubt he would be my nighttime swing partner. By the next morning, I needed Mitchell to have a lasting impression of me and a sexual experience he would think about for days and weeks to come. Indeed, I had to give him another fucking he would not soon forget.

I also needed to make mental notes on everything about him: who his friends and associates were, how close he seemed to be with various individuals, how he liked to spend his time, what he liked to talk about, what he enjoyed doing, what his personal tastes and quirks were and his attitudes on politics, women, unions, wages, the economy, the military, and the government.

The fancy-dress Gala was going very well. Lorraine Hesten was quite the hostess, very beautiful and elegant. Most of the guests, I would say, were in their late 40s, 50s, or early 60s. I was taken by surprise when Naomi showed up escorted by a relatively young, good-looking guy. I figured he must be the one that just uses his two initials; the guy we saw very briefly at a party a few weeks back. Apparently he caught Lorraine's eye too, because they strolled arm-in-arm much of the evening while she introduced him to various guests.

Meanwhile, Naomi was off chatting with different groups, and at one point had several couples all around her, hanging on her every word. Taylor was abducted by Vivian, who obviously had chosen him for the night. The other two host couples seemed to have everything under control. That left Mitchell, one of the official hosts for the evening, to escort me, introducing me to nearly all the guests.

When Lorraine Hesten introduced the writer to Mitchell and me, I was momentarily thrown off guard. He was one of the few relatively young guys there, appealing, and someone I could be interested in. I had plenty of training about how to behave in these kinds of situations. But it is difficult to train your emotions, especially if you haven't experienced this situation on the job. Well, now I have. I caught his name, though: ZZ.

I didn't want to become too well-acquainted with ZZ because I had to guard against getting caught up in a personal attraction. That would completely divert me from what I needed to accomplish that evening, so I was rather mysteriously cold.

Sure enough, at Gala's end, just as Vivian had told me, there were six couples: Mitchell and me, Vivian and Taylor, Jeff and Naomi, Lorraine and ZZ, and the two other host couples.

Most of us began stripping down fast to get out of our fancy, restrictive clothing. I thought we were all going to have a little naked sex party right there. But couples started going off in different directions, claiming their respective bedrooms for the night.

Now naked, as I was, Mitchell declared that as a host, he had reserved one of the largest and fanciest bedrooms for the night. With his arm tightly around my waist, leaving our clothes behind, we ascended the arched stairway and ambled down the hallway to our bedroom. It was indeed magnificent. I had to make sure Mitchell would not want to leave this bedroom for any reason until the next morning. For the next eight hours, I would have his undivided attention.

I just let him talk about anything and everything, interspersed with kissing and affection, flirtation and teasing, a little snoozing, and a sexual night I am confident he will never forget.

Mitchell was a good talker and an affectionate sex partner. He never had much to say about work, and that was one area I did not want to inquire about. He spoke often about his wife, Lorraine, in the most affectionate and respectful terms. That was a very attractive quality about him. And he spoke about genetics, robotics, and machines that could think. Mitchell was impressed that I had some detailed knowledge of these topics and could intelligently discuss these subjects with him.

In all, the night went well. We enjoyed each other and I got to know him. I found his thoughts to be insightful, sensitive, touching. He caught my fascination. My assignment was clicking.

That following Saturday, March 22nd, Taylor and I had a mission. We were to attend the Alice and Denny party to meet Marcel and Yvonne Auric, my contacts in Paris. Alan had told me that they were a respected Parisian business couple who do some work for the FBI. They were also members of the Chaillot Gardens swing club in Paris. "Both speak near-perfect English with a slight but discernible French accent," Alan told me. "Both had been exchange students. They met in the U.S., married, and lived in Washington, D.C. for some years before returning to France. You should openly do your thing with Marcel at Alice and Denny's party; it's mainly for show. Make sure people see you together. He will openly give you his card, so when you are in Paris, call them. They can help you. Use them."

Trying to get close to Mitchell Hesten, I learned, could be very challenging. He seemed to be completely faithful to his wife outside of swinging. So it might be only through swinging that I would be able to see him alone and get to know him. I would have to make the most of these opportunities.

"Fortunately," Alan said, "he is a very regular swinger. The Hestens reportedly attend parties at Chaillot Gardens just about every Saturday night that they are in Paris. Marcel will be available to escort you."

A few weeks after the Gala, as I was preparing my things for my trip to Paris, I gave my sister Monique a call. I asked her about a distant relative I met years ago. "Do you remember Jacques Pinard?" I asked her. "He stayed at our house when he was touring the U.S. I remember he was 20 when I was 14 and you were just 10. I had such a crush on him, but he never paid any attention to me. Well, now that I am 30 and he is 36, that sounds perfect. Do you think he is available?"

Monique thought he may have married some years back, but would inquire about his particulars with other relatives in the region and obtain his phone number for me. "And what is new with you and Stuart?" Monique asked.

"Oh, nothing has changed. I just don't think I am ready for marriage yet. And Stuart wants to wait too, so that works out fine."

A few days after my conversation with Monique, I received a surprise phone call from Mitchell, requesting that I accompany him and his wife and his guest, ZZ, to an upcoming dinner-dance-swing party at Chaillot Gardens. Apparently, I was going to be escorted by ZZ himself. Whatever happened to Naomi, I wondered? I understood that the Hestens had personally selected ZZ and Naomi to travel with them to Paris and accompany them to social and business gatherings.

I was now told by the bureau that Naomi had accepted a contract offer to do some film work for Sid Colesome, leaving ZZ without a weekly swing partner. How fortunate for me! But, I had to wonder, did the bureau have a hand in Naomi's departure? Alan told me that Naomi sent Sid pornographic tapes of herself that included a soundtrack— very important because of her sexy voice. Watching Naomi on tape after having personally experienced her at parties, Sid became obsessed with the idea that Naomi was key to the success he had envisioned. She was the special person he needed to make his *Queen of Erotica* film and others he was working on. Colesome needed to sign Naomi, only to find out she had just signed with Mitchell and Lorraine. Colesome needed to be decisive and was willing to offer Naomi a contract that could be worth as much as a million dollars.

Sid got Naomi under contract, and now I was going to get ZZ as my personal escort in Paris! Everything was going very well.

ELEVEN

The Group Room

Renee Clare's Fourth Report
Paris
April 12 – June 20, 1980

O N ONE OF my very first evenings in Paris, I had a scrump-
tious dinner with the Aurics at one of their favorite restaurants. Over dinner, they explained the manner in which they would
serve as my contacts while I was in Paris. As a Chaillot Gardens
member, Marcel would be available to take me to Garden parties if
I did not have an escort. Both he and Yvonne were available, they
said, especially on weekends, to assist me with anything. "Keep in
mind," Marcel remarked, "both of us are tailors. You know what
that means," he chuckled. "We tail people."

The plan was for me to schedule lunch with Yvonne at least one
day each week, whereupon I would disclose everything I could think
of in relation to my assignment. Yvonne would record my remarks.
After lunch we would stroll by the post office, where she would mail
the sealed tape in a security envelope addressed to the U.S. Embassy
while I casually mailed a few letters. From there, time allowing, we
would visit a museum.

I also arranged to have dinner with Jacques that first week in Paris. He accompanied me to a very fine and exquisitely-decorated restaurant. The setting told me that Jacques was available for romantic interests.

Over dinner I learned that his wife had left him about six months prior, taking their two children with her to their country home. She had since filed for divorce. Jacques spoke of this in tones that indicated that he was not happy at all with these developments. It was evident that he still very much loved her, and missed her and the children. He seemed lonely and lost.

I told Jacques about the painful crush I had on him when I was 14. He had no idea, he said. For the next several hours we engaged in focused conversation, totally fixated upon each other. After dinner, I invited him home, where we enjoyed another hour or so of flirtation and adoration before embracing in a sizzling, steamy night together. It was such a pleasure to be sexual with someone I was romantically interested in.

On April 19th, as previously agreed to in California, I had a date with ZZ and the Hestens to dine, dance, and swing at Chaillot Gardens, an extravagantly stylish swing club in the Paris suburbs. My job that night was to thoroughly entertain the Hestens' business associates and to get sufficient time alone with Mitchell Hesten to further my relationship with him. I was to learn all I could about him and Lorraine.

I was told by the bureau that there was no real expectation that in the next few months I was going to uncover any big secrets pertaining to the Hestens' spying activities. I was mainly there to observe, but also to be the human element, developing personal profiles of the Hestens, adding a face and personality to the pictures obtained mainly by electronic surveillance and computer analysis; and to help develop the web of their personal and business contacts.

I was to observe everything and watch for details, however insignificant they might seem. The government was confident that somehow, in a very uncanny manner that no one had been able to detect, this man — perhaps his wife too — were passing secrets to the Soviets. My assignment was to find out all I could.

Because so many business people attended them, an international swing party was an ideal setting for the exchange of information and even documents. These parties provided a unique opportunity for interaction among various international groups for business, social relationships, swinging, and perhaps even espionage. What would espionage activities look like? What would I be looking for? I was told to note the passing of information in the form of briefcases, envelopes, mail, and items such as keys. These forms of exchange could take place right out in the open, with everyone watching and no one suspecting, or in secluded areas such as restrooms or dressing rooms. That seemed like an impossible task! But I only needed to note such things in relation to the Hestens. The "tailors," Marcel and Yvonne, would be close by to assist me with these observations.

The swing portion of the party offers its own challenges. Advantageously, everyone is naked. All work items and materials are locked in a personal dressing room. Thus, it would appear that the swinging environment is materially exchange-free. However, ingenious methods and devices have been discovered in years past for secretly passing something to another person while completely naked and empty-handed. In short, the Aurics and I had to observe as much as we could — everything, everywhere.

For this first party I had some additional goals. First, I had to impress the Hestens in my role as ZZ's escort by contributing visually, sensually, and verbally during the dining and dancing portion of the evening; secondly, to delight the Hestens' business dinner guests in all ways possible, particularly sexually; and finally, to spend the night with Mitchell Hesten.

Chaillot Gardens more than lived up to my expectations. The second floor of the villa is a plush, sensuous swing club while the first floor hosts a fine restaurant, complimented by an Art Deco lounge and an inviting dance floor. The group room in the swing area offers a rich spectrum of scents and color. Sinewy naked bodies slithering upon each other in the glow of the warm orange light present a compelling invitation to join the group. Wall-to-wall mirrors, as well as those on the ceiling, reflect these images. The floor is padded throughout. In each corner of the room as well as at the center of each wall, huge, exotically-perfumed plants plume up to the ceiling, producing the room's hypnotic fragrance. This sensuous setting is hallucinatory, infusing one with sexual desire.

I noticed no suspicious "spy" activities during my inaugural party at Chaillot Gardens; no shady foreign characters or obviously strange activities (not counting swinging as a strange activity). After that first week at the Gardens, we attended two Paris parties. ZZ glided about at all three parties, speaking to anyone who spoke some English. He said he was busy gathering facts and impressions of each party for his book. At one party, he opined that society was now enjoying the golden age of sexual freedom. With birth control pills eliminating the fear of pregnancy and advanced antibiotics removing fears of most sexually transmitted diseases, all of us now could enjoy sex as freely and easily as we enjoyed food and drink.

Initially, ZZ was continually engaging and flirtatious towards me. At our first party, he hardly ever took his eyes off me. I knew he would have liked some swing time with me and I would have enjoyed that too — very much! But I had work to do. I couldn't start having sex with ZZ at these parties. I had to focus on Mitchell and his business associates. Consequently, at our second party, I made the very difficult decision to inform ZZ that I was engaged to my high school sweetheart and therefore, to avoid any ongoing emotional attachments, I would swing only with married men. At that point, the sparkling, sizzling zap developing between us fizzled.

After three weeks of parties, I was beginning to know and understand the Hestens. They seemed to be quite an impressive pair, a couple to emulate. I must have succeeded in my goal of securing my presence at the Hesten dinner table, for they invited me to one swing party after another. Fortunately for me, the Hestens had a penchant for swinging, faithfully attending parties nearly every Saturday night. Mitchell once remarked that they could take in the sights and charms of Paris nearly every night of the week, but Saturday nights were reserved for business, dining, and swinging.

The May 10th party at Chaillot Gardens was the first in which I felt I was on the verge of discovering key activities in Mitchell's espionage operations. The Aurics were there too, seated unobtrusively close by. Yvonne kept an eye on Lorraine whenever she went to the ladies room. The dinner and dance activities proceeded much like my first party there. Having finished my sexual routine with Mitchell's main associate of the evening, I wandered into the intoxicating group room, looking for Mitchell. And there he was. Watching from an adjacent corner, I witnessed a particularly interesting encounter between him and a dark-haired, fleshy beauty whom I had not seen previously, or since. From another vantage point, the Aurics observed too.

Aided by the mirrored walls and ceiling and the orange glow permeating the room, I watched the encounter unfold. Initially the woman was lying on her side, unattended, curled up, and motion-less. Mitchell, lying somewhat behind her, scooted over to her from behind. He approached her gently, possibly whispering something in her ear. He seemed careful not to place his hands on her as he pressed his abdomen against her butt. He then attempted to enter her.

She did not appear to know him. But without looking behind her or saying anything discernible, she assisted him until they were thoroughly genitally engaged. The rest of their bodies, however, were totally disconnected. I could soon hear the slap of his abdo-men rhythmically hitting her fleshy butt as his shaft periodically plumbed and reappeared from within her. In rather quick fashion, Mitchell ejected his semen into her while she lay there, somewhat motionless,

When they were done, she scooted away, remaining on her side until she was a fair distance from Mitchell. Without even looking behind her, she arose and left the room.

Because it took place at a swing party, this event would not have stood out except for the fact that it was repeated in exactly the same way the following week. This time, Mitchell connected to a cute young blonde who behaved like the woman at the previous party. There was practically no interaction other than Mitchell inseminat-ing her.

Again, Mitchell and the woman were never face-to-face, and she didn't turn around to glance at him. He probably never saw her face either. She never said a word to him as far as I could tell. He may have uttered a few words in her ear; that I could not say. The whole encounter seemed to be devoid of sexual pleasure, which was why it seemed so strange here, where the objective was to enjoy sex.

I recalled Lorraine commenting that Mitchell likes anonymous sex. But this seemed rather extreme — no conversation, no recognition. So this could all mean absolutely nothing. But I became concerned that these encounters could be significant. What if these two women were Russian agents, or working on behalf of agents receiving important information? Impersonal sex at a swing party would be an ideal manner in which to engage a foreign agent. The couple is naked, hardly communicating, having sex in the open for all to see. She is barely receptive and does not look or speak to him. He is hardly touching her. To all watching, no information has been transferred.

"Look, no hands," Mitchell seems to say. Is he the deceiving magician, transferring important information before our very eyes, leaving us to wonder how he did it? Very possibly, yes.

At the next party, it was time to get the Aurics more involved. It was time for the "tailors" to do some tailing. If there were to be more of these group-room encounters in the following weeks, we would need to know who these women were. The Aurics were to tail any future women to ascertain their identity. But the first two women had come and gone; we would not be able to find out who they were. Privacy at Chaillot Gardens was very strictly enforced and no one was going to reveal any information. If there was a third woman this week, we would have to determine her identity.

Not wanting to raise suspicion by looking for Mitchell in the group room for a third consecutive week, I asked the Aurics to observe instead. I told them that if Mitchell repeated the sex act in a manner similar to the previous two weeks, they were to follow the woman home and secretly obtain her identity. They were not to confront her, ask her any questions, or make themselves known in any way. As private citizens with no authority, the Aurics would have to work completely behind the scenes. If necessary, agents of the U.S. government could discretely follow up.

And so the Aurics observed the group room. Marcel reported that there was indeed a third woman! When he and Yvonne had entered the group room, he said, there were actually two young women lying on their sides in a curled-up position. Mitchell had not yet arrived. But when he did, one woman, looked right at him as he walked in and did not appear to know him. Mitchell saw her too, but there did not seem to be any recognition on his part. However, after he passed her, he suddenly approached her from behind so that she would not see his face. Was this spontaneous, anonymous sex? It appeared to be. But then, like the previous two women, after insemination, she rose and left the room without looking back. Marcel mentioned that he thought he noticed Mitchell utter something in her ear when he first approached her; perhaps a code word so that she would know it was him.

The Aurics later followed the woman and her escort home, obtained her name and address, and ascertained that the woman was married and attended the party with her husband.

So this was an ongoing situation! What could this mean? To a casual observer, the group-room encounter appeared to be spontaneous and anonymous. But to me, who had been watching and noting Mitchell's every move, these sexual encounters seemed to have been pre-arranged. But why? It couldn't be that Mitchell, a swinger at a swing party, was paying these women for sex. He has me and Lorraine, two of the most beautiful, sexy women on the planet. For free!

I told Yvonne that if there was a fourth woman, we would need to establish around-the-clock surveillance. We would need to know where these women go during the week. Who did they see? What did they do?

Trained to remember the smallest of details, I now recalled that the very first woman wore a dangling silver charm bracelet and that the second wore a distinctive dangling anklet — possibly the very same piece of jewelry adjusted for length. I asked the Aurics if the third woman wore any type of jewelry. Yvonne had noticed that the woman's pendant and earrings did not seem to match her bracelet, but didn't recall the specifics. Perhaps Mitchell looks for a woman wearing the bracelet or anklet. That was something to look for during more of these group-room encounters.

Marcel and Yvonne were again assigned to observe Mitchell in the group room. If woman No. 4 appeared, they were to proceed as they did the prior week: obtain her identity and then get the American crew to begin around-the-clock surveillance.

Marcel reported that, again, he and Yvonne arrived in the group room well ahead of Mitchell. And yes, there was a woman wearing the identifiable piece of jewelry. "I was very tempted," he said, "to creep up on her and screw her myself. But I thought better of it; I didn't know the password whereby she would receive me. Perhaps it was 'open sesame' or something like that!"

The Aurics waited for Mitchell to arrive. When he did, she was the woman of the evening. After having apparently spotted her dangling silver charm bracelet, Mitchell approached her, taking a circuitous route in order meet up with her from behind and assure that she would not see him. He must have uttered the magic words, for the woman assisted him in entering her. He then dispatched his semen into her in a businesslike fashion, after which both, independently and without acknowledgment, arose and departed the room.

On Friday of that week during my lunch out with Yvonne, I learned that the woman was married, attending the party with her husband. They were identified as a young, middle-class couple of modest means living in the Parisian suburbs. They had no identifiable close ties with anyone outside France. They had departed Paris very early Sunday morning, just hours after the Saturday-night swing party, and had returned Wednesday night from a three-night stay in New Delhi, India.

Equally surprising, we learned that the couple we had identified the prior week had also left Paris only hours after their party. They had gone to Sydney, Australia, returning the following Wednesday night.

I told Yvonne I was onto something significant. Mitchell must be paying for these trips, but why? These group-room sexual encounters had to be business arrangements of some kind. These women must be delivering something to somebody after they land, or perhaps making arrangements for operatives in these cities. It appears Mitchell Hesten had serious reasons to be so dedicated to Saturday night swing parties; it wasn't just business opportunities, social aspects, and sexual variety. No! The driving force seemed to be a secret agenda.

At four consecutive parties at Chaillot Gardens, Mitchell Hesten had four somewhat strange sexual encounters with four different women in the group room. At least two of the women flew to some far-off bustling city for a three-day trip with their husbands just hours after their swing party. What was the hurry to leave Paris? What did the couples do when they got there?

I couldn't tell if Lorraine knew of Mitchell's schemes. She accepts that he is going to engage in some kind of group-room activity each week. Beyond that, I had no insight into her knowledge or involvement.

To get answers, we needed to follow the next couple on their trip. I would not be able to go. I had to assume that I was always being watched; and the Hestens knew all my comings and goings (later, I found out they did). But, quickly now, Marcel and Yvonne had to obtain documentation to travel as U.S. Embassy personnel. Fortunately, they had time to do so; Mitchell's plan for the upcoming weekend was to return to one of the Parisian city parties, giving us another week to prepare for possible woman No. 5.

I was excited that my assignment was going to produce more results than just personality profiles! Now I felt justified in putting in a request to extend my initial six-month assignment. Yvonne said she would relay my wishes to headquarters.

Meanwhile, there was much going on in my personal life. My relationship with ZZ had rekindled. Back in April, we began the traditional French goodnight: quick pecks on the right cheek, left cheek. But that quick kiss slowed down each week and our parting kiss at my door got longer and more affectionate. And last week we spontaneously added a quick kiss on the lips! As I have been getting to know ZZ, I am finding him more and more appealing.

On another front, my childhood crush on Jacques had been fulfilled. My time with him was mainly devoted to easing the pain and suffering he was experiencing from the separation from his family.

I urged Jacques to try to reconcile with his wife. I suggested that he write to her, requesting that they meet in August for the traditional French vacation. He said that he would.

Interestingly, I hadn't known until a few weeks prior that Jacques was one of Mitchell's chief chemists! Jacques, of course, knew about my FASTEC background, having met my uncles 16 years ago. I told Jacques, "Let's never talk about your work. I'm interested in you, not what you do." And that was the last we ever spoke of it.

Meanwhile, back in Silicon Valley, the Swains were planning a big party in August in honor of Bob Swain's 60th birthday. Pressure was mounting on his son, Stuart, to announce our engagement at that party.

Now into June, the Aurics finally received the documentation they needed to board whatever plane the next couple took and follow them throughout their trip. We must know where they go, who they see, and what they do.

The next Saturday night, June 14th, we all returned for another party at the Gardens. I was so excited about the prospect of another rendezvous that I made certain I was in the group room, too. The Aurics were there, of course, watching and ready to travel just about anywhere.

And sure enough, there was woman No. 5, dangling silver charm anklet and all. I couldn't believe it! For the rest of that party, Saturday night into Sunday morning, I wondered where they all might be headed.

By Sunday afternoon, I just had to know; I wasn't going to wait until Friday lunch with Yvonne. Marcel had said he would leave their travel information with his concierge. Unable to contain myself any longer, I took the Metro to their apartment, where the concierge told me they would be back Wednesday night. They had gone to Rio de Janeiro, Brazil.

On Friday Yvonne was giggling with excitement, fresh from Rio, wearing a hat and a Brazilian outfit. She and Marcel had a wonderful time, she reported.

Yvonne revealed in her charming, slightly French accent that upon arriving in Rio late at night, they followed the couple by taxi, expecting that the obvious destination after a long plane flight would be a hotel, where they could check in and go to bed. "But surprisingly, it was not. Instead, we followed them to a rather far-off location, arriving eventually at a maternity hospital, where the couple, entering together, approached the front desk. The hospital, I noted, was open 24 hours a day, seven days a week."

Yvonne said that an official, apparently summoned by the desk clerk, ushered the couple down a corridor to a room with signage in Portuguese. "I don't understand Portuguese," Yvonne continued, "but my knowledge of Latin is good enough that I could decipher the sign. It said something like, 'Private Womens Rest Room. Lab Personnel Only'. The woman entered alone, then re-emerged in about 10 minutes. The couple left the hospital and returned to their awaiting taxi. Marcel and I tailed them, of course. From the hospital, we proceeded on another long drive to a totally different part of the city. Finally, we arrived at what was to be our hotel for the next three nights.

"It was obvious we had gone far out of our way to go to that maternity hospital. It also became evident in the next few days that their whole mission to Rio had been completed at the hospital. For those next three days we followed our couple from one tourist destination after another, immersing ourselves in the local food, drink, dancing, shopping, and tourist attractions. On Wednesday our couple flew back to Paris and we did too."

So what was Mitchell's interest in this trip? Was it just those 10 minutes at the maternity hospital on Sunday? We couldn't know all the facts at that point. But the next day was Saturday. Yvonne had to get packed, ready for another party and another trip.

TWELVE

Romance

Renee Clare's Fifth Report
Paris
June 21 – July 27, 1980

O N SATURDAY NIGHT, June 21ˢᵀ, we again staked out Mitchell in the Chaillot Gardens group room. But there was no sixth
woman. Mitchell was lingering there, apparently waiting, but a
woman wearing the identifiable piece of jewelry never showed up.
Evidently, we all got stood up. The woman must have changed her
mind, or just could not make it for some reason.

Quickly now I grabbed Mitchell for the next hour. Since Mitchell
was unable to deliver anything to anybody in the group-room, I assumed he still possessed it, whatever "it" was. I suspected he was
sexually depositing secrets into these women, to be delivered at the
other end of their plane flights. Because Mitchell was now due to
meet up with me for our weekly rendezvous, I was now in position
to get it!

I know Mitchell looks forward to the hour or so we have at each
party after his quick group-room time. One would think that sex

with Lorraine and me would be plenty for any man his age, but he still manages to come big time with these group-room women, afterwards dripping all over the place. Tonight, I had to make sure I got all that drippy stuff.

Fortunately, as a result of sex school, I had such a wide repertoire of sexual activities to draw from that I could always tune into his mood and guide the activities accordingly. Sometimes he was pensive and quiet; other times, verbose and energetic. I made sure each week with me was unique, suited to his mood, and sexually vivid in some way. I had to make certain we didn't fall into a predictable routine and that everything was a little different each week; something new and exciting.

But this week I had to make sure that he came deep inside of me and I got everything he had to give. He didn't seem concerned and he didn't hold back. That night I went home with a vagina full of Mitchell's semen, very possibly containing secret information meant for woman number six. Of course, I had to struggle to keep as much semen inside of me as possible; I was constantly leaking.

I went to the American Embassy as soon as it opened Sunday morning. I was eventually able to see someone with authority, but I had to wait for the technical staff to arrive so I could remove my diaphragm and leave it for analysis. Normally, there is not much in or on my diaphragm when I remove it, but this time it contained a small, gooey glob. I told the technician that I wanted the semen to be analyzed not only for fertility but also for any kind of irregularities. I requested that in addition to ordinary analysis, I wanted the samples to be investigated with a powerful electron microscope capable of detecting irregularities as small as one micron (a millionth of a meter).

If ever asked, I needed to explain why I went to the Embassy that morning. So I renewed my passport, which was fortunately due to expire in a few months.

A few days later, I received the lab results for Mitchell's semen. Fertility analysis indicated that he could possibly father a child, but would probably need hormone intervention. The electron microscope analysis indicated many small, mysterious specks sprinkled throughout the specimen. What that indicated, no one would speculate.

I asked what it would take to enlarge these specks. The response was "Equipment and techniques not yet invented."

This statement brought to mind the conversation I had with Uncle Lou back in February. He had said, "I know of no process by which words shrunk to a microscopic dot could be magnified back and still be readable." Was I being overly obsessed with this "secrets-in-the-semen" idea, or was I on the verge of discovering an entirely new concept of espionage?

I felt that the urgency and brevity of woman No. 5's visit to the maternity hospital in Rio was important. Perhaps she, like me at the Embassy, had deposited samples of Mitchell's semen for microscopic investigation while they were still relatively warm and fresh in her vagina from the previous night.

The urgency with which the previous couples departed for New Delhi and Sydney supported this hypothesis. If Mitchell is having his semen analyzed by experts in New Delhi, Sydney, and now Rio, is he concerned about his fertility or is he passing secrets?

I suspected he was depositing secrets into these women and sending them off with their husbands to various corners of the globe. I think Mitchell had an intermediary set up each group-room encounter. The contact needed to wear a charm bracelet or anklet so he would know her. He whispered a password into her ear so she knew it was him. He didn't want her to be able to identify him in case she was picked up by the police. Perhaps she would just as soon not know who he was, either. My guess is that these women were members of one of the city swing clubs. Although new to Chaillot Gardens, the women did not seem to find these parties abhorrent or distasteful. They seemed comfortable enough to have sex in the group room where anyone in the swing area could watch.

Yvonne thought I was getting carried away with the secrets-in-the-semen theory. She thought it was imaginative, but farfetched and completely without basis. "Why India, Australia, and Brazil?" she inquired. "They are allies."

"Because they are allies, because they're our friends, these traveling women would hardly be scrutinized," I replied. "Once at their destination, these women can transfer the acquired information to agents who then take it to the Soviet Union."

Yvonne laughed. "Mitchell could have much more easily mailed a miniaturized version of any document on one piece of paper to each woman's apartment. The women then could carry their mail with them to their destinations. He doesn't have to resort to microscopic techniques. Why all the unnecessary intrigue of swing parties and laced semen?

"And besides," she continued, "you know, better than I, that there is also the technical and scientific problem of how someone could lace secretions such as semen, with a foreign substance. Secretions are manufactured within the body and not exposed to the outside world until the body ejects it. So, how can one put anything encoded into it? I know you would say that Mitchell, a leading scientist in the tech world, could probably jump over that hurdle if he had to."

On Saturday, June 28th, we were again at Chaillot Gardens. And this week there actually was a woman No. 6. The Aurics swung into action, so to speak. I just knew that within hours they would be flying to some distant destination. This week I had the patience to wait to see Yvonne on Friday and hear all about it. Besides, my personal life was in a tizzy and needed some of my emotional attention while I awaited Yvonne.

As ZZ and I had been saying goodnight at my door, the quick kiss on the lips we had initiated a few weeks prior had been getting slower and slower. And he had begun embracing me ever so lightly and gently. The sexual attraction between ZZ and me had increased alarmingly. It just isn't natural for two young, sexually-active people to accompany each other to a to a weekly dressy dinner dance, then run around naked having sex with everyone around them to the exclusion of one another! This situation was getting out of control and developing into a serious romantic problem. I was falling in love with him. As I got to know him better each week, I felt more in love. What was I going to do? I felt I had to keep a lid on it, at least for the next few parties. I had to concentrate on what Mitchell was doing and come up with some answers.

That Friday, July 4th, one year after my initial nude swim party, I met Yvonne for lunch. "Where did you go this time?" I excitedly asked.

"Tokyo!" Yvonne exclaimed, pulling out a kimono she had purchased. "The nature of this trip was strikingly similar to the previous one. Upon arriving in Japan, now Monday morning local time, we did not go to our hotel but instead proceeded on a long drive to a women's health clinic.

"Marcel and I followed the couple into the clinic, where they were escorted to a particular room. Like the woman in Rio, she entered the room alone and exited a few minutes later. Apparently, her mission was completed. Like the previous couple, they had nothing else to do during the next three days except be tourists. We followed them around and did likewise. The four of us returned to Paris on Wednesday night."

Now into July, we noted that there were only four parties left. There are no parties in August because practically all of Paris shuts down and nearly the whole country goes on vacation. We had to wrap up our observations and analysis soon and develop our report. The Hestens and ZZ would go back to California, not to return to Paris until after the New Year. I, too, would return to the U.S. in late August. I had to stop any and all plans for my engagement party. *I couldn't marry Stuart!*

I told Yvonne the detailed plans I had laid out in order to continue the assignment into next year. She related them to the bureau.

Saturday, July 5th. Time for another party and possibly another trip for Yvonne and Marcel. Indeed, this was the case. On Friday, July 11th, Yvonne reported to me at our weekly lunch that she and Marcel had gone to Athens, Greece. Everything about woman No. 7 followed the script. Their first stop after their flight, now late Sunday evening, was a general hospital, where the woman, like her predecessors, was ushered into a private room. After several minutes, her mission was seemingly complete. Then it was on to their hotel, located in the vicinity of the Parthenon. The Aurics befriended the couple, traveling with them to visit ruins, museums, restaurants, and souvenir shops. The four returned to Paris Wednesday night.

That next night, on Saturday, July 12th, we did not go to Challiot

Gardens, but rather back to the City party. It was fun, but appeared to be uneventful as far as the case was concerned.

During that week, Jacques informed me that his wife had agreed to try reconciliation. She invited him to join her and their children at their country home during the month of August, when he, like all good Frenchmen, would be on vacation. Jacques had accepted the invitation and I hope that all goes well for them.

Also that week, I phoned Silicon Valley and informed Stuart, my childhood sweetheart, my lifelong friend, my gay fiancé, that we couldn't get married! We had always placated our family and friends by saying we were waiting to launch our careers before marriage. But both our careers had long been launched. I told Stuart, who was still masquerading as a straight man, not to worry; I would be there to break our engagement. I would tell everyone how I loved him more than anyone in the world, which was true. Then I'd say that, being the selfish person I am, I needed more time to travel the world while Stuart stayed in the Valley, helping shape the future of the FASTEC corporation.

My concern now was with ZZ. By mid-July, my attraction to him had grown to a painful level. His strong magnetic appeal seemed to be an undeniable force, drawing me in. We were on the verge of a complete breakdown of formality. It seemed like only a matter of time before one of us succumbed and this façade would be over.

At lunch with Yvonne on Bastille Day, Monday the 14th, I decided that we should file our tentative conclusions about Mitchell's activities. My report was verbal, as usual, with Yvonne recording. My conclusions were as follows.

<u>Regard as certain</u>: During a nine-week period in the summer of 1980, Mitchell Hesten was observed inseminating seven women

in plain sight on seven separate occasions in the group room of the Parisian Chaillot Gardens swing club.

Regard as certain: (Observed the last five occasions.) The morning after the swing party, on Sunday, each woman and her husband flew from Paris to a cosmopolitan city and returned the following Wednesday night.

Seems to be likely: Mitchell Hesten is having his semen analyzed and scrutinized by experts at each destination. This conclusion is based upon observing that each couple's first destination upon landing in their city is a health care facility that is always open. There, it is possible and very likely, that each woman deposited samples of Hesten's semen that were fresh in her vagina from the previous night.

We can only speculate as to the purpose of these acts.

1) The Hestens, possibly feeling a need to fill a void in their very accomplished lives, want to have a child together. Lorraine, 47, has two grown daughters by a previous marriage, ages 28 and 26. Mitchell, 51, has one daughter (age 29, married).

2) Mitchell Hesten has somehow imparted secret information to these women, which they carry (knowingly or not) to operatives at their next location.

On Saturday, July 19th, we returned to Chaillot Gardens. There would be no woman No. 8. Mitchell did not even go into the group room that night. The evening was uneventful as far as I could tell. But for me, the important part of the evening was with ZZ. Would it go beyond my front door and into my bedroom?

It turned out that the answer was no. All emotions would be on hold until our last party that following week.

Monday, July 21st, lunch with Yvonne. The bureau reported back to us regarding Mitchell's activities with the group-room women. Based on our report and the surveillance operations they made over the past year and a half, there is a strong possibility that the Hestens are trying to have a baby. It seems that Mitchell Hesten wants to father a child with Lorraine and that Lorraine wants to give birth.

One significant achievement missing in the Hestens' list of personal accomplishments was having a child together, especially a son. The effort and expense would be enormous and could involve medical procedures never done before. But the Hestens were always on the pioneering edge of technical advances. This is where they excelled. They had the necessary means and funds, and more importantly, the wherewithal to get it done. It was expected that in-vitro fertilization, a new experimental procedure by which infertile women could become pregnant, would soon become available. The Hestens seemed to be very involved in this pursuit, even investing in a new medical corporation formed by the Paris, Athens, and West German fertility facilities!

The bureau revealed that over the past 18 months, the Hestens visited many of the foremost childbirth physicians in the world. While living in Silicon Valley, they frequented those in San Francisco, and while on business trips, those in New York and Washington. During the last few months, they frequented prominent physicians in Paris, Athens, London, and West Berlin. In addition, last year they traveled to see physicians in Sydney, New Delhi, Rio, and Tokyo.

It appears that Lorraine Hesten is very dedicated to giving birth and that Mitchell Hesten is intent on producing a son. It could be that the Hestens want to produce a child involving all the latest and innovative technological advances; a child, especially a male, who would owe his very life to technology, and be produced by techniques rarely seen before.

The bureau believes that this is the process Yvonne and I have been observing. They further believe that, as of this date, the Hestens have not shared their quest to have a child with anyone outside their intimate circle. The Hestens are accustomed to secrecy; it is how they operate. If they are successful in this endeavor, it could be historic.

Of course, all of this could just be a charade to cover their espionage operations. "Keep a close eye on all this and note all details," they told me.

Apparently, the bureau was very impressed with my tenacity and detective skills during this assignment. So much so that they enthusiastically endorsed my detailed plan to continue the assignment beyond August.

July 26th was my last party of the summer with ZZ. He and the Hestens were leaving in the next few days for meetings in Brussels, Copenhagen, and Amsterdam. From there they would go back to California and not to return to Paris until after the new year, more than four months from now. I certainly wasn't going to wait until then to renew my observations of the Hestens or be with ZZ. I was going to San Francisco in late August to see the Swains about canceling my wedding . After that, I could feel free to pursue my romance with ZZ.

I didn't notice anything out of the ordinary at this party. The Hestens had their dinner guests as usual. Having already eavesdropped on many of the business conversations in the lounge, I noted who was sitting with whom in the dining room. By now, I knew most of the regulars by name; those I didn't know, the first- or second-timers, I felt compelled to watch closely. Mitchell was usually very sedentary at dinner. He rarely spoke to anyone other than his business guests, giving them his full attention. Lorraine liked to use the ladies lounge to freshen up and I was often tempted to go with her, but I usually stayed at the dinner table. Yvonne kept an eye on her.

The after-dinner dancing would often present a challenge for me to keep track of everyone. Who does Mitchell dance with other than Lorraine, me, and his female guests? Who does Lorraine dance with? ZZ was usually the hardest to keep track of. He was always conversing with new people and presenting his business cards to them, presumably for purposes of his book.

And then later, as always, I tried to observe who was swinging with whom, who was conversing in the hospitality suite, and, of course, who was swinging with whom in the group room. So much to remember after each party! I always tried to notice and memorize as many details as I could. Then I rattled the whole list off at lunch with Yvonne, who recorded it all.

Now, as ZZ and I headed home after the party, my thoughts turned to ZZ, and only ZZ. After a four-month, naked-close association, my feelings had developed into sexual, romantic longing. These last moments of our summer in Paris were going to be definitive.

And now, the time had come for our goodnight kiss...right cheek, left cheek...lips, more lips...a tight embrace. My thoughts raced to taking him into my bedroom and embarking on that passionate, sexual relationship we both knew we were destined to have.

But I broke off the kiss. I began telling him in a low whispery voice, "You know that right now I am engaged to someone. You are going to hear about my impending marriage. Disregard what you hear. I am going to call off my wedding plans. I am not going to marry him. It is YOU I want to be with. I want us to be together. But for now, I am very sorry, but I have to say goodnight."

And with that I gradually withdrew from our embrace, then physically separated from him, puckering a kiss to him in the process. We parted and I went inside my apartment, leaving him at my doorway.

I felt terrible, wrenching with sadness. Our parting was definitely not a fitting end to a whole summer of sharing intimate evenings. In my heart, I knew we should have at least spent that last night together. But I just couldn't. When that moment arrived during our kiss, I couldn't bring him through my front door. It just did not feel right.

Technically, I was engaged to Stuart. After demanding ZZ's respect the last three months for my engagement, I wasn't going to cheat on Stuart now by getting in bed with ZZ. I did not ever want to appear to be disloyal to Stuart in anyone's eyes. Stuart was my first love, a true love. And I still loved him dearly. But he is gay.

By Labor Day, I will have broken off my engagement with Stuart. ZZ will be attending the annual Labor Day weekend swinger's convention, very conveniently held this year in San Francisco. I will be there too, as a single, available female. Then, if he takes me in his arms, sparks will fly, and I will be his. My hope is that we will become a couple.

A most fortuitous confluence of romantic interests and job necessities has brought me to this very promising situation. At this point, it will be part of my job assignment to be romancing ZZ. Establishing that couple status will be of prime importance, and I will need ZZ's unwavering support.

The main barrier to my romantic relationship with ZZ thus far has been the Hestens. Had ZZ and I began a serious relationship near the beginning of the summer, they would have strongly disapproved, because of their suspicions that I was spying for their main competitor, the FASTEC Corporation. Would ZZ have stood by me? I don't think so. His ambition to be the international authority on swinging would have prevailed. But if he'd stood by me in spite of the Hestens' disapproval, he would have been dismissed, and my assignment would have been completely botched. Either way, beginning a relationship with ZZ at that time would not have been beneficial. So it was essential to postpone it, and I did. But now the time is becoming right.

ZZ is now a fixture in the Hesten organization. And over the weeks, I have repeatedly demonstrated my immense worth as ZZ's partner to the Hestens. At this point, I believe, ZZ's attraction to me has intensified to an undeniable level, as mine has to him. I do not believe that he would easily give me up. The Hestens would have to accept me or face the possibility of losing us both.

I know the Hestens have had ambivalent feelings about me. But I am confident I have been winning them over. My forthcoming announcement that my engagement has been broken can be viewed as my complete and final break with the Swains.

I know the bureau wanted to protect me on my initial assignment. But I could not have been training all last year, day in and day out, just to accompany my assignee at a party one night a week. Now I need to be where all the action is. I will need to be there every day and night. I will need to be where ZZ is as part of the inner circle.

ZZ's quest to become the international authority on swinging gives him close access to Mitchell and Lorraine. As ZZ's girlfriend, I will have that access too.

And what about love?, I ask myself. Could this steamy romance I am anticipating possibly lead to love? I indeed hope so. But for now, no. Love demands deep understanding of and empathy for the other person. Love demands that we know each other. And we won't, at least for some time. I would like to think that ZZ could possibly fall in love with me. But right now, it would only be my façade he falls in love with. Not the real me. Not Agent Clare! And in fact, I don't know who ZZ really is either.

Oh, ZZ! I have read some of your published works. You are no great writer, but what cover! Traveling around with the Hestens, writing about international swing parties!

I would be crushed if it turns out that you are an espionage collaborator; the go-between, an invaluable gear of Mitchell's espionage machine, the guy who floats freely through each party, receiving and imparting important information for each operation, and who, if convicted as a co-conspirator, might not be able to publish anything about it for the next 30 years!

But, hopefully, you are a fellow agent (or would-be agent) like me, but with a much better vantage point, enjoying the trust and confidence of Mitchell and Lorraine. Perhaps you are assisted by the government in your publications just as they might have assisted Naomi in launching her acting career.

I am romantically hoping for the latter. I will see you again in about five weeks; I have told you how much I want to be with you.

Wait for me!

THIRTEEN

Coupling

Renee Clare's Sixth Report
San Francisco / Yugoslavia
July 28 – October 6, 1980

A T THE CONCLUSION of my last report, it was late July, 1980, near the end of my six-month Paris assignment. This report picks up from there, at the beginning of my renewed assignment. Because this is a report, not a romance novel, I won't go into all the sexy and steamy details of the beginnings of my relationship with ZZ except to say that we met up again on Labor Day weekend at the 1980 swinger's convention in San Francisco. Not having seen each other for over a month, we produced quite a display of fireworks. Enraptured with one another, we practically hid out at my apartment for the first two weeks of September, hardly communicating with anyone in the outside world except for Lorraine and Mitchell. We had a San Francisco honeymoon. It was the most "in love" sensation I had ever experienced. Besides our sizzling physical attraction, we always seemed spiritually connected, whether we were eating out, running in the park, working out, or just enjoying the

City and each other. It was a little scary. Such a new experience for me. How was I going to handle this?

During our first week together, ZZ revealed that Lorraine had spoken to him at the end of August, expressing how ecstatic she was to hear that I had canceled my plans to marry Stuart Swain. Lorraine and Mitch were hoping, he told me, that I would want to travel with the three of them. They planned to offer me a one-year contract that would commence on the first of October.

I was flabbergasted! This is exactly what I wanted. Never in my wildest dreams did I think Mitch and Lorraine were going to offer me a contract so immediately! "Tell them yes!" I exclaimed excitedly to ZZ. But he seemed slightly hesitant for a moment. (Did our couple status give him pause as to our traveling plans?) "Surely you are going to travel with them," I went on. "You have to travel with them if you have aspirations of becoming the international authority on swinging. And now I get to officially travel with you. Tell them I say YES!"

I don't think ZZ needed any encouragement to romance me once we met again, but getting the green light from Mitch and Lorraine certainly could have eased his mind about it. Their early endorsement of me was a surprise given their previous reservations. They must have realized just how important I had become to their business operations — too important to let me just slip away. (At this point, like ZZ and Lorraine, I had begun to refer to Mitchell as "Mitch".)

One of the first serious discussions I had with ZZ was how were we going to feel about swinging in the manner we had become accustomed to this past spring and summer. As we discussed the topic, it became clear to both of us that our new bond as a couple should have no effect on our swinging style and, likewise, party swinging should have no effect on our relationship. "When we swing at parties, it should be no different than other couples flirting at cocktails parties. There is no seriousness to it; it is just social. And in the service of Mitch and Lorraine, swinging is also good business. That is what they are paying us for. I have no problem with that," I explained to ZZ.

ZZ actually seemed relieved at my proclamation. Perhaps he was feeling apprehensive that I might be more possessive of him. But we each had our own personal reasons for wanting to continue to swing. For ZZ, it was his book; for me, it was to have more intimate time with Mitch. So swing we would. I suggested to ZZ that we follow the Hesten model. We should expect loyalty and fidelity in our relationship outside of swing parties. But at a party we should each behave as we have in the past.

And what about sexual sessions with Mitch or Lorraine outside of parties? I told ZZ, "You have a very special, very beautiful relationship with Lorraine; of course you should not give that up." And I was thinking that I had to keep my personal relationship with Mitch active. It was going to be important for me to get his thoughts and reactions to various events as they occurred. I suggested we should each inform the other in advance of any separate sexual plans we might have with Mitch or Lorraine, but hopefully, these needs could be met at swing parties. In general, I was against separate overnights with either of them, and ZZ agreed.

After ample discussion, ZZ returned Lorraine's call in my presence, excitedly telling them that we had become a couple. I could hear that they were genuinely pleased. We met them for dinner the next night at one of our favorite San Francisco restaurants.

At dinner the Hestens were indeed excited to see us both, wishing us all the best. They inquired as to what we had been doing since we saw them last. I didn't mind telling them that we had hardly gotten out of bed!

"But at the swinger's convention," ZZ interjected, "we had some very interesting experiences. Did you ever hear of the *human car wash*?" Lorraine and Mitch expressed a puzzled "No."

"Yes, let's tell them about it!" I insisted.

ZZ began. "One workshop was a nude, couples-only massage session. It was well attended, about 25 couples. Everyone stripped down. Massage oil and mats were available. The session was led by a therapist couple who gave us detailed instructions as we went along on how to massage every area of the body — no sex stuff. First the women massaged their male partners lying on the mats; head to toe, front and back. Then the women lay on the mats and it was the men's turn to oil them up, massaging as they went along. But the highlight of the session came at the end when we all participated in what was called the human car wash."

"I'd like to tell them about that part," I said. "Couples lined up side-by-side and face-to-face with their partner, forming two long lines, each line alternating male and female. Everyone stands with their partner across from them and someone of the opposite sex on either side. So I am holding hands with ZZ across from me with men to my right and my left holding hands with their partners on either side of ZZ. Remember, we are all well-oiled. We raise our arms high and close ranks so that we are pressed closely together. We drop our arms and place them around the waist of the person beside us. So each guy beside me has an arm around my waist. My body is rubbing against ZZ in front of me while also rubbing hips with the guys beside me. That was a lot of fun by itself. But now the car wash begins.

"The couple at the head of the line starts, their arms raised high, her first and him following. They slither through all those oily compacted couples, stopping along the way when they find someone in particular they want grind against for a few seconds. Remember, their hands are raised, so it is just body against body, When the first couple reaches the end of the line, they take their place at the end, standing across from each other as the second couple comes squealing and squirreling through. It's like a sandwich where you are the meat. When it was my turn to wiggle through, it was such delicious fun!"

After dinner, the discussions turned more serious. The Hestens expressed their gratitude for the unofficial work I had already done for them in the past few months in Paris. They said how delighted they would be if I accepted their offer to travel with the three of them.

"Yes, I accept!" I interjected.

Mitch laid out their travel plans for the next 12 months, beginning with a week-long scientific conference in Yugoslavia the first week in October. Their hope was that we could begin work by attending it with them.

"Of course," was our immediate joint reply. There had to be swinging somewhere along the trip, since that was my specialty in the Hestens' eyes. Wherever the Hestens go, there is always swinging: good for ZZ's book and good for me too, since I get to interact very personally with Mitch's associates and possibly Mitch himself.

The Hestens proceeded to outline their plans for conferences and meetings in cities including Yugoslavia, Greece, Brazil, Hong

Kong, and Japan. They said I needed to be under contract with them so that I, like ZZ, could get the proper travel documents and visas.

I was astounded at the amount of money they proposed to pay me. Mitch said he would have to up ZZ's contract yet again to equal mine. Everything seemed to be moving so well and so quickly.

I signed my contract. I had to be a part of the Hestens' business delegation to travel in communist countries. My title was International Corporate Counsel. The first trip was in Yugoslavia from October 6-10, where Mitch was to give a keynote address at the annual biotech conference. From there we would fly to Athens, where Mitch and Lorraine had key business meetings arranged. In November, we would be going to Hong Kong and Japan. In early December, we were off to a conference in Rio de Janeiro, Brazil. Over the course of three months, we would attend conferences on three different continents!

Next we discussed swing parties. Mitch and Lorraine wanted to hear assurances from us that, having become a romantic couple, we would not be inhibited from swinging in the same flamboyant and exuberant style that distinguished our behavior in Paris. We assured them of how much pleasure and gratification we derived from past parties and that we looked forward to continuing in our same, sexy style.

Mitch went on to explain the nature of the parties. "Some, perhaps even most, of the swing parties we will be attending are private parties organized by Lorraine and me in conjunction with our hosts. Our hosts receive these parties as one of the perks of doing business with us. And don't think for one moment that communist countries are not prospective clients. They need technology. We anticipate they could be huge clients. And we want their business!

"As usual, Renee, your assignment will be to entertain our business prospects. In these cases, that would be our conference hosts. I hope you are not going to find this job demeaning or repulsive in contrast with your very prestigious career as an attorney. You need to feel that this is exactly what you want to do at this point in your life, and you need to be clear about what's in it for you.

"For ZZ, this is an excellent opportunity. He gets to write about swinging wherever we go. He gets to become the international authority. Essentially, we want to hire you, Renee, because you're a young, beautiful, sexy redhead who will have our horny hosts drooling at the idea of just being in the same room with you. If they think there is even a remote possibility that they could end up naked in bed with you or have sex with you — well, then, there is no telling how much more inclined they might be to engage us in business.

"That's what's in it for *us*. What's in it for *you?*"

I replied, "Don't think I wouldn't enjoy all that adoration! I love it! And I can handle it. But let's be clear, I probably would not be doing this if it weren't for ZZ. I know this is an excellent opportunity for him. And right now I want to go wherever ZZ goes.

"Obviously, I'm not looking at this job as part of my career path, although 'International Corporate Counsel' should look quite snappy on my resume. With the kind of money you are paying me, I should be able to stash away a bundle. That should give me greater latitude later in life to work on cases I feel passionate about without having to worry so much about income. So while I still have my youth, good looks, and sex appeal, I plan to cash in! Why not?"

"Fair enough," Mitch replied. "And naturally, if this job is not working out for you or for us, either of us can terminate the contract."

Mitch continued, "Our objective is to have a party at each city we visit. We could very well be the only swingers our clients have ever met. For them, hooking up with us could very well give them the sexual opportunity of a lifetime. Other companies may offer sex with prostitutes, but you, Renee, the young, beautiful corporate attorney, the high-class peer, are the experience of a lifetime."

"OK, I'm game!"

At that moment, I couldn't help but recall how the FBI referred to me as the complete package: youth, beauty, brains, and sex appeal. It certainly helps to be so well-endowed.

Near the end of dinner, Lorraine asked me in a rather whimsical fashion, "Renee, can you keep a secret?" Then she answered herself. "I know that you can, being the lawyer you are. So I am going to tell you a family secret. Mitch and I are trying to have a baby!"

"How wonderful," I chimed in without asking any questions.

"I know it may seem somewhat ridiculous for a couple of our age, each of us with adult children, but having a baby now is something we both want very much. We have our hearts set on it. You know, there are marvelous new techniques and procedures being developed where a woman can become pregnant with an implanted donor egg fertilized by her husband. With the recent successful birth of a baby conceived this way, totally new ways of conceiving are becoming possible for women who otherwise could not have children. I am very optimistic that I will be pregnant within the year."

"Oh! That's wonderful Lorraine!"

"I mention all this now because you will be hearing so much about it as we travel around. Wherever we go, Mitch and I will be seeing some of the foremost fertility physicians in the world. On this October trip, we have appointments with Dr. Papalexopoulos in Athens. On our Asian trip, we'll see Dr. Myakama in Tokyo. And then it's on to Dr. Silva in Brazil."

I reflected on the bureau report I received in July that cited Athens, Tokyo, and Rio as three of the cities the Hestens had been frequenting for fertility advice and treatment. Athens, Tokyo, and Rio were also the three cities where Marcel and Yvonne Auric followed couples the morning after a Chaillot Gardens party. The Hestens were also investors in a new medical health corporation that included three of Lorraine's fertility doctors. I could see where these upcoming trips could be very important and enlightening.

"You know," Lorraine went on, "for swing parties, I use a fancy new type of diaphragm. I'll show it to you sometime. I recommend that you get one too. They are easy to put in for the evening, easy to take out the next morning. Let's make an appointment for you with my fertility doctor in Paris, Dr. Laplace. He can fit you for one when we return."

"Thanks, Lorraine, I look forward to it. I have been using the same diaphragm for years. Time to get a new one. And birth control pills don't always agree with me, messing with my estrogen levels, giving me headaches and nausea."

How perfect, I thought to myself. Lorraine just gave me an excuse to inquire about their fertility involvements, starting with Dr. Laplace. Perfect!

At the conclusion of dinner, Mitch and Lorraine expressed again how happy they were for us, and how fortunate they were that I was joining their team. They predicted extraordinarily fun times for the two of us and very profitable business deals for the two of them.

In the days that followed, ZZ and I continued to share our feelings for each other and how we wanted our relationship defined.

I tried to present as much of my real self as I could without any indication of my involvement in the FBI. I knew it would be much easier over time to just be myself. And I wanted ZZ to know the real me as much as possible.

I realized through these conversations that, although we had walked around together physically naked during four months of swing parties, our inner selves were always fully clothed. We hardly knew anything about each other!

But we did know each other's natures. We found each other very attractive. I told ZZ as much about myself as I could: my family, my college days, law school, and my work as a civil rights attorney. ZZ told me more about himself: growing up in Los Angeles, studying journalism at Berkeley, and working as a tech writer in the Navy Department. He said he had been struggling as a professional writer, but seemed to have found an audience with his stories of swingers.

He expressed serious concerns that by accepting this job with the Hestens, I was swerving off my career path as an attorney (job title aside). ZZ said he was happy I was willing to put my career path on hold so we could be together, but that he was concerned for me.

That was so sweet of him to say. (Little did he know!) I expressed how much I appreciated his concerns and how thoughtful he was to consider my needs. But, emphasizing how hard I had been working for the past dozen years at Berkeley, Harvard, and the Justice Department, I explained that a break from the academic path was just what I needed right now.

ZZ seemed pleased with my explanation. He didn't want to feel that I was sacrificing my needs. Perhaps he was feeling that I might expect a sacrifice from him at some future point. I didn't know.

These are the typical types of evaluations two people try to make when they don't know each other well. It feels awkward.

As ZZ told me about himself, I listened intently, trying to evaluate exactly what he does. Is he just a writer, as he says? Could he be a federal agent like me? Could he be part of Mitch's espionage organization? I had developed strong feelings for ZZ at this point. I was going to be seriously disappointed and upset if he were up to no good. I was so much enjoying the "love is blind" sensation.

About the third week into September, I had an appointment to visit Alan, my boss at the Federal Building. I told ZZ I planned to visit my old friends and co-workers at the Justice Department for a long lunch to tell them all about us.

This was actually my second meeting with Alan since my return from Paris. My first was in late August before I met up with ZZ at the swingers convention. At that meeting, Alan, Mary Jo, and Kathy discussed and evaluated my initial assignment. "You did a great job in Paris," Alan declared, "absolutely fantastic; everything we had hoped when we assigned you to this project."

At this September meeting, I formally resigned my position as a civil rights attorney at the Department of Justice. Now that my six month leave of absence was over, and I was employed by Mitch's company, I could not have it appear that I had any connection with the Justice Department. Of course, I was still secretly employed by the FBI. Also at this meeting, I informed Alan of all that had transpired since my return to San Francisco: my new relationship with ZZ, my new relationship with the Hestens, and the upcoming travel plans.

"Fantastic," was Alan's response. "You will be in a prime position to observe everyone the Hestens do business with.

"Wherever you travel, learn all about Hestens' associates, friends, and contacts. Learn their routines, activities, places they frequent. Memorize information about everyone and everything. I like your laundry list method. (That's where I memorize a whole string of related information and assign a single letter to it. Then I memorize a different string of information and assign a different letter to it. Eventually, I have a whole list of single letters that help me conjure up everything I have memorized. It looks like a Chinese laundry list.) When you return to Paris after a trip, meet with Yvonne like before and rattle off your laundry list of information. When you return to San Francisco after a trip, make an appointment to meet with Mary Jo or Kathy for lunch at a diner and do the same.

"Your main objective is to discover all the operatives who are links in the chain that plots against U.S. interests and disseminates secret material. We want to know everyone who is involved. You are in the position to get that information. We want to be able to build a viable case: names of those involved, actions observed, dates, and more.

"We need to determine if Hesten is acting with a few key people or working with a whole network of spies. We would like to get some definitive evidence implicating him. Months back, you recall, we made available to him phony secret documents. If any of these ever show up in the Soviet bloc, it would be definitive evidence that he passed them on. So far, nothing has materialized. Meanwhile we're going after the whole operation.

"You are going to be in a lot more danger on this assignment, and may have to call upon your training. You are going to be in foreign countries where you do not know a soul. You are going to attend private swing parties where the rules can be a little vague and loose. There will be alcohol and drugs; stay clean. Parties could get out of hand. Remember all your defensive sex techniques and be ready to use them. Be on guard.

"You can expect that the four of you and your luggage will be well searched any time you fly out of the States. But even if Hesten is carrying secrets with him, I am sure they will be well hidden.

"So, Renee, tell me, what are your general impressions of your three companions so far?"

I replied, "I'll start with ZZ. I really like him. He seems like such a great guy. I feel in my gut that he is. But I fear that he could be naïve, and possibly get caught up in some of Mitch's operations without realizing it. I sure hope everything turns out okay for him. I am going to be seriously disappointed and brokenhearted if it ends up otherwise.

"As for Lorraine, I sure admire her; she's everything a woman should be (unless if she's passing secrets, that is). She is elegant, beautiful, intelligent, sexy, and financially savvy, a full partner in her marriage and their business. She seems to be a loving, devoted wife and mother. Her older daughter Jasmine, who is two years younger than I am, is in charge of their Paris office.

"And then there is Mitch. Well, you know about him: an entrepreneurial genius as both a scientist and a businessman. He is very smooth, very likable, and has so much talent. He treats everyone he meets with dignity and respect. He knows how to operate to get people to do just what he wants them to."

Alan replied, "From what I hear about them, your descriptions seem right on. I am sure you will have no problem turning them in if the evidence points in that direction. Just keep an open mind about everything."

"This is a real fun assignment. Much more depth and intricacies than I expected. Thanks so much."

"You trained for it and earned it. Happy and safe travels."

* * * * *

On a beautiful sunny day a couple of weeks after that, we were in Dubrovnik, Yugoslavia. It was Saturday, October 4th, 1980, the 23rd anniversary of the launching of Sputnik, and five months after the death of Marshall Tito, the country's communist hero, without whom the country might not hold together.

We stayed overnight in Dubrovnik, sightseeing, eating out, and enjoying the picturesque, Venice-like city. The next day, Sunday, we arrived in Herceg-Novi, a quiet little town and the site of this year's Eastern European Biotech Conference. We were met by the conference organizer, a pleasant-looking, rather jovial heavyset man about Mitch's age, Mr. Busjindrankovic, whom everyone called Mr. Boss, or just plain Boss.

The rugged hills of the countryside reminded me of California. The grounds of the conference center resembled a small university campus, with cottages and dormitories. We were shown our cottage, settled in, and then strolled about the grounds. Later the four of us joined Boss, Mrs. Boss, and several scientists and their wives for Sunday night dinner at the conference center.

I had yet to get any sense that we were in a communist country. A "decadent" Elvis Presley film was playing at a local movie theater, Coca-Cola machines seemed to be everywhere, and the evening and nights spots were alive with Western-style disco and rock 'n roll music.

On Monday, the annual Eastern European Biotech Conference

began. There were about 40 participants from many parts of the world, mainly from Eastern Europe. I was surprised to learn that it would be conducted entirely in English, despite the fact that the four of us were the only native English speakers in attendance! There were no other Americans present; no British either. The Americans and British generally feel that it is best not to bestow prestige upon these conferences as a result of their attendance. The Hestens are an exception. Mitch says, "Thank you, America; I'll just go myself and take all their business." I don't think the State Department is pleased.

All talks were presented in English; all questions, answers, and discussions were also in English. English had become the official international scientific language. A scientist, therefore, must learn to think and converse in these terms.

And so there we were: the French, Italians, Germans, Greeks, Yugoslavs, Romanians, Hungarians, Austrians, Czechs, and others, all speaking English.

Most of the participants were young, in their 20s and 30s. About one-third of them were women. As an elder statesman in the field, Mitch gave one of the opening talks. He spoke about recent advances in the biotech field and new trends developing. He made predictions, some of which should become evident in the next five to ten years.

Then Mitch spoke of how, by the very nature of human beings, there will always be a fervent drive for new technology. "Our rich culture," he said, "is derived from the complexity and subtleties of our brains. Language," he said, "is rich with verbs describing variations and subtleties of action; adjectives and adverbs express all possible shades and nuances of actions and objects. All cultures of the world have a rich language because every human on the planet thinks in these terms.

"Music is the richness of language and emotions expressed through the sounds of the voice and instruments that we invent to help us express this melodiousness. Art is the richness of language and emotion expressed through visual stimulation, usually in the form of paintings and sculpture. Dance, opera, and ballet are combinations of both the visual and the auditory. Other species do not have language, music, art, dance, and so forth because their brains lack the capacity to think in such subtle terms. It is not so much that they physically couldn't develop these skills; it is more because they have nothing to say. We are very special creatures. The tech industry thrives and will continue to thrive because creatures like us are always looking for new ways to express ourselves."

As examples, Mitch spoke about some of the latest discoveries and patents, one being digital camera technology that stored photos on a memory chip instead of using photographic film. He talked about how that field has developed and blossomed since its discovery about five years ago. Tools such as these help us in our research. And Mitch spoke about the various genetic diseases that our field works endlessly to eradicate.

Mitch's thirty-minute speech was very well received and generated great interest, many questions, and much discussion. His talk was accented with numerous slides and references to other talks and literature. A printed copy of his speech was passed out to everyone in attendance. And, as an added touch, each participant received several souvenir flashlights with the inscription *1980 Eastern European Biotech Conference, Herceg-Novi, Yugoslavia.* "Take a souvenir for yourself and one or two for your friends and family," Mitch declared.

Lorraine walked among the delegates, personally distributing the souvenirs.

All-in-all, it was a delightful day: fun to see Mitch at work, animated and energized; and enjoyable to see him receive so much respect and adulation. I thoroughly enjoyed observing all this, but my nature and training gave me the sense throughout that something more was going on beneath the surface of what I witnessed. Just what, I had no idea. But I grabbed up several souvenir flashlights and a copy of Mitch's speech.

Later, I mentioned to Lorraine that throughout the meeting, I felt I was being starred at.

Lorraine concurred. "You have to realize that many of these people have never met an American!"

I particularly noticed a young, handsome Romanian scientist who could hardly take his eyes off me all day. And to a lesser degree, a young Bulgarian scientist.

That evening, we had dinner with Boss and his wife. Around dessert time, I was surprised at the direction taken by the after-dinner discussion. Boss mentioned that he had met the four of us before. (I thought I had recognized him.) It was at Chaillot Gardens back in June. "We spoke briefly," Boss said.

"Oh, yes, I recall," Mitch replied diplomatically. I don't know if he really did remember Boss or not. But I did. Someone had introduced the four of us to Boss and his wife in the cocktail lounge. I remember Boss giving me quite a sexual look-over, but we had no further contact with them that night.

Boss then asked, "How about if I arrange a small private swing party at the end of the conference to celebrate our good times and friendship? Are you open to such a party?"

Mitch replied, "I think the four of us would enjoy that very much. Do you have people in mind?"

"My wife and I, of course. After that, I know many participants here would love to be in the company of you four stimulating Americans."

Lorraine suggested, "Yes, the Romanian and Bulgarian scientists who have been eyeing us all day, and the Czech woman who seems to adore ZZ."

"Shall we plan then for Friday night?" Boss asked.

Mitch replied, "No, many of the participants will be leaving late Friday afternoon after the last session. Lorraine has to leave Friday morning to make a doctor's appointment that afternoon. Thursday night would be much better."

"Okay," Boss agreed, "Thursday night it is."

Later that evening at our cottage, Mitch went over our personal strategies for the rest of the week. He would be attending all the talks and would socialize with everyone. Lorraine would attend the talks that interested her. ZZ and I should be available to socialize during breaks and at lunch. "Turn on the charm, be friendly, even flirt, but discreetly."

At the swing party, I was to thoroughly entertain Boss. "Take plenty of time with him. He is an important person we will want to deal with in the future. The Romanian and Bulgarian guys will have to settle for Lorraine," Mitch said with a wink and a smile.

"After you are finished with Boss, Renee, if there is still time or interest left, you can take on the two scientists or anyone else." For himself, Mitch thought it would be appropriate to be with Boss's wife, unless she took to ZZ. "We need to spread ourselves among all of them; no swinging among ourselves."

Mitch stressed the importance of us making a very strong, positive impression at the swing party. Word gets around, he stressed. This party is very important.

Borrowing a phrase from Taylor, I told my three companions, "Don't worry. I'll give Boss a fucking he will never forget!"

FOURTEEN

Spy Alert

Renee Clare's Seventh Report
International Travels / Silicon Valley
October 7, 1980 – February 24, 1981

THAT IS HOW the week in Herced-Novi played out. The Thursday evening swing party developed as planned. There was a four-room recreation cottage available and we had plenty of snack food. I immediately played up to Boss and led him into one of the far rooms. I felt a bit nervous: my first private party without Taylor and in a foreign country. Boss' wife could conceivably come in, jealous and angry, yelling things at me, none of which I would understand, and possibly even physically attacking me. I recalled my job training and acted accordingly.

I chose a room that was logistically the most suitable and a position in bed that gave me a full view of the entrance. As it turned out, everything went well. I did a lot of flirting and teasing with Boss. I let him fondle me and lick me all over. And I called upon much of the subtle oral sex skills I learned during training, greatly raising his level of excitement. I was always in complete control, preventing him from coming until I wanted him to. I took plenty of time with him, teasing, flirting, kissing. I shimmied my breasts and wiggled about. I drove him crazy. I let him fondle me and lick me some more. He was panting and gasping.

Finally, when I could tell his sexual desire was at its height, I chose the woman-on-top position and kept the sexual movements slow for a while. When I sensed the moment was right, I began moving more vigorously, bouncing up and down, my tits going wild. He came big time, creating a roar that I'm sure his wife could hear several rooms away. It was several minutes before he could get up. I think I did it! In all, I gave him a fucking he will never forget!

While I was doing my thing with Boss, Mitch was delighting Mrs. Boss in one of the front rooms. ZZ was with the Czech woman. As it turned out, she was the only woman scientist willing and available on this short notice. So Lorraine took on both the young Romanian and Bulgarian scientists in the bedroom next to mine. The Romanian watched intently while the Bulgarian was engaged with Lorraine. But not for long. As Lorraine had noted to me earlier, these young scientists are usually rather inexperienced sexually; they do not have much staying power and blast off rather quickly. The Bulgarian came fast. Then it was the Romanian's turn.

After everyone was spent, the two scientists still wanted to have some contact with me. After Boss left the room, I motioned for the two guys to come in and join me in bed. The three of us hugged and rolled around together for a while. I kissed them both and let them fondle me. "Maybe next time we can do some screwing," I told them.

They smiled. Their eyes lit up. "Some screwing! Da! Da!" they exclaimed.

On Friday morning, we took Lorraine to the airport so she could fly to Athens to make her appointment with Dr. Papalexopoulos later that day. The three of us stayed until Sunday and then joined Lorraine.

This trip was the first of many trips we took to various parts of the world. Some of the patterns we established in Yugoslavia persisted in following trips. Mitch and I usually swung with the host couple and Lorraine and ZZ with the other couple or couples. The sense was that the leader gets the young, beautiful woman (me!), but his wife would be more comfortable with a man more her age group (Mitch), rather than the young, handsome man (ZZ). But if she gravitated toward ZZ he took her.

In Athens, Mitch and Lorraine had meetings scheduled with a scientific business group on the first three days of the week. As the foreign secretary and corporate counsel, ZZ and I attended the first day of every meeting, leaving the rest of the week for sightseeing. On Wednesday night we participated in our requisite swing party, where I, of course, entertained the business host. Mitch and Lorraine both had fertility appointments on Thursday with Dr. Papalexopoulos, and Friday we flew back to San Francisco.

For the last two weeks of October, we were in the San Francisco area. Mitch and Lorraine were busy at their Santa Clara headquarters; ZZ and I were hanging out at my City apartment. I arranged to have lunch one afternoon with Kathy, where I related everything that happened during my two-week trip.

While in the Bay Area, I dedicated myself to locating and reading every reference in Mitchell's speech. Most of them were quite technical. I barely understood what they were about at this point. But in the months to come, I came to understand the basics and significance of each reference. But the most fascinating reference on the list had to have been there by mistake. Perhaps it had been planted there by someone to embarrass Mitch. I understood this reference completely! It was all about the sex practices of some ancient Asian noblemen, most notably the practice in which the man inserts a small pearl into his penis before sex, then passes the pearl to the woman during orgasm. It is said that the sensation of the pearl ejecting from the man's penis during ejaculation greatly enhances his orgasm. Fascinating!

My initial reaction was to inform Mitch of the irrelevant reference. But I couldn't do that! Why would I have been so interested in his references? So I never mentioned it.

The first two weeks in November the four of us went on our Asian trip. Before leaving, I had lunch with Kathy and rattled off everything that occurred in my presence while we were in the San Francisco area. The first week of our Asian trip, we attended the 1980 Asian Biotech Conference in Hong Kong. The second week Mitch and Lorraine had scientific-business meetings in Tokyo. Lorraine had fertility appointments on both Fridays with Dr. Myakama in Tokyo.

The Asian Biotech Conference was similar to the conference we attended the previous month in Yugoslavia. Again, the total conference was conducted in English, and Mitch's talk was very well received. His speech was like his previous talk in Yugoslavia, but included topics more attuned to Asian interests. Again, Mitch spoke energetically about the emerging field of digital photography. And again, he distributed copies of his talk and Lorraine walked around the room giving out souvenir flashlights with the inscription *1980 Asian Biotech Conference, Hong Kong.*

The sightseeing in both Hong Kong and Tokyo was gorgeous and, of course, I had my usual laundry list to memorize. But personally, the most interesting aspect was the format of the private Asian swing parties. It was totally different from Western parties.

In both Hong Kong and in Tokyo, Mitch had reserved two adjoining suites on the same floor as the suites at our hotel. In both cities, the two most senior Asian couples joined us for dinner at the hotel, after which we all adjourned to our respective hotel rooms, where we showered, groomed, and dressed in hotel robes. They called for us when they were ready, whereupon the four of us, wearing only hotel robes, walked down the hall to their rooms. The four of them greeted us; they also were dressed only in robes.

We immediately paired up with our chosen partner. I paired up with our Asian host and escorted him back to my bedroom down the hall. Lorraine escorted her partner to her room; Mitch took the host's wife into one of the rented suites; ZZ stayed in the other suite with the other Asian woman. The interesting aspect was that each couple had their own private suite for an hour or so, and was only nude in the presence of their partners. There was no group nudity or sexual activity: it was all very civilized, very respectful.

The first week of December we had a third conference to attend. This one was in the summer weather of Rio de Janeiro, Brazil, a very exciting city. As far as Mitch's talk was concerned, it was everything I had come to expect, including emphasis on digital photography and the distribution of an ample supply of souvenir flashlights embossed with *1980 South American Biotech Conference, Rio de Janeiro, Brazil.*

I found this experience of traveling with Mitch, Lorraine and ZZ surprisingly delightful, exciting, and exhilarating. It was a new life unfolding for me, in the constant companionship of such intelligent, sophisticated, dynamic people. The bureau had cautioned me about the "Patty Hearst effect," referring to how the heiress, Patty Hearst, began to sympathize and identify with the band of criminals who had kidnapped and ransomed her, eventually joining their cause. But I had to admit that the more I was with Mitch and Lorraine, the more I admired and respected them.

I know ZZ felt the same way. He said he was in constant awe of them. I had come to the conclusion that if any of these three were involved in espionage activities, it would be for one reason only: they felt it was the right thing to do. They would have to believe that morally, they were making the correct choice. And now, getting to know ZZ so completely, I just couldn't see him making a choice for communism. Naturally, there could be a whole side of ZZ that I didn't yet know, just as there was a side of me he didn't know. But these unknowns would have to fit in with the person's basic makeup. Knowing him as I did, I could state that in my professional judgment, ZZ would not knowingly betray his country.

But I couldn't say that about the Hestens. My everyday experience with them told me that the Hestens are moral people. But they are innovators and leaders. If they believe in their hearts that communism is the way of the future and in the best interests of the people of the United States, I could envision them feeling it was their duty to pave a path for the rest of us in that direction. My fear, then, was that ZZ could be an unwitting accomplice of that operation.

During Christmas week, ZZ was with his family in Los Angeles and I was with mine in Santa Clara. During this time I made a point of apologizing again to all the Swains about ending my engagement to Stuart, who appeared to be very fatigued from the grief they had heaped upon him in the last few months regarding the wedding cancellation. I emphasized to everyone what a great job opportunity I had as the company's international corporate counsel, traveling all over Europe, Asia, and South America, having a good time and being paid fantastically well. I emphasized to everyone that the timing just wasn't right for me to get married. I never mentioned anything about ZZ.

I told my parents about ZZ later that night. They were relieved to learn I was actually working and that I had a boyfriend. They feared I had given up my legal career and was just running around.

Privately, I confided in Stuart about ZZ. I know he was very happy for me. I asked how he was doing. He said okay, but not great. He apologized profusely for putting me in the position of having to cancel our wedding plans, but once the wedding idea got started by others in connection with his father's 60th birthday party, he just could not stop it.

Also, during Christmas week, I spoke to Uncle Lou about digital camera photography. What I learned was that normal photography works by exposing a segment of film to the variations in the light on your subject, producing a negative of the picture. With this negative you can get a print of your original picture.

Digital photography works on an entirely different principle. A digital camera is like a TV camera in that the image is composed of a digitized array of dots, or pixels. This digitized picture has to be read by another instrument in order for the viewer to see it. In a TV system, your television is the reader. It receives the image from the TV camera and reproduces it on the screen. (Ever notice how your TV picture is made up of lots of little dots?)

In digital photography there is no film, no physical picture.

Instead, what is produced is an electronic picture like that produced by a TV camera. It is possible to store these photos in the camera on a removable component — what you might call a memory chip. This component can be taken out of the camera and read by some other device. There is no film to develop; rather, you need an instrument that reads the memory chip and displays your pictures on a screen.

I thanked Uncle Lou for this information.

The first few weeks in January, the Hestens were traveling. They went to several conferences, one of them being a small conference in Moscow. Having only been hired three months prior, I was not yet on the Soviet approval list as part of the Hesten delegation, so I could not go. ZZ could go, but elected to stay behind with me, stating he could not bear to be away from me that long. He was so adorably sweet.

During this time, I had revisited the references I had noted in October. All were repeated in the November Tokyo list and then again on the December Rio list. Even the reference about how an ancient nobleman enhanced his orgasm by ejecting a pearl from his penis.

Aside from this fun reference, I now better understood the others. One was a reference to a seminar Mitch gave in Silicon Valley back in March. He spoke about the graininess of photos taken at the current level of digital photography technology. But, he said, written text of any size, be it typed or handwritten, can be computer enhanced and therefore easily read. He also mentioned that using a small round memory chip enables the photographer to take about seven photos.

When the Hestens returned to the U.S., the four of us began packing, preparing for our year anchored in Paris while traveling around Europe. Our first stop after leaving California was New Orleans. Mitch had obtained four tickets for that year's Super Bowl. We arrived on Monday the 19th and had all week to enjoy the city in anticipation of the big game on Sunday.

As it turned out, I was so happy to still be in the U.S. that week. On Tuesday the 20th, President Reagan was inaugurated. But equally significant, it was the day our 52 hostages in Iran had been released after captivity of well over a year! All of America was celebrating, and New Orleans went wild! It was fun, fun, fun all week. America was excited, displaying yellow ribbons everywhere inspired by the popular song about "tying a yellow ribbon around the old oak tree to welcome me home." America was tying yellow ribbons around everything.

That Sunday afternoon, the most exciting moment of the football game was the sight of a huge yellow ribbon around the entire dome of the stadium. It was breathtaking.

After the game we went on to New York, and then finally, after a five-month hiatus, we were back in Paris.

I set up house with ZZ in his apartment. My sister, Monique, was back occupying the Parisian apartment that I had so much enjoyed last summer while she was in San Francisco.

The three of us arranged fairly quickly to have dinner together after our arrival in Paris. I was anxious for ZZ and Monique to meet. I had instructed Monique not to mention Stuart, as I knew that ZZ, not knowing my true relationship with Stuart, felt a little awkward and sensitive about him being my previous fiancé and almost my husband. The three of us got on quite well, as I knew we would. I am very fortunate that my sister Monique and I have such an easy time together.

Also during my first few days in Paris, I arranged to have lunch with Yvonne so that I could fill her in on all I had been doing from September to January. I told her everything was working out well with ZZ. And I told her that, true to the bureau's assessment, the Hestens were apparently trying to have a baby. Lorraine had told me all about the hormone shots she and Mitch receive and the technique of implanting a donor egg into Lorraine so that she can become pregnant by Mitch, then carry the baby and give birth. She had explained to me that she always uses a diaphragm when she has sex with other men so she can be sure that if she gets pregnant, it will be Mitch's baby.

I told Yvonne that Lorraine had already visited three fertility specialists during our recent trips to Athens, Tokyo, and Rio. Yvonne chuckled, recalling the trips she and Marcel made to those sites following women who were apparently producing samples of Mitchell's hormone-enhanced semen for analysis.

I explained to Yvonne that I had already been debriefed on those three trips, but I needed to tell her about people and events I experienced in the last few months while anchored in San Francisco. Yvonne and I were both so very pleased to be resuming our weekly lunches, agreeing on a date, time and place for the next week's meeting.

I was beginning to meet ZZ's friends, business associates, and office associates; people I had just barely heard about last year. I particularly enjoyed meeting Jasmine, Lorraine's older daughter, who was only two years younger than me. I found it so amazing that mother and daughter could look so much alike and that even their mannerisms and speech were similar. Jasmine absolutely fascinated me. I felt I was with a young Lorraine!

SECRETS

It wasn't long before Lorraine made a date to take the two of us shopping. Lorraine loves to buy beautiful clothes and accessories, and now she had two young ladies in Paris to treat. The company pays for all my clothes and Lorraine and Mitch get to dress me for each occasion in the exact style they wish me to project. She even arranged my appointment at Dr. Laplace's office and paid for my new fancy diaphragm.

My life in Paris was becoming very full. It was much more fun and exciting than just going to Saturday night parties, and so much more complete living with a boyfriend, having breakfast and dinner together every day, and some sort of sexual play or contact most every night.

As an agent, I was in a much better position to learn important information. I was seeing much more of Mitch and Lorraine, having dinner with them, their guests and associates a few times a week and meeting their Parisian friends and office workers. I was getting to know Mitch and Lorraine on a much more personal level.

One day when I had time to myself, I happened to take out the stash of souvenir flashlights I had brought with me. When I casually threw them all on the table, I was in for a surprise. They all flashed briefly, just like an array of flashbulb cameras! I picked one up and turned it on. It flashed again and went off. This seemed more like a flashbulb camera than a flashlight. I looked for other moving parts. There didn't seem to be any. It seemed to be entirely factory-sealed.

I checked the other souvenirs. They all just flashed. They could be toys that did nothing but flash, But my instincts and training about such things had me suspicious.

I could not find any part of the souvenir to twist open or pull apart. There was nowhere to replace batteries. There was no place

- 216 -

to put in film, if it were a regular camera. There was no memory chip for a digital camera. I was about to give up when I noticed that under the leather strap there was a small hatched door about the size of a thumbnail. It was so well-camouflaged that it was very difficult to see unless the flashlight was turned at a certain angle.

I flipped open the hatched door. There, suspended in the chamber by two prongs, was a small, round, shiny white ball bearing about the size of a BB. Could this be the memory chip that holds all photos from a digital camera?

I was nervously excited. I removed the shiny white BB from the chamber. But after holding it in my hand for about 10 seconds, it melted into a thick, sticky white goo. It looked like some guy just came in my hand!

At my next meeting with Yvonne I gave her a couple of Mitch's flashlights to bring to the bureau's lab in Paris for inspection. At our meeting a week later, my suspicions were confirmed.

"These flashlights are not flashlights," she said. "They are high-tech digital cameras! When you turn one on, it snaps a picture. When you turn it off, it is then in ready mode to snap another picture."

This was mind-boggling. Mitchell Hesten was definitely up to something — but what? Why all the deception, pretending the souvenirs were flashlights, not cameras? Questions abounded. Who were these cameras for? Obviously not for everyone at these conferences. Mitch would have discussed the cameras in his speech if they were meant for everyone. Who was in the know — a few attendees or many? What was the intended use of these cameras? Was it for spying?

The fact that these cameras were distributed on three continents was part of the bureau's concern. Perhaps Mitch was recruiting and setting up a worldwide spy network. They could take candid pictures, photographing others without their knowledge! They could photograph anything without anybody's knowledge! And there was no film for processors to see.

It appeared that Mitch had designed these cameras himself, because digital cameras were not yet commercially available. The design is not known to exist, although it was similar to those used by industry and the military.

But the clincher for the FBI was the identification of a Hesten associate, a vociferous Venezuelan delegate at the Rio conference, as a Cuban native and an avid Castro supporter. The specter of a Cuban-style revolutionary movement hatching in Latin America and elsewhere, buoyed by digital photo imagery, was cause for alarm within the bureau. Digital cameras could be instruments with which spy networks communicated worldwide. The FBI alerted American interests around the world.

Yvonne informed me of word from the bureau that Mitchell Hesten was a person of interest at government agencies in addition to the FBI. Therefore, all information regarding his activities would be flowing into the Coordination Committee, a government oversight committee with representatives from the FBI, CIA, and other agencies within the Defense Department and State Department. The Justice Department was sending this report over to the Defense Department as well as all of my previous reports. By pooling information from all agencies, they should be able to see the total picture.

Something big is going on!

FIFTEEN

Discovery!

Renee Clare's Eighth Report
Continuous Updates to the Coordination Committee
European Travels
February 25 – October 9, 1981

THE ALARM HAD been sounded. U.S. intelligence agencies around the world had been alerted to possible activities of international spy rings aided by digital camera technology. For myself, my job hadn't changed on the day-to-day personal level. I was still here in Paris with ZZ, Lorraine, and Mitch to discover and report any relevant information.

I have to say that my outlook changed immensely after the alert alarm. I now found it difficult to just have fun and enjoy myself with all this happening. But there wasn't anything I was supposed to do differently. Quite the contrary. My job was to act the same, be the same, be with the Hestens and ZZ, be on the inside and note everybody and everything. This I continued to do.

In the days that followed, I tried to make sense of it all. I, a non-scientist, could rather easily deduce that these souvenir flashlights were probably digital cameras. So wouldn't just about every scientist who obtained these cameras come to the same realization?

No! The distribution process that we employed for the flash-lights would repress that discovery. If all the souvenirs had been stashed under the delegates' chairs ahead of time, the situation could have led to camera discovery. At the end of the session, almost everyone would have picked up their flashlights at about the same time, intentionally or unintentionally turning them on, filling the room with flashbulb camera-type flashes, and perhaps planting the idea that these souvenirs could be cameras.

But that scenario did not take place. One delegate at a time is handed a couple of flashlights. Receiving two or three at the same time, the delegate has his hands full. He probably does not even try to turn one on. He just puts them away. Now the next delegate gets his, and so on.

Who knows under what circumstances delegates would pay much attention to their souvenirs. Perhaps later in the confines of their sleeping quarters or in the next day or two before the conference was over. But perhaps they didn't take their souvenirs out of their travel bag until they returned home and then what? They get placed in a drawer or given to kids or family members. In all these scenarios, it's most likely that the camera aspect of their flashlights will go unnoticed.

But some delegates — the ones who are part of the supposed spy ring and those who are joining it — will know what the flashlights are for. But then, I wondered, why didn't Mitch just distribute the cameras personally to those who were supposed to receive them? Well, he certainly wouldn't want to single them out, and perhaps, I thought, he didn't even know who they were!

What I needed now was to discover when, where, and how these cameras were going to be used.

At this point in my report, I think it would be appropriate for me to present how I viewed the interaction between the four of us at that time.

ZZ and I were at our sixth-month anniversary. The very strong magnetic feelings we initially had for each other had enhanced; we were feeling amazingly close. ZZ seemed to really know me, although he was lacking some very important information. And I felt I knew him, even though I wasn't sure, exactly, what ZZ had been doing professionally the last few years. ZZ is one of the sweetest guys I have ever known. He has none of the macho behavior that plagues many men. He is very comfortable with who he is and feels no need to put on false displays of masculinity. I wonder if being a swinger has anything to do with that. Mitch is the same way! I haven't known any other swingers (that I am aware of), except for Taylor, who is bisexual.

ZZ was learning a lot about biotech from his many conversations with Mitch. I hadn't realized before that he and Mitch talked regularly for hours. Mitch treats ZZ like the son he never had. But I have to wonder if all their conversations were just good, social fun. Or are they plotting things I should know about? ZZ is a good-hearted person; I just hope all this stuff the four of us are doing is going to work out for him and me. I was worried that ZZ could be a bit naïve and, unwittingly, could become involved in unsavory areas without realizing it. As far as I know, he didn't have a clue that his lover was an FBI agent. Likewise, he may not know that his employers could be enemies of our country. I was beginning to get very worried that ZZ, unknowingly, could become implicated in Mitch's big plans.

ZZ has many conversations with Lorraine, too. But I think the basis of their relationship is sexual. I think ZZ fantasizes that he is in love with her. He knows he can't have her in the traditional sense, but he has the next best thing: he gets to be with her day after day, and even have sex with her from time to time. That's pretty good! ZZ would never admit to me how much he loves her; he might not even admit it to himself. I felt it was OK for ZZ to feel he was in love with Lorraine. If he is truly in love with me, she will fade into a fantasy. I'm the real thing!

I feel a strange attraction to Lorraine myself. I am completely fascinated by her. If I had a much older sister, I would want her to have all the qualities that Lorraine has.

And I think Lorraine has come to feel the same way about me. I think she knows me as well as ZZ does. She understands me as only a woman could. I know Lorraine appreciates my attributes: my style, my intelligence, my chutzpah. She smiles at my ease with women and my influence over men. She confides in me (or so it would appear), asking my opinion on one thing or another. She tells me all about her quest for pregnancy: the injections, possible egg implant procedures, new ideas on the horizon, and all the problems involved. She assures me she always uses a diaphragm when she has sex with other men so she can be sure that if she becomes pregnant, it will be Mitch's baby. I feel we have become very close.

Lorraine confided that for now she is limiting her physician visits to just Dr. Laplace in Paris, Dr. Mann in West Berlin, and Dr. Papalexopoulos in Athens. All three have similar philosophies and technical expertise and all three were comfortable with Mitch and her visiting any one of them at any time. Those are the three doctors who have incorporated, the bureau informed me! Sometimes she feels discouraged, she confided, by the apparent lack of progress, but she is buoyed by the fact that all of this is completely innovative and there are many directions in which to proceed. She and Mitch are completely optimistic. Is that why they have become personal investors in the medical corporation?

As far as ZZ is concerned, I think Lorraine sees him mainly as an amusement. She is very flattered that a handsome, desirable guy ten years her junior finds her so attractive in so many ways. ZZ gets along well with the three of us because he has such an accepting nature. Besides, he is in love with Lorraine, thinks he is in love with me, and absolutely admires and respects Mitch.

Mitch is the patriarch and he calls the shots. He has a can-do philosophy. What other man would deposit so much capital in producing secret cameras or place so much time, money and faith in new fertility projects in an effort to engineer a baby? And he is extremely appreciative of Lorraine. I have never heard him utter a derogatory remark about her or put her down in any way; quite the opposite. He always speaks very highly of her and he has the utmost respect for her. I think Mitch has disciplined himself to never be out of control. He never losses his cool. Rather, in a confrontational situation, he becomes verbally assertive; totally in control.

It is interesting how the four of us get along so well. I think that is because, foremost, we are in an employer/employee relationship. It's clear that Mitch and Lorraine make all the decisions; ZZ and I simply follow them. And, intelligently, ZZ and I have kept it that way. But aside from that, our four personalities blend naturally and smoothly. I, of course, get along with everyone; that's my job!

In late March, after the Hestens returned from their annual Gala in Los Gatos, it was time for our Italian trip. We enjoyed a week of meetings with businessmen and scientists in Rome, Florence, and

Sienna, then another week in Naples, Genoa, and Milan. At the end of both weeks, Lorraine flew to Athens for her fertility appointment with Dr. Papalexopoulos.

At all these meetings throughout the year, the Hestens were looking to acquire or partner with appropriate laboratories with talented personnel that could merge into the company's basic genetic research operation. They were also looking to buy or lease facilities that could support their medical equipment manufacturing unit.

In April, the four of us took a 10-day business trip to Belgium, Holland, and Sweden. Here we attended regular club swing parties at the Candy Club in Amsterdam and the Sextant in Brussels. At the end of the trip, Lorraine visited Dr. Mann in West Berlin.

Much of the time that ZZ and I were in Paris, Mitch and Lorraine would return to Silicon Valley, juggling business in the U.S., Paris, and now other European cities as well. When not traveling with Mitch and Lorraine, ZZ had a lot of work to do at the Paris office. Effectively, he was second in charge after Jasmine in seeing that Paris-based activities functioned effectively.

ZZ was getting a lot of work done on his book, having interviewed various party people at the clubs during our travels. Now he was writing up the dynamics of the various clubs and the styles of the private parties. I hadn't experienced any adverse moments at any of the private parties, but I always had to be on guard, ready to use the defensive sex techniques I had learned during my training.

I must say that ZZ has impressed me with his vast knowledge of many subjects such as literature, the arts, and science. I have studied all that stuff too, but he really knows it. He insists that although he is well-versed in many subjects, he is master of none. The only area in which my sophisticated knowledge is about equal to his is in the sciences. ZZ says he really learns all this information by writing about it. He reminded me that he had a civilian job with the Navy Department as a tech writer.

Then I asked ZZ what kind of work had he been doing since he left the Navy Department six years ago. Just writing, I had supposed. ZZ told me he had left that job so he could write full-time, but to augment his income, he would accept consulting assignments from private companies. Then, to my horror, ZZ mentioned he once wrote up a tech-spec detailing specifications for a high-tech digital camera similar to the ones that Mitch often talks about at conferences and seminars! My heart skipped a beat, maybe two. I was horrified! I felt absolutely heartbroken. ZZ could be implicated and indicted! I wished I had never asked him anything about this!

All spring I had a nagging feeling about the flashlight cameras. Did ZZ know the souvenirs were digital cameras? Did he have any involvement in designing these souvenirs? I had to know! Occasionally, at our apartment, I would leave a flashlight or two lying around so that I might observe ZZ's reaction to them. I was so relieved when he never showed any interest in them whatsoever, nor did he display any strange reaction to them. One day I asked ZZ why he thought Mitch always distributes these flashlights at conferences. His response was that Mitch is "Somewhat of a showman and likes to make a lasting impression, even planning swing parties, for example." I could agree with that. But still, as time went on, I was getting more and more worried that ZZ had become seriously embroiled in Mitch's schemes.

Throughout the spring, I never heard any developments concerning the alert the FBI put out in February concerning worldwide distribution of digital cameras. Of course, I just kept doing my job. Through Yvonne, I was told what a terrific job I was doing. The bureau was encouraging me to continue in strong fashion. They emphatically emphasized that the work I was doing was vitally important!

In early June, Mitch was invited to speak at several mini-tech conferences. The concept was that, since funds were not readily available for all interested parties to travel to a main conference, these mini-conferences served to bring the speakers to the audience. The speakers would present a brief advance rendition of their talk at one or more of the sites, and in the process, they would obtain feedback, field questions, and hear suggestions from the other scientists at the various sites. As a result of these mini-conferences, the presenters could modify their presentations after taking the questions and suggestions into account.

The schedule for the June mini conferences was as follows.

Week one: Monday and Tuesday in Budapest; Thursday and Friday in Prague.

Week two: Monday and Tuesday in East Germany; Thursday and Friday in Vienna.

Wednesdays and Saturdays were travel days. Mitch planned to speak at all four sites. Lorraine planned to use all four of the travel days to go to West Berlin for appointments with Dr. Mann.

It was then that I came to the realization that Lorraine always has a fertility appointment on the day after a swing party, reminiscent of Mitch's women all leaving Paris the day after their swing parties at Chaillot Gardens. What does this mean? I could only speculate.

It had to be significant that Lorraine always arrived at her fertility appointment with a vagina full of party semen. Why? Are the swingers possible sperm donors? My understanding was that it was of utmost importance for Mitchell to be the father of Lorraine's baby.

The swinger semen, then, could not be for Lorraine's personal treatments. Then why? Then I recalled that she and Mitchell were investors in the medical corporation her doctors formed. Could it be that Lorraine was supplying the corporation with donor sperm? Could sperm, sitting in Lorraine's vagina for 18 hours or so, be useful as donor sperm? Could digital camera technology somehow involve the international fertility field?

I speculated further. Perhaps what Mitchell received in exchange for secrets was a steady supply of Eastern European women smuggled from East Berlin into the West for the purpose of in-vitro fertilization experimentation. With a steady supply of female test subjects, the Hestens' medical corporation could easily outpace all competition and thereby obtain international patents, producing huge profits.

After all this speculation, I had to now focus on the upcoming mini conferences. So that I might observe each delegate's reaction, I had told Mitch that I would be happy to distribute the souvenirs at each of the four mini conferences. Mitch agreed. He liked the idea of me, the tall, buxom, redheaded, American beauty parading around during his presentation.

As I distributed the flashlights at each mini-conference, I carefully observed each recipient. Everyone took a few flashlights and tucked them away with their belongings. I did not get the sense that they were of any particular significance to anyone. After each of Mitch's speeches, I took one of his handouts and checked the references at the end. The reference list had not changed! It was exactly the same as last year. The reference about the ancient noblemen passing pearls during sex was still there!

At all four sites, the organizer insisted that he and Mitch organize a late-night swing party for a select few. I was beginning to wonder if we were getting invited to all these meetings for our scientific and business input or for our sexual output! Since meeting organizers consult with each other and compare notes and since Boss was the organizer of last year's annual meeting, I am sure our reputation as lively swingers preceded us.

Lorraine quipped to me, "As soon as they catch a glimpse of you and me arriving in town, they can't wait for that party!" I believe she was exactly right. Lorraine re-emphasized that at the swing party, I was to entertain the organizer for as long as he wanted to be with me. "The organizer gets the young beauty for as long as he likes. Do your stuff," Lorraine told me. "I've seen you in action; he won't sleep a wink all night thinking about you!"

"The night before or the night after?"

"Both!"

Lorraine said she could take on as many as three scientists while I am with the organizer. "These young guys come rather quickly. They don't have much lasting power."

Everything went well at all four sites. Budapest, Prague, and Vienna are beautiful old cities. East Berlin is downright depressing, but the scientists we met there were exceptionally interesting. We interacted mainly with Koch, the organizer, and Schiller, the head scientist. Both were rather young for the positions they held. Koch and Schiller informed us that, because of the devastating world war, most current-day German scientists had entered their field in the 1960s, leading to a relatively young leadership.

Of course, when it came time for our swing party, I entertained Koch, the organizer, who was probably about Lorraine's age.

Lorraine went with the young, very handsome Hans Schiller. I later had the sense from Lorraine that she found this party with Schiller to be exceptionally pleasurable. She seemed very happy about it, significantly so.

In July, Mitch and Lorraine expressed their delight with how magnificently ZZ and I were performing our duties by extending our contracts for an additional year at yet another hefty salary increase. I could not imagine how we could possibly be worth that much money!

Then it happened. The most tragic day of my life, July 28, 1981, my whole world came crashing down. I would never again be the person I was. I start crying every time I think of it. I am crying now as I relate this to you. I feel now just as deeply as I did then upon hearing the news. I received a long-distance phone call from my mom in California. She was crying. "Cheri," she sobbed, "I am so sorry to have to tell you this, but Stuart died this morning in his sleep."

"WHAT? WHAT?" I never heard of such a thing! A young man, 31 years old, dies in his sleep! I knew he had been quite ill the last several months, but not gravely ill. No one expected that he might die! I just couldn't understand what happened to him. Mom continued, "He just wasted away, caught pneumonia, and couldn't recover." I was so completely devastated, I couldn't even function. ZZ had to make all the arrangements and put me on a plane for California, where the funeral was being held. I cried for two weeks.

Stuart was part of me, my twin. Part of me died with him. I would never be the same. I began to feel very guilty about having called off the wedding. Perhaps I should have married him and had affairs. Everyone in the family would have been so happy if we were together. Perhaps he would not have died. Perhaps I could have made a difference. We could have had children and raised a nice family. I didn't know what to think, and all I could do is regret what never happened between us.

After two weeks, I returned to Paris. I was immensely grateful for the support I received from Lorraine, Mitch, and ZZ. The Hestens reduced their travel schedule significantly so they could be around as much as possible. With Stuart's death, I had the sad realization that I might not ever again feel as spiritually close with anyone as I did with him.

But ZZ rescued me. He brought me out from the depths of hell. It was during this period that ZZ completely captured my heart and I fell deeply in love with him. It must have been torture for him to see me in such mourning over my previous fiancé, one whom he would naturally assume was my previous lover. He told me that sometimes I even cried in my sleep. Yet I could not ever tell ZZ the truth. Even though Stuart was dead, he took his secret to the grave. His family never knew, and certainly should not find out now. I feel I am forever bound to my promise to Stuart that I would never tell a soul.

I am telling you on the committee, but you are bound by oath not to reveal these secret documents. And now, as I write this report, I wonder if Stuart died of the new disease striking gay men: Acquired Immunodeficiency Syndrome, or AIDS. Stuart was cremated, so, thankfully, we will never know.

During this dark period of my life, ZZ was very creative, keeping everything light and sometimes even silly. He said I was "The most beautiful creature he had ever been genitally connected to." I had to laugh! ZZ did everything imaginable to cheer me up and to help restore me to my natural self. He was so amazingly sweet.

Then he proposed to me. "I want you to know how much I love

you and adore you," he said. "I want to marry you. I am proposing to you now so you know how strong my love is for you, but I don't want you to answer yet. I know you are mourning from a great loss and you need to have time. Answer me in the future when you are ready. I would like to see you back doing serious work — you are much too brilliant to be doing this. After our contracts are over next year, we will have an enormous amount of money. I'll have plenty of material to work with for my book and you can return to practicing law. We could be enormously happy together."

Now I was crying out of happiness as well as sadness.

I just loved him for that. This is the guy I am going to marry, I had decided. I might not ever have to tell him I am an agent. If manageable, it's better if spouses don't know. I realize this is often the case. The fewer people who know, the more secure the agent is, as well as all those who interact with him or her.

But then a wave of terror struck me. What if ZZ was indicted along with Mitch and Lorraine? I couldn't bear to lose him, especially right after Stuart. I had to speak to Yvonne!

At our next meeting, I told her my feelings, my hopes, and my fears. I asked her to review ZZ's file with the bureau and told her to relay all my thoughts to Alan in San Francisco. I desperately needed some reassurance that everything was going to be okay.

I thought the week between meetings with Yvonne would never pass.

When we met the following week, Yvonne reminded me that ZZ was a tech writer for the Navy Department from ages 28 through 33. He possessed an extremely high security clearance.

"Yes, but that was five years ago. What about now?"

Then Yvonne told me, "Wait to you hear this! Alan informed me that you and ZZ, together as a couple, have been pre-selected for a very high-level, extremely sensitive project. Alan doesn't know anything about it. It is so super-secret, he is not even entitled to know!

"Alan said you have no reason to worry about ZZ; the government would not have considered him for such an important, highly sensitive assignment if they had any doubts about him. Of course, you cannot say anything to ZZ about this possible assignment."

"Oh, Yvonne, I am so happy! Thank you! Thank you!"

Yvonne reminded me that my one-year assignment for the FBI had ended. "But don't worry," she said, "your assignment has been extended for the duration of the case. And they wanted me to emphasize that your work is vital, vital! Just keep doing what you have been doing."

We were now into September and the annual biotech conference was approaching. I suggested to Mitch and Lorraine that the four of us go out for a special dinner; we dined at one of our favorite restaurants. As it turned out, all four of us had something special to say.

During dinner, I announced that I was ready to resume work and thanked everyone for being so understanding and so wonderfully good to me. Then I announced that ZZ had proposed to me, asking that I hold off my decision until I was ready.

"I would like to say, before all of us gathered here this evening, that I love ZZ with all my heart and accept his offer of marriage." ZZ gave me a big, big kiss, with Lorraine and Mitch cheering us on.

Then ZZ had a surprise of his own: a beautiful engagement ring he had been carrying around just in case. He gracefully placed it on my finger. It was stunningly beautiful. For me, it was wonderful to feel so happy again. ZZ and I kissed again, as Mitch and Lorraine toasted us. Then ZZ said, "I would like to announce that I love and adore this woman."

Later at dessert, Mitch announced that the West Germans had invited us to do a mini-conference in Hamburg sometime in the next few weeks like those we did in Prague, Budapest, Vienna and East Berlin. Mitch explained that because of politics, the West Germans rarely attended meetings in communist countries, especially if the East Germans were attending. Not to be scientifically left out, the West German scientists invite many of the presenters to come to West Germany some time before or after the October Biotech Conference to discuss the main topics.

Lorraine's announcement was that she was ecstatic about Dr. Mann's new breakthrough fertility procedure. It had worked very well for a woman a few years older than Lorraine, but the woman, unfortunately, suffered a miscarriage at six weeks. Still, the procedure seemed very promising. Lorraine and Mitch arranged appointments with Dr. Mann for the Thursday and Saturday we would be in Hamburg and again two weeks later, when we would be in Prague.

On Monday, September 21, the four of us arrived in Hamburg, West Germany for meetings with scientists at the Hamburg National Laboratory. The lab is primarily a physics laboratory, but chosen nonetheless because of its excellent meeting facilities. There were eleven West German scientists visiting the facility and seven visiting contributors, including Mitch.

Mitch gave his talk on Monday, the first day of the meeting. It was similar in length and style to his speech of the previous year, but the content was quite different except for one point: the development of digital camera technology and the storage of photographic images on a removable chip. And once again, during his speech, I distributed the souvenir flashlights.

Monday evening, we attended the formal dinner and dance at the lab's banquet hall. I dressed in a long chic white gown, Lorraine in pastel tangerine, the guys in tuxedos. The dinner was a very fancy presentation, and even the dancing was rather formal, mainly waltzes and foxtrots. This was quite an impressive evening; they don't have a formal dance at the actual conference.

At the end of the evening when the four of us were alone, Mitch said he had been approached by Hartmann, the meeting organizer, to see if we would participate at a swing party they were arranging for late Wednesday night. We agreed we would.

But Tuesday night was extremely interesting. The four of us joined Hartmann and four other swingers for sightseeing in Hamburg's famous red-light district. I didn't know if prostitution was legal in this area or just ignored, but the activities were blatant. Walking down the main street, we saw a provocative woman standing under every light post. Passersby are encouraged to look her over, make conversation, and perhaps make her a proposition. The buildings on the street all contained naked women standing or sitting in the open windows.

There are cabaret shows in the red-light district. We attended one and got two tables close together, with the four of us at one table and the five Germans at the other. The show consisted of several totally naked women strutting about on stage, making crude remarks and gestures, some of which were very funny. Meanwhile, a few other totally naked women worked the audience, prancing around, making advances on the guys. Interestingly, they avoid tables where women are sitting, so they didn't come our way. But the five scientists seated nearby received a lot of attention. The women walked around their table, played with their hair, kissed them on the cheek, and even sat on their laps if the guys let them. There seemed to be no boundaries, so my guess was that they were available right then and there for sex, probably in the side rooms. (I learned later that prostitution is indeed legal in this part of the city and that the health of each prostitute is checked regularly by the government.)

I had never seen a show like that in the U.S. It would be illegal, I'm sure.

That next night, Wednesday, September 23, we had our swing party. But it was a bit strange. Hartmann brought five women as he said he would, but they seemed to be right off the street of the red light district we had visited the night before. I think he purchased them for our party. Should be interesting for ZZ and Mitch!

After the party, I asked ZZ about his experience. He stated that the woman took a condom out of her purse and requested that he use it. She told him she never has sex without one.

"I agreed to use it, of course. But I found using a condom some-what strange. I don't think I have used one in 15 years. It was an interesting experience though," ZZ commented. And that was our Hamburg experience.

Saturday, after Mitch and Lorraine's fertility appointment with Dr. Mann in West Berlin, we all flew back to Paris for a restful week before the upcoming Prague conference.

So ended my first contract with the company. Now I'm ready to begin another. Meanwhile, Lorraine has become enraptured that perhaps she is, or is about to become, pregnant.

Monday, October 5, 1981: Prague, Czechoslovakia, site of this year's Eastern European Bio-technical Conference. The Prague conference was huge, with over 60 participants and more than 20 countries represented. Conspicuously absent were the East

Germans. Mitch told us at lunch break that he had made an agreement with the East Germans that we, along with a few other groups, would come Friday to participate in a mini-conference.

It was a pleasure for ZZ and me to be back in Prague, the Paris of the Communist world. The city is so alive, so beautiful. There was still so much we wanted to see and do, so we were hoping we would not have to spend too much time at the conference. But of course on Monday, we needed to be around most of the day to meet everyone and make ourselves desirable in every sense of the word.

I heard Mitch's speech again, during which I walked about distributing the souvenir flashlights, now with the inscription *1981 Eastern European Biotech Conference, Prague, Czechoslovakia.* Naturally, Mitch had me dressed in "conservative-beautiful." He delighted in this opportunity to present me to everyone in attendance. I used the opportunity to observe each recipient. Again, I didn't notice anything significant.

Many of this year's participants were in attendance last year. The Bulgarian and Romanian scientists of last year joined Lorraine and me during snack time, and I saw ZZ chatting with Milada, his Czech woman of last year. Boss was there, ogling me whenever he saw me. I could see he was already thinking about the farewell swing party.

Conference sessions on Tuesday and Wednesday went very well, but ZZ and I just could not slip away long enough to fully enjoy the majesty and beauty of Prague. But then Mitch made us a grand offer. "In celebration of Renee's highly successful completion of her first-year contract, ZZ's continued excellent performance, and your engagement, we propose to send the two of you on an all-expenses-paid one-week vacation in Prague sometime in the next few weeks as a present from Lorraine and me."

ZZ and I hugged and kissed. We were very touched.

The Wednesday night swing party went as planned. Everyone seemed to have a very good time.

Thursday, October 8th, the day after the swing party, was the last official day of the conference. ZZ and I got in a little sightseeing, Mitch attended the conference, and Lorraine flew to West Berlin for the day to see Dr. Mann. She returned in the evening to join us and ecstatically told us she could be pregnant!

Early Friday morning, October 9th, the four of us flew from Prague to East Berlin for our prearranged mini-conference. We were picked up at the airport personally by Koch, the organizer, and Schiller, the lead scientist. They were the two guys Lorraine and I swung with when we were there back in June.

During the limo drive, Koch asked us if, at the end of the meetings, we would be interested in a repeat performance of our intimate June swing party. Inga and Eva would join us again; just the four of us with the four of them. We agreed.

At the June party, I had been with Koch, the organizer. Lorraine was with the younger, very handsome Schiller. ZZ was with Eva and Mitch was with Inga. I remember that Lorraine was particularly pleased after her swing session with the handsome Mr. Schiller.

In regard to today's mini-conference, I rather mindlessly floated through it. But, now that the meetings have concluded for the day, it was swing time. Time for me to do my swing performance, which I always enjoy!

According to plan, the four of us proceeded to the designated suites reserved for swinging. The Germans were there to greet us. Mitch and ZZ went off with Inga and Eva to the suite on the left; Lorraine and I with Koch and Schiller to the suite on the right. I

headed straight for the back bedroom, which is the one the organizer gets. Surprisingly, Koch stated, "In order to have had the experience of both of you two beautiful Americans, I would like to
have this evening with Lorraine."

Lorraine seemed very surprised, but said, "Fine!" I know she
felt disappointed not getting Schiller again.

And I was equally surprised to be getting the young, very handsome, Mr. Schiller, who also seemed a bit confused.

"Don't worry, I'll take good care of you," I declared, smilingly
reassuring him as I took his hand, ushering him into the back bedroom that I had already claimed. It had been a long time since I had
been swinging with anyone this appealing. I was looking forward to
this one.

He seemed a bit shy, even a little nervous, as we stripped down
and got in bed together. To get started, I took his hands and placed
them on my breasts. He told me I had the most beautiful breasts he
had ever seen. "They are like two big eyeballs, staring right at me.
Naturally," he said, "I have to stare right back."

"Go ahead, stare and play with them," I said flirtingly.

He cupped them in his palms and licked them, first one, then
the other, then both quickly back and forth. Then I swished them
back and forth over his face. He was delighted and began chuckling,
"If I had a couple of these, I would fondle myself all day!"

He then surprised me by kissing me tenderly on the lips. And
then again. Soon we were kissing like lovers do and rolling about
the bed. I could see how much he enjoyed just playing with me and
viewing my naked body top to bottom. He said I had such a beautiful body, that he wanted to have a lot of time to enjoy it. He didn't
want everything to be over so fast.

"That's fine. Take your time," I replied.

After a while, he told me he once heard an off-color joke told by a comedian in English, so he didn't understand it at the time, but now he did.

"The comic said that there was a famous actress known for her beautiful legs. She had named one of her legs Christmas, and the other one Easter. Then he said that he would love to take a trip up between the holidays. And everyone laughed."

"Yes, well you can take a trip up between my holidays."

"Well, I would enjoy that very much," he declared, as he lowered himself down on the bed, placing himself between my legs at about knee level.

Raising my thighs and spreading them, he guided his face up between them until his lips became firmly planted on mine, his tongue twirling inside of me. His delicate touch and caressing style sent me swooning into my orgasmic, rhythmic song.

I was ready. He was ready. With great emotion, he pulled up his body over mine, raising my legs, spreading them wide. As his arrow pierced my body, an inexplicable exaltation engulfed my entire being. I quivered with excitement as he thrust himself deep within me.

Suddenly, I flashed on those references about ancient noblemen ejaculating pearls. Those references are NOT mistakes! They are INSTRUCTIONS!

The digital camera memory chip is the PEARL! And I am about to receive one; a memory chip pearl containing encoded information!

I became physically wild with excitement, enraptured with intense pleasure. I cried out in delirious orgasmic delight, as the defining moment was rushing to its conclusion. "This is it! This is it!" I shouted to myself.

And when he came deep within me, my whole body quaked with pleasure. It was an orgasm of my total self: mind and body. I was so elated, so ecstatic, I could hardly believe it. It was the most spectacular moment of my professional career: the sheer joy, the euphoria, the exhilaration that I experienced that evening in East Berlin was pure ecstasy.

I was so dazed, I could hardly say goodbye to Schiller. He hoped, he said, that I would return soon; he so looked forward to seeing me again. Then he left the room.

Several minutes later, Lorraine came in and ran over to me, hugging me as I got up. "Are you all right, Renee?"

"Yes," I replied in a daze.

"You know, Mitch and I are going to need you to attend and participate in my fertility appointment tomorrow. Is that OK?"

"Of course. I am so excited!"

"Oh! Terrific! I am so relieved to hear you say that! And I will have to ask you not to remove your diaphragm until we are at the doctor's office. Agreed?"

"Agreed."

"Oh! Renee! You have no idea how important this fertility appointment is going to be!"

SIXTEEN

Mitchell

Mitchell Hesten's Account
East Berlin / West Berlin
Friday, October 9 – Saturday, October 10, 1981

ONE LOOK AT Renee and Lorraine standing there, hugging at the end of the swing party in East Berlin, told the story. Renee had apparently caught on to some aspect of our operation. Didn't really surprise me — smart gal. Lots of brains in that beautiful package of hers.

So we had come to a crossroads. In the weeks and months ahead, we would either have to go it alone without Renee and ZZ or continue with their full knowledge and support. The decision would be theirs.

Just how much of our operation Renee had come to know, I had no idea. While it was certainly a good sign that she appeared quite accepting of it, I found it somewhat disturbing that she was able to discern anything at all. I was curious what Dr. Mann's take would be on this development. It would be a remarkable piece of intelligence work for her to understand very much.

Then I heard Lorraine asking Renee if she would be willing to participate at her fertility appointment and then telling her how important it was going to be.

"Of course!" Renee replied. "I am so excited!"

Apparently, Koch had switched partners on them at the party. Schiller had sex with Renee, not Lorraine! Renee's discovery, then, had become somewhat of a moot point. We would have had to tell her something, anyway. We needed her participation at Lorraine's appointment tomorrow. I planned to call Dr. Mann as soon as we are in West Berlin to inform him of this development.

Once out of our hotel suite, ZZ and Renee walked arm-in-arm and exchanged the usual type of after-party chatter.

The four of us were quiet while being driven through East Berlin by our escorts. Perhaps we were all into our own thoughts. Me? I was trying to picture our future operation without Renee and ZZ. We could do it, sure. But we would lose much of our pizzazz and appeal. I was encouraged by Renee's accepting reaction. But what about later, when she understood what we were doing more fully? ZZ hadn't a clue. But he is a joiner and he is very adventurous. I thought we could count on him to stick with us if Renee was in.

Koch had arranged for us to be driven to Checkpoint Charlie, one of the points where one can cross through the Berlin Wall from the Communist Eastern sector into the Western sector. There were a plethora of armed guards and officials on both sides, numerous questions asked to each of us, and plenty of official papers to be inspected and stamped. But before nightfall, as Koch had promised, there we were in West Berlin.

The first thing I did was to call ahead to Dr. Mann, informing him about Renee's participation tomorrow. Exhausted from the very long day, we arrived at our hotel and arranged to meet in the morning to go to the American Hospital for Lorraine's appointment.

That next morning, Saturday, October 10th, Dr. Mann was there to greet us in his outer lobby. I began, "Thanks for meeting us, doctor. This is the couple I told you about: Miss Renee Clare and Mr. Zillary Zahn."

"Good morning. I am extremely pleased to be meeting you both. Let's go into my office where we can chat."

"Your English is so perfect," noted Renee as we walked along. "You sound just like an American."

"I am American, Miss Clare. Fertility is an international enterprise."

Renee, I could see, was getting very excited about the situation. I wonder what she thought we were doing.

We made ourselves comfortable in the doctor's office. The doctor sat behind his desk and the four of us took seats in a semicircular fashion, facing him. The doctor began.

"So, Miss Clare, do you understand why you are here?" he asked in a very smooth, professional voice.

"No one has told me anything, but I have some idea."

"Do you care to share your idea?"

"I think I have semen in me that was meant for Mrs. Hesten, so I am here to make a donation."

"That's correct. You can make that donation all by yourself in the privacy of the room across the way; just remove your diaphragm very carefully and deposit it in the container on the shelf."

"Oh, I would much rather you do it; I understand that this is going to be very important. I don't want to mess up anything."

"Fine, if you wish. I will need you to sign a consent form, and I will ask Mrs. Hesten to be present during the removal."

"Oh, I have no modesty among these three. I want everyone to be present, particularly my fiancé. I want him to see everything. Whatever this is all about, it has to be very interesting; I want to share my experience with him."

"Very well. I will list Mrs. Hesten as the official witness, and ask both of you to sign this form where indicated."

Dr. Mann passed the form on a clipboard over to Renee, who glanced over it and signed. Then she passed it onto Lorraine, who signed it and gave it back to the doctor.

The doctor looked it over, checking to see that it was all signed properly, and then pronounced, "Fine, let's all move to the examination room."

At that point, we moved into the adjoining room, where Renee playfully hopped onto the patient exam table. It was clear that Renee was very pleased to cooperate. Lorraine, ZZ, and I sat in chairs provided in the room. ZZ had been listening and watching intently all this time, trying to understand the significance of what he was witnessing. Dr. Mann entered the room last and began explaining. "Miss Clare, the dressing room is over there. In it you will find a dressing gown. Put it on and remove all clothes from the waist down. You can leave your clothes in the dressing room."

Returning from the dressing room, Renee hopped again onto the patient exam table, quickly placing her legs in the stirrups. Putting gloves on each hand, the doctor continued. "Are you okay and comfortable?"

"Yes, but wait! I want the others to actually see what you are doing. I particularly want ZZ, my fiancé, to see everything. To me this is like giving birth."

"Very well. Everyone gather around and watch." Lorraine and I made sure ZZ had the best location to see as much as possible. "Are you ready now Miss Clare?"

"Yes, yes! Definitely, yes!"

The doctor reached into Renee's vagina and carefully pulled out her diaphragm, showing it to everyone before taking it into a previously-unseen side office.

ZZ looked absolutely mesmerized, wondering, I am sure, what was this all about? Renee looked peaceful and very happy.

Returning a few minutes later, the doctor commented to Renee, "Thank you Miss Clare. You may get dressed now and meet us back in my adjoining office."

The three of us, along with the doctor, moved back into his office and awaited Renee. When she returned, she took her seat.

"Thank you, Miss Clare, for contributing today in our work. We appreciate your enthusiasm. I understand that you, yourself, realized you needed to participate with us today. I am curious to know, if you don't mind telling us, just what is it that you think we are doing?"

"I don't know exactly. But I had a realization during sex with Schiller. My mind went into freefall and in a flash, I understood many things. First of all, Schiller was a bit nervous and confused to be getting me instead of Lorraine. That alerted me that something was going on; that got me thinking. I don't usually get these young virile types. I get the older organizers. And that makes sense. My role is to absolutely delight them so that they will spread the good word about our parties. And although this role is very important — essential actually — I realized that there is another aspect to this division of clients between Lorraine and me. It's important that Lorraine get these young virile men. Why?

"Previously, I had realized something else. After every swing party, without fail, Lorraine has a fertility appointment the very next day! Throughout this whole year, she has been flying off somewhere for her appointment as soon after these parties as she can. It fascinates me that Lorraine always goes to the fertility doctor full of party semen. Why? The simplest reason could be that these swingers are possible sperm donors. And conveniently, you would be reasonably assured of good genetics. And also conveniently, you would never know who the true father was: maybe Mitch, maybe not.

"I had previously understood that it was important that Mitch be the father of Lorraine's baby. I would think that would still be the case. So, I am becoming increasingly convinced that there are some other very exciting answers to my observations.

"Perhaps the semen is not for Lorraine at all. Perhaps it is for other women who come here in hopes of becoming pregnant. Aren't you part of a medical corporation with the Paris and Athens offices specializing in in-vitro fertilization? The motives of scientific and financial gain could certainly account for Lorraine's dutiful delivery of swinger sperm.

"But then I thought that it is doubtful that doctors could or would want to impregnate a woman from sperm that has been sitting in another woman's vagina for 12 to 18 hours.

"So now I think, perhaps, all this has nothing to do with semen; nothing to do with semen at all!

"I think this is about something else altogether. I think this is about retrieving something else that has been deposited there. I am almost certain I sexually received something like a pearl from Schiller that was meant for Lorraine. When you retrieved my diaphragm and showed it to us, I thought I saw a gooey blob adhered to the fabric of the diaphragm; that's not usually there. So, I am eager to know what this is all about.

"I must say, the number of parties we put on does seem excessive. And the number of young men that Lorraine takes on at each party is two or three times the number of men I have sex with. Just three nights ago in Prague, Lorraine had sex with all five available young guys!

"I don't think that anything I just described is an exaggeration or that anything is just coincidence. I am right, aren't I?"

Renee just about left us all speechless. That was quite an account!

Lorraine finally replied. "You never cease to amaze me, Renee. Yes, you are on the right track. But it is a lot more complicated than that."

Doctor Mann picked it up from there. "We are involved here in a great experimental enterprise. We have come to a decision point in terms of how you might participate with us in the weeks and months ahead. In the future, we could operate exactly as we did today. You come in when necessary, remove your diaphragm, and give it to us for examination. No questions asked. No answers given.

"Or we could operate in an entirely different manner; one in which both of you are fully informed and included in everything that we do here. The Hestens have told me that they would prefer this latter avenue and have asked me to explore it with you."

"I would very much prefer having full knowledge," Renee jumped in. "I feel as though I have just given birth. Now, I want to see my child!"

"Very well put, I understand. What about you, Mr. Zahn?"

"If Renee wants to participate, I'm all for it."

"All right, but I must tell you that inclusion comes with a very stiff price, so you will need to listen and consider carefully. In order for you to learn about our program, you will need to sign an oath of secrecy. This oath will mean that you can never tell anyone about what you learn here. That is a very stiff price to pay."

"You mean to tell me that these fertility procedures are top secret?" ZZ inquired.

"Yes, they are," said the doctor. "This secrecy oath could be particularly difficult for you, Mr. Zahn, since, as I understand it, you are a writer. What we do here could be a very interesting story. But you will never be allowed to write about it: no articles, no books, nothing."

"Never?"

"Well, for at least 30 or 40 years, and very possibly never. How does this secrecy aspect strike you, Mr. Zahn?"

"Whatever Renee wants to do, I'll abide by. I know she wants to be included in whatever discussions and actions you are going to do, so yes, I'll sign."

"Excellent, Mr. Zahn. Now that you have both indicated your initial inclination, let me be more specific. The business in which we operate involves a good deal of international intrigue. You have to understand that there are extremely harsh penalties for violation of the secrecy oath — hefty fines and years of imprisonment. I won't specify them now; just know that is the case.

"You both need to consider very carefully. You two can walk out of here now: no oath, no knowledge. Whether you two would be allowed to continue in your employ with the Hestens under these conditions is not for me to say. That would be for them to work out with you. But I know their preference is for the two of you to sign on and continue with them in the exact same capacity as you have been up until now. But to do that will require an on oath of secrecy. What do you think, Miss Clare?"

It was obvious Renee did not want to force ZZ's hand. She wanted him to decide. "I'll defer to my fiancé," she replied.

Then ZZ got more assertive. "Yes, we'll sign. We have no compulsion to go around blabbing things. So, doctor, let me see if I understand this correctly. By signing a secrecy oath, we get the satisfaction of participation in all aspects of a great human endeavor, but that satisfaction will be coupled with the frustration of never being able to tell anyone about it."

"Oh, I think satisfaction is much too neutral a word, Mr. Zahn. I think what you are going to experience is much more like elation. I would say you are going to experience the thrill of participation coupled with the frustration of perpetual secrecy. You may never be allowed to tell a soul about it."

"Okay," ZZ decided, "if that's the way it has to be, we will accept that. We will sign," he declared assertively.

"Okay!" The doctor broke into a smile, not seen yet this evening. Lorraine and I were smiling too. "There is just one more piece of information to disclose, probably the most important disclosure. I am going to hand you the official oath to read and sign. Here you are," he said as he gave an oath to Renee and then one to ZZ.

I noticed Renee hardly gave her oath a glance, but smiled glowingly having received it. But ZZ's face lit up when he saw his. "This is an oath to the United States government!"

"That's right," the doctor affirmed. "Now that you understand how serious this is, you can still back out."

"Of course, I will take an oath to the government of the United States. Why didn't you say so in the first place?"

"I first had to find out your willingness," the doctor replied. "I will now ask you, and then Miss Clare, to stand, raise your right hand, read your oath out loud, and then sign it." ZZ did this, followed by Renee.

Lorraine interjected, "I would like the honor of signing as a witness to Renee's oath," which she did.

I followed, stating, "And I would like to sign as witness to ZZ's oath," which I promptly did.

Then, with both ZZ and Renee still on their feet, the doctor pronounced, "And now, in my capacity as an intelligence officer of the government of the United States of America, I will sign each of your oaths, completing the process.

"Welcome, Renee and ZZ, to our enterprise, codename 'The Rose.' The Hestens first informed me about the two of you several months back and, as a result, you have both been thoroughly investigated by the government. When I received their report, I was in for a very pleasant surprise."

The doctor continued. "Among other things, I was assured that the addition of Renee and ZZ to The Rose would enhance it magnificently. In fact, the report refers to the two of you as the prize acquisition. So we are, indeed, very pleased to have you join us. We feel confident that once you understand the significance of The Rose, you will want to participate at a very high level. If, for some reason, you do not wish to participate at all, that is your prerogative. However, regardless of your level of participation, you are forever bound by your oath of secrecy. You can never speak to anyone about what you will learn here unless he or she is a U.S. government official with a secret clearance and official need-to-know. Is that understood?"

"Yes, of course," both ZZ and Renee agreed.

"Now, let's have some champagne and a little celebrating," the doctor pronounced. "I know you are both anxious to know all about The Rose before adjourning for today. Here is a brief report that tells all about it, one for each of you. We will be in the outer office. Let us know when you have finished and are ready to talk about it. Make yourselves comfortable. I will have some sandwiches and salads brought to you. We'll see you in a little while."

He poured each of us a glass of bubbly and we left Renee and ZZ alone in Dr. Mann's office to read the report.

SEVENTEEN

The Rose

Part 1: Mitchell Hesten's Report
Silicon Valley / International Travels
1973 - 1978

THIS IS A brief report about The Rose, an undercover operation of the United States government to provide a safe, secure and secret channel by which Soviet Bloc dissidents could transfer highly sensitive, secret information to United States intelligence.

I am Mitchell Hesten, CEO of one of the leading high-tech companies here in Silicon Valley. I understand that the Coordination Committee, in an effort to obtain a clear picture of pertinent events in the development of The Rose, is interested in my personal story and that of my wife, Lorraine. She discussed in some detail our non-classified stories with a writer, Zillary Zahn, who we had hired to work for our company in 1980. As a starter, I attach those personal articles. *(Author's Note: These appear as chapters three through seven.)*

I probably first appeared on your radar in 1973. That was the year I met Lorraine, my future wife and business partner. I think it would be fair to say that, unofficially, The Rose had its beginning at about that time or shortly thereafter, when my wife and I decided to have a baby. Between the two of us, we had three adult daughters by previous marriages; we now wanted to have the experience of raising a child together, preferably a son, but a fourth daughter would have been just fine.

It never occurred to us that there could be any problem for Lorraine to conceive.

At age 40, Lorraine was still fertile, and, having already given birth twice, she assumed becoming pregnant again would not be a problem. Should be easy, we figured. We discussed our desire to have a baby with family and close friends, but did not mention it within the company or to the outside world. Our decision seemed a bit odd to some at first, since we already had three daughters in their 20s. Why would we now want to start all over again? But each of us had a compelling desire to form a new family together, a binding, biological tie.

True, we would be traveling a lot. But that seemed to be a benefit, not an obstacle. We had the financial resources to hire nannies, au pairs, teachers, whoever was needed. The child would grow up in a very cultural environment, much more so than any of our daughters.

In 1974, our company continued to obtain military contracts from the Defense Department, mainly from one particular agency, DARPA (Defense Advanced Research Projects Agency), whose mandate was to seek out new technologies that could effectively be used by the military.

There was one project that was particularly challenging and therefore extremely rewarding in its success: moving storehouses of classified and sometimes highly-secret documents from one part of the country to another. There were two natural ways to do this: loading the material onto trucks and hauling it for days to the desired location, or moving the information electronically from a computer at the original site to a computer at a new site, then printing it out at that new location.

Eventually, when computer information could be transmitted securely from one location to another, there would be no need to physically transport it. But in the 1970s nothing transmitted from one computer to another was secure against hackers. Therefore, transmitting secret information could not yet be done entirely by computer. I was asked to come up with another technique. So I helped invent and patent a method of continually shrinking the size of information on a printed page until entire storehouses of information could be flown by military jet from one location to another.

In addition I helped develop a machine that could read all this compressed information, enlarge it using computer enhancement, and then print it. It took two years to get this technology operational. DARPA was extremely happy with my work.

1975 was a big year for me personally and for our company. Lorraine received her master's degree in finance and since we were no longer tied to San Francisco, we moved to Los Gatos in Silicon Valley. Living there was much more convenient for work, and we began to see much more of our dear friends.

Another important development for us in '75 was our company going international. Lorraine, coming from a rather wealthy family, decided that she wanted to invest as much of her own money into the company as I had over the years. With this addition to the company's resources, we went international with Lorraine and me as equal partners. We traveled about a third of the year, setting up operations in Paris as our European base. I called on our friends and business associates, Ed and Dianne, to assist in these international ventures, which they did most efficiently.

In 1976, after several years of trying to conceive, Lorraine, now 43, was beginning to wonder what the problem was. So was I. We began to work with our family physician in order to know exactly when Lorraine was ovulating. We sought assistance at fertility clinics in San Francisco, New York and Washington, D.C. when we were there on business. No one could see any obvious problem. So we kept trying.

Also that year, my secret supercomputer project with DARPA was concluding. It was then that I had my initial contact with another defense department agency, the Defense Intelligence Agency (DIA), whose mandate is foreign military espionage. One day while at work in Silicon Valley, I had an appointment with a gentleman I had never heard of, Philip Keslyn, who had convinced my secretary that he needed to see me. He was a tall, lanky guy; clean-cut, nice-looking, about my age. He identified himself as a DIA agent and wanted to see me about doing some work for the agency. He knew all about my ongoing work with DARPA and the success I had there.

Keslyn told me the DIA had determined that I, as an astute scientist and entrepreneur, could be of invaluable assistance in obtaining information from behind the Iron Curtain, as the Soviet Bloc countries were referred to.

Keslyn also said, if I agreed to the DIA plan, he would request that during future visits to Communist country seminars and conferences, I would offer the Communists altered U.S. intelligence documents approved by the DIA for distribution in return for "favors". Those favors were to be continued and increased invitations to their conferences and preferential treatment when the Communists selected partners for future business operations with the West.

"In other words," Keslyn said, "You will be offering them your services as a spy in return for huge amounts of future business. Our hope is that by ingratiating yourself to them, you will be in a position to learn things and come by subtle information to pass on to us.

"We know that, as the intellectual scientist and engaging businessman you are, you would be able to pick up on even the most subtle, nuanced bits of information around you. You would be able to observe what others wouldn't, and interpret what others couldn't.

"If you are successful, our project will continue to get funding, which in turn will pay for all your trips abroad as well as your entourage.

"What do you think of this general idea?"

"I'm open to it; sure."

"Good. Discuss this with your wife, but no one else. I have seen Lorraine, of course. But I have not formally met her. She is a very impressive person, like you, and I know what an asset she is to your operation here. If she agrees to our plan, we will go ahead with it. But if she doesn't, the plan is off. We need both of you together.

"If Lorraine is interested, let's meet in a few days. Here is my card. It just has my name and a phone number where you can reach me; nothing official, naturally. I'll make a tentative appointment with your secretary on the way out. If that time is not good with Lorraine, change it to a more suitable one.

"We at the Defense Department are very impressed with your capabilities. If you are inclined to help us further in these observational ways, your country would be most appreciative. Thank you for your time and we will be in touch."

Lorraine very much liked the idea. She is always excited by action: international business, finances, having a baby, now this. I don't know how she existed in her previous conventional marriage, but she says she is not that person anymore. She has changed significantly from those "obedient wifely days". I have meant so much to her, she says, in helping her achieve her full potential.

I understand how she feels. Because of Lorraine, I am now far more than just an overachieving scientist.

A few days later, Lorraine and I met with Mr. Keslyn in our Silicon Valley office. After discussing what Keslyn and I talked about previously, we shifted to the topic of Lorraine's quest for pregnancy.

"I understand," Keslyn began, "that over the course of the coming year, you will be setting up ten DARPA supercomputer sites in cosmopolitan cities around the world, producing a secret worldwide communications network for transference of ultra-sensitive information. The sites chosen were San Francisco, Washington D.C., London, Paris, West Berlin, Athens, New Delhi, Tokyo, Sidney, and Rio de Janeiro.

"If I understand correctly, each supercomputer will be placed in a secure wing of a health facility that never closes, to provide easy access for U.S. Embassy and consulate personnel, intelligence officers, and military personnel.

"But if you are going to be passing documents to the Communists, you can be sure they will be checking up on you. They will want to know why you are spending so much time at these hospitals and health facilities all over the world. What we would like them to observe is that you and your wife are consulting with worldwide fertility experts.

"The DIA plan is to give additional office space to the local fertility specialist at each of the ten data centers in the secure wing of the health facility where the supercomputer, receiver, and printer are going to be assembled and operating. Then, during the days that you are going to be working on the machines, you can also have extensive fertility appointments. Anyone checking on your whereabouts will know that you are going to these sites for fertility tests and advice. Excellent cover!

"In order to request funds and set up a budget, our project needed a code name. I chose The Rose.

"DARPA is going to need U.S. intelligence officers at each of the data centers to receive the secret information and act upon it, if necessary. To accommodate your fertility requirements, I have selected three doctors, presently serving in the military, whose expertise is in the general field of fertility, pregnancy, and childbirth. These doctors will be trained to become intelligence officers and will undergo intensive training with specialists around the world to learn the latest fertility methods in the field. They will be experts among specialists.

"These doctors are natives of the country in which they will be stationed, and are bilingual in English and their native language.. We expect to have Dr. Mann in West Berlin, Dr. Papalexopoulos in Athens, and Dr. Laplace in Paris. At the hospital sites, these doctors will partner with the specialists presently in these cities."

And so, with the establishment of The Rose, the U.S. government had entered the international fertility business.

That following year, 1977, turned out to be busy on many fronts. Lorraine and I had begun to attend swing parties, mainly at Alice and Denny's when we were in California, and Challoit Gardens when we were in Paris. Much of the year we were shuttling back and forth between Silicon Valley and Paris in our endeavor to set up the Paris office as the center of our European operations. Ed and Dianne, our friends and business associates, joined us in Paris that year and part of the next. The four of us discovered international swing clubs to be invaluable in making important business connections. These international parties furthered business relationships and provided an ongoing social network.

All during that year, when not attending conferences and not engulfed in our work in Paris or California, Lorraine and I would fly off to one of the ten DARPA sites to seek professional help from the fertility specialist, who now had an additional office at the local American hospital or affiliate health facility. While there, we would complete the assemblage and testing of the site's new supercomputer system.

We also attended important conferences that year. With the Warsaw high tech conference approaching, Phil Keslyn flew out to Paris to meet with us. He brought two altered copies of documents describing several U.S. military projects. Using the new secret international communication system, Keslyn sent the documents from Washington to the American hospital in Paris, where they were printed out on the new supercomputer.

"As you know, these are not photocopies," Keslyn emphasized. "You cannot cleanly alter photocopies; the alterations will always be evident. But using the new supercomputer data system, documents are computer-copied. If you alter a few words here or there, completely changing the meaning, the alterations will not be perceived! The machine-copied altered words will look no different than the originals. The pages will look exactly the same. There is no way to tell that these are not photocopies except by comparison with the originals. Great system!

"Give these to the Soviets," he said. "They will know these are official U.S. projects. You can't fool them on that. Take them with you to the Communist conference in Poland. Give one set to the official at the customs office; he will pass it up the ladder until it reaches the appropriate authority. Give the second set of documents directly to the person in charge of the conference. Let's see what happens.

"At all these conferences, you both have to try to pick up on little things from scientists and officials. Note things, no matter how insignificant they may seem. Never write anything down. Then compare mental notes when you are walking in the grounds; expect that your room will be bugged. And expect that your room will be searched when you are out.

"Be careful about your clothing and accessories. They can attach little microphones to your sweaters, jackets — just about anything. After you have thoroughly checked your clothes, discuss what you have seen and heard. Discussions will help you remember details and make connections between them.

"Most likely nothing will come of this venture in the beginning. It takes time to understand what is out of the ordinary. We are looking at this as a long-range project over a period of years, if you are willing.

"I will talk to you upon your return to better assess how to do this more effectively the next time around. Good luck to you both."

And so, Lorraine and I, along with Ed and Dianne, attended the 1977 high-tech conference in Warsaw, Poland. I gave one set of my altered, machine-produced "secret US documents" to the customs official and the other set to the conference organizer. I just said, "I'd like you to have these." That's all. Because Ed and Dianne were not to know anything about all this, these documents were distributed when they were not around or were unaware.

Nothing was said back to me at the time, but on the last day of the conference I was summoned to have a chat with the chief of police. Why was I handing out these documents, he demanded to know? I explained that in my work I come across many such documents.

"I brought copies of these to demonstrate my willingness to share some secret U.S. information. I am not seeking cash in return. What I am seeking is a rather large share of future business your country must do in my fields of operation."

"All right," he said. "Keep bringing them and we'll see what we can do for you. You understand we will have to check these documents out to see if they are really worth anything to us. If it turns out that you can provide a steady supply of important documents, I am sure we can come up with an equitable business arrangement." And so went the 1977 Polish conference.

After going through US Customs upon our return to California, Lorraine and I were ushered into a private room where we spoke with two officials. They flashed their ID, identifying themselves as DIA agents.

One of them declared, "Mr. Keslyn asked that we speak to you about your trip. Do you have anything to report to us? Did you see anything, hear anything, find out anything that might be of interest to the US government?"

We were embarrassed to report, "No, on all accounts."

"Don't worry. This is just the beginning. It takes time to get used to these environments, to even know what is ordinary and what is not. Keep at it. We thank you, and your government thanks you."

Later that year, Ed, Dianne, Lorraine, and I attended a computer technology conference in Budapest, Hungary, at which I presented a short talk and provided "secret documents" to the conference organizer and to the customs officer. Also present at this conference was a Viennese swinger couple we had met recently at a Chaillot Gardens dinner-dance-swing party. They informed us that they were trying to arrange a small swing party in their suite one evening during the conference. Were we interested?

"Of course," we replied.

The party consisted of us two American couples, the Viennese couple, two Hungarian couples, and one Polish couple. All through the party, individually, and very privately, amid all the nakedness and sexuality, the Poles and a couple of Hungarians were attempting to tell us things we could hardly understand. It is not very often, if ever, that these people come in contact with Americans. Obviously, they did not want to be overheard by others present for fear of informers. It was also clear that they were talking politics. Each spoke in soft muted tones, in a clipped manner, and in English that was difficult to understand because of their thick accents and limited knowledge of the language.

Unfortunately, we understood virtually nothing. It was a very frustrating situation for them and for us.

After the party as Lorraine and I strolled about the hotel, she expressed her frustration. "Mitchy, we were in a perfect situation to pick up interesting political information and possibly help these individuals, but all we could do was NOTHING!"

Eventually, we discussed this situation with Keslyn back in Paris. He, too, expressed his frustration that nothing came of the information we were given, but was excited over our close access.

"With swing parties, you will be in a prime position to receive information that very few others would be able to obtain," he said. "Obviously, this is the path you should pursue at future conferences. You need to be very open about the fact that you are swingers, gain a reputation for it. Try to arrange a party at every conference. Invite key people, perhaps even the conference organizers — get them aboard!"

We discussed the possibility of Lorraine and I wearing jewelry containing very small, undetectable recording devices whose content could be determined later by language experts. Keslyn immediately ordered some for our upcoming Moscow conference.

By the end of 1977, all ten DARPA sites were in operation and could securely communicate ultra-secret information with each other. Lorraine, however, now 44 years old, was still not pregnant.

But at nearly all the sites we attended, there was a buzz among the fertility specialists that researchers everywhere were attempting in-vitro fertilization, a process in which an egg, either from the mother or a donor, is fertilized by the father "in vitro" (outside the body). This fertilized egg would be inserted in the woman seeking pregnancy. If the egg lodged appropriately, the woman becomes pregnant.

Our three doctor-servicemen were learning as much about the process as they could. Lorraine opined that as she aged in the next few years, her prospects of becoming pregnant could become greater because of new technological developments.

Next up was the Moscow conference, where I had been invited to give a talk. Ed and Dianne were part of our delegation. For the occasion, Keslyn had sent us especially enticing documents to present to the Russian officials, which we did with great delight.

Our experience there turned out to be even more frustrating than the Hungarian one with respect to being able to privately communicate with the citizens. No Russians were allowed to enter our hotel without an official pass. All service personnel who had contact with guests at the hotel were foreigners, mainly Eastern Europeans. We never came in contact with Russian citizens except those who were hired by the government to serve as our tour guides.

At the conference sessions, the Russian delegation was seated apart from visiting delegations. Mixing was discouraged between talks. During breaks, it could be very unpleasant for a Russian scientist to be conversing with the non-Russian attendees. Everyone was constantly being watched. But there was one breakdown in this official segregation policy. Apparently, the Budapest organizer, having obtained information concerning our little swing party organized by the Viennese couple, informed the Russian organizer about it.

Were the Russians going to consider hosting a bourgeois, decadent, capitalistic, American-style swing party? Damn right they were! Ah, the power of sex! When the opportunity to engage sexually with foreign women arises, rules are occasionally broken and barriers sometimes break down.

The organizer wanted to know if the two beautiful American women accompanying me would be available at the party. When I said, "Yes, definitely," that seemed to seal the deal.

At the swing party, the organizer presented himself and three very physically appealing comrades to match up with the four of us. These were a very attractive older female scientist, a young handsome male scientist, and a young, alluring, large-titted female scientist. The party was held in a hotel room devoid of any furniture.

Upon entering the foyer, we were confronted by two uniformed guards. The male guard assisted the men in undressing completely. The female guard assisted the women, who also had to undress until they were completely naked. Even their jewelry had to be taken off and placed in a safe.

Everyone was given a complete look-over. The guards wanted to ensure that nothing could be passed from one person to another.

The eight of us, completely naked, were then allowed to enter the room. I didn't feel too put out by all the stripping and look-overs. But I could imagine that the women could have felt this procedure to be completely humiliating. It sure didn't feel like this was going to be much of a fun party.

But we paired up, each taking one of the four corners of the room: I was with the alluring young female scientist and Ed was with the older woman; the organizer was with Dianne, and Lorraine was with the young male scientist. There was no bedding; just heaps of large pillows in each corner of the room. I was surprised that the young woman I was with quickly took charge and moved me slightly such that the organizer, at the opposite corner of the room, would not be able to see us very well. I was transfixed just looking at her, but she was very intent in conversing with me. She whispered rampant political statements in my ear in very good English, telling me how so many young scientists want to defect to the West. After grunting my understanding, we proceeded to engage in exuberant sex. Her passion, I'm sure, was emanating from her impression that somehow I was going to be her liberator.

Lorraine had a similar experience with the young scientist she was with. She caught a similar gist. But knowing he was being watched, he spoke very softly in poor English with an unintelligible accent.

Although sexually very satisfying, in all, the party was a very sad, frustrating experience.

Back at the hotel, knowing that our room was undoubtedly bugged, Lorraine and I strolled about the deserted lobby. Lorraine was extremely agitated. "Mitchy, that was so depressing, so AWFUL! These scientists are pouring their hearts out to us. We can barely understand them and can offer them NOTHING, no hope of anything! This is downright discouraging. We have to do something! We are in a very opportune position, one that very few Americans ever find themselves in. Through swinging, we are in position to obtain information from behind the Iron Curtain at its source. We can't waste another opportunity like this! You're the genius in the family, INVENT SOMETHING!"

Back in Paris we had a lengthy phone conversation with Phil Keslyn in Washington, relating our experiences and frustrations. As a result of our last swing party in Hungary, Keslyn had been quick to recognize our unique position. However, the small concealed recording devices we had attached to our clothes were, of course, of no value at a party in which we had to leave all our clothing behind. Keslyn had nothing to offer us that could be of any use at a completely nude party.

"You are as good an inventor as anyone working in the Defense Department," Keslyn told me. "Put your brilliant mind to work and see if you can invent something whereby in the future, you will be able to capture what these people are trying to tell you, even if everyone is completely naked.

"If you devise something, don't worry about the costs. My superiors are already anticipating the great rewards The Rose can present. Whatever you need, we will provide!"

In the days that followed I thought about our experience at the Russian conference. What would we need at future Communist Bloc conferences and seminars in order to obtain information that would be complete and understandable? Verbal communication, we learned from experience, was just not going to work. What we needed from a delegate was a statement, clearly written, typed or printed, in the delegate's own language or clear English, prepared in advance in the privacy of his or her home or office. The question is, how can he or she secretly transfer this written information to us?

Then the idea hit me! Digital photography had just been developed a few years ago. One advantage of digital cameras over standard ones is that they use no film. Instead, photos are stored on a removable memory chip that can be viewed by a reading device such as one of the supercomputers we set up around the world. If a digital camera was confiscated by Communist officials, they would have no way to view the coded photographs. Hence, no evidence. No one could get caught passing information.

All a conference delegate had to do was take a photograph of his or her typed, printed, or handwritten statement. The photo would not be very sharp due to the crude nature of the camera; objects are hardly distinguishable. But written or typed text could be computer-enhanced at one of the data centers. The computer would determine what language was being used and the alphabet of that language. Using context, the computer determined what each word is, then replaced each letter with a sharp image. Thus, photos of text would come out clear and sharp and could be printed, while photos of people or objects were very grainy and generally of little use.

At this point, digital photography had only been used by industry and the military. Keslyn could, therefore, be of great help in providing past designs that the military found effective.

When I ran these ideas by Lorraine, she was wildly supportive. "I knew you could come up with something, Mitchy! You are so inventive! But how are we going to decide which delegates get cameras, because we can never know, really, who in a delegation will want to communicate with us? And how can we possibly distribute these cameras without the authorities noticing?"

In the ensuing discussion, we came up with the idea of disguising the cameras so that they would look like something else. What if they looked like flashlights, we wondered? We could stamp the name of the conference and the date on each one and distribute them as souvenirs. But we still faced the same problem: Among the delegates, who should we alert that the flashlights were really cameras?

After some discussion, we decided to tell no one.

Most of these delegates were geniuses who thrived on mind games and experimenting. Over time, the desperate and the inspired, the clever and the inquisitive, would discover that they possessed the means to pass vital information to the West. And when we returned some months later and were in their presence, they would realize we were giving them the opportunity to complete that communication.

By telephone, Lorraine and I discussed these ideas with Keslyn. Because of the large costs involved and other issues, he needed to present them to his superiors. A few days later, he returned our call, saying his superiors were awed by the concept and the enormous possibilities it presented. They enthusiastically endorsed our plans. Keslyn suggested we schedule an appointment with him in Washington sometime soon. That we did.

At our meeting, Keslyn expressed his deep concern over our high degree of vulnerability. He felt that giving everyone a flashlight-camera presented too high a risk of being discovered. "Loyal Communists can also be clever and inspired. We don't need to unnecessarily expose ourselves to the authorities, to officials, to delegates meandering about, and to those delegates not sufficiently involved. They don't need cameras! Let's give them toy flashlights. We can manufacture some that look and feel exactly like the real ones, just missing a key part. You will not be able to see or feel the difference.

"At a conference, open the box of toy flashlights first and distribute them according to plan. Then distribute the box of cameras to delegates who are seated and involved." Keslyn laid down several designs that could be used to make a cylindrical camera look like a flashlight. He had also brought camera parts the military had used before.

"You are welcome," Keslyn said, "to take these drawings and parts with you and see what aspects of these designs you want to incorporate into your 'flashlight.'"

Then we talked some about the general plan and other aspects of The Rose. Mainly, we expected the project to be a slow, but extremely productive, long-range program. We would not expect more than one or two delegates per conference to discover our communication process and comprehend enough to transfer information.

Upon leaving our meeting, Lorraine and I were experiencing a tremendous high from the excitement of producing something that could yield a significant contribution to the fight to win the Cold War. At the same time, we could feel the huge expectations of the federal government. These were exciting times. The Rose was budding.

But what about Lorraine's quest for pregnancy? A dramatic, historic event occurred in July 1978 in that regard. For the first time in human history, a baby was born as a result of in-vitro fertilization. The fertilized egg was inserted in the mother, where it lodged appropriately, and developed into a child that was born full-term: a truly historic event for mankind. Suddenly, the world of human fertility changed forever. Now even infertile women could expect that pregnancy was possible.

As a result of this discovery, our doctors and their staffs in Paris, West Berlin, and Athens were motivated to band together to form a medical corporation with the goal of developing successful medical techniques leading to pregnancy via in-vitro fertilization.

Lorraine and I became investors in that corporation.

By the end of 1978, I had built a prototype flashlight-camera. Keslyn approved it. The camera we designed would look like a flashlight, except that there would be no way to change batteries. One of the movable parts would be the off/on switch. When you turned the flashlight on, it would shine a light on the subject, snap a picture, and automatically turn off.

The only other movable part would be the thumbnail-sized door that could swing open, revealing the chamber in which the removable memory chip was attached to the flashlight proper by two prongs. This door would not be visible to the casual observer; it would be covered by the leather strap embossed with the conference name and date.

For starters, we would use the military-designed memory chip. But now we needed to act quickly to design a memory chip that could be transferred without any possibility of being detected, even if everyone was completely naked!

The questions for us now were *where* and *how*.

Where, on or in his body, could a delegate hide a memory chip full of statements and documents damaging to a foreign regime? Where could he or she conceal it before entering a party so it would not be discovered upon a thorough strip- search?

And then *how* would a delegate transfer the hidden chip to an American at a completely naked swing party in full view of Soviet authorities?

These were the questions we had to address.

EIGHTEEN

Erotic Sex

Part 2: Mitchell Hesten's Report
Silicon Valley / International Travels
1979 – February 26, 1981

IN ADDRESSING THE memory chip design, I reminded Lorraine of the fantastic story we had both read recently. It detailed a sex practice popular among ancient Asian nobleman. A nobleman of those times would, on occasion, insert a tiny pearl in his penis immediately before sexual activity. It was said that the sensation of the pearl shooting out of his penis upon ejaculation greatly enhanced his orgasm.

Lorraine and I thought about adapting this fantastic idea to fit our problem of how to secretly pass on a memory chip at a completely naked swing party. We wanted to use the concept that a male delegate could somehow store digital photos in his penis and ejaculate them into Lorraine, where they could be stored and later retrieved and analyzed. How to accomplish all this was our number-one problem.

If we solved this problem, then we needed to develop a plan for problem number two: how to lead delegates to the path by which they could transfer information at a swing party.

Having accomplished this, we would need to adjust the ten supercomputers scattered all over the world so that they could read the text in photos that were transferred to us. Right now, the supercomputers were tuned to read condensed text sent from another computer. This was problem number three.

Lorraine and I began with the first problem: developing a memory chip a delegate could plant on his body and transfer to Lorraine at a completely naked swing party. In order for a conference delegate to associate a memory chip with the pearl in the referenced story about sexual practices of ancient noblemen, we would want to design the chip to resemble a shiny white pearl. But a pearl provides evidence that authorities could find in the man or woman, raising possible accusations of spying against the regime. We had to keep in mind that all of this was very dangerous!

A key aspect of our design had to be leaving no evidence of the process of transference from the delegate to us. We decided that, when this pearl-like memory chip was removed from the camera, it should melt into a sticky, white, putty-like substance in about ten seconds, rendering it useless to transfer to anyone else.

If the memory chip was placed at the tip of the penis within the ten second phase when it is solid, it should begin to dissolve first at its warmest spot. Held in place with a cold finger, the memory chip would melt into sticky goo, slowly draining into the penis and coalescing near the tip, creating an erotic sensation. Upon ejaculation, the sticky memory chip goo mixed with semen should spurt out mainly intact, creating another erotic sensation.

Once in the vagina, there was the problem of containment. Some of the goo mixed with semen would certainly leak out. To limit leakage as much as possible, we thought of magnetizing the pearl to attract it to a specifically-designed magnetic diaphragm containing adhesive fabric. The goo, once in the vagina, should be magnetically drawn to the diaphragm and adhere to the fabric. Thus, the original pearl would now appear as a blob of goo stuck on the diaphragm.

Still, some of the goo might be lost as leakage. But if the leakage was minimal, it should not result in the loss of any photos, just the loss of pixels, which could reduce intensity and blur the image. The photos would still be viable, as long as there was enough clarity in the text for computer enhancement at our supercomputer data centers.

If most of these ideal design features could be met, sexual transference of a delegate's photos could take place at a swing party, raising few, if any, suspicions. Therefore, establishing a precedent of having a swing party at the end of a conference was vital to the sexual transference scheme.

Lorraine and I recognized that it was not going to be easy to obtain all the design features we wanted. It could take many months, even years. Perhaps it was not feasible at all! But the whole notion was so intriguing, we just had to pursue it.

If we were successful, we would then need to lead delegates to discover how to follow the steps required for sexual transference. This rather tedious procedure, we had hoped, would discourage any officials who happened to tinker with a flashlight-camera.

A persistent delegate would have to make two major discoveries regarding his flashlight-camera. These were difficult enough that we did not expect more than one or two delegates per conference to make them. (If one happened to be an enthusiastic Communist, we would surely be arrested.) The small number of participating delegates would enable Lorraine to have sex with all of them during the swing party and also helped insure that the process was kept secret for years to come. Thus, we were looking to have a small number of prolific sources provide a steady stream of information over time.

The first discovery a delegate would have to make was that his flashlight was a camera — not difficult for a scientist interested enough to tinker with his souvenirs. This leap would be assisted by the remarks in my speech concerning digital photography. Discovering the memory ball chamber would also help the delegate understand the purpose of the flashlight-camera.

At this point, the delegate could use his camera and pass photos to Lorraine or me just by giving us the intact flashlight-camera. We found that it wouldn't matter much if his photos had been sitting in his camera for days, weeks, or even months; the photos would come out sharp as long as the camera had been kept in a cool, dry place. This was undoubtedly the easier transfer procedure. But it was only feasible at a large gathering, where returning a flashlight or exchanging it for another might go unnoticed by authorities. At intimate gatherings, sexual transference became the important mode of communication.

For a delegate to engage in sexual transference, he would need to make the second great discovery: how to secretly transfer the memory ball to an American when we were all completely naked. We expected this discovery to take some time, and it would require several flashlight-cameras. He would also need to read all the references in the written version of the talk passed out during my presentation.

To begin this process, the scientist should associate the memory ball with the pearl in the story. But when he removed it from the camera chamber, he'd see that it melts into putty-like goo. At this point, a persistent delegate will not give up, but continue experimenting with other flashlights in his possession and perhaps others obtainable at his work lab and from friends who have no interest in them.

With continued experimentation and information provided in the references of my talk, the scientist should realize that he needed to photograph statements and text and then get involved in a swing party attended by the Americans. Just prior to the party, he would insert the memory ball into his penis and then experience that erotic orgasm with Lorraine at the party, transferring photos to her.

But what if the delegate is a woman who was desperate to communicate, like the one who confided in me at the Moscow swing party?

We didn't yet have a good answer. She might have to convince one of her male comrades to use the memory ball. That could be a risky process because she would have to know who to trust.

Perfecting this sexual transference procedure required many, many repetitions of inserting a particularly designed pearl into my penis, experiencing that erotic sensation, ejaculating the pearl into Lorraine, then having her diaphragm read in case the transfer was not visible to the naked eye. We did most of this experimentation when we were in Paris, very close to Dr. Laplace's office and the adjacent supercomputer, which we relied on.

Each time I placed the memory ball at my penis tip, I would watch it melt and feel it coalesce inside me, creating a sexually-arousing sensation. Upon ejaculation inside Lorraine, I indeed experienced an enhanced, erotic orgasm! Lorraine reported feeling nothing special. Sometime later, we would place her specially-designed diaphragm in the Paris data center's reader. For months, we got negative results. Nothing!

After many more months of experimentation with sexual transference, we were beginning to get a flicker of success. It could definitely work. But we were at the point where Keslyn wanted to go ahead and have eighty flashlight-cameras produced for the upcoming Moscow conference. Using the best memory ball we had at that time, Keslyn had his expert technical writer supervise the production of the specifications document, which I brought to the manufacturer.

By early 1980, we were getting good results with sexual transference as long as the diaphragm was removed and read within 24 hours after being deposited with goo. Another limiting factor had to do with the necessary small size of the ball and its required composition. Only about seven pages of type could be stored. When the memory ball was full, the light of the flashlight would no longer go on. These features and limitations were discussed in one of my references listed at the end of the printed copy of my talk.

At the 1980 Moscow Tech Conference, Lorraine and I had a total of eighty flashlight-cameras and toy flashlights to distribute to the less than thirty delegates and officials. Each flashlight had a leather strap attached that covered the hatched door of the memory ball chamber and insulated it from heat. The strap was embossed *1980 Moscow Tech Conference.* Lorraine showed the open box of toy flashlights to the officials, giving a couple to each of them, then requesting permission to distribute them to each delegate. Permission was granted. The toys were distributed to all officials, others in authority, and delegates on the periphery who were not very involved with the talk. After all the toys were distributed to the appropriate people, Lorraine opened another box and distributed the cameras to the remaining delegates.

During my scheduled address to the delegates, I briefly mentioned the new digital camera technology as one of the examples of the developing high-tech industry. During my talk I said, "My wife has passed among you, distributing souvenir flashlights commemorating our meeting. She has more, should you want some." I mentioned that "Copies of my talk, complete with references, will also be passed among you."

My presentation, including the souvenir flashlights, was well-received. Lorraine and I were nervously excited. The Rose was now operational! Flashlight-cameras were everywhere throughout the room. We weren't expecting any secret communication at this conference, but now delegates had cameras to experiment with and perhaps a statement to prepare and deliver to us on our return visit next year. We both felt dizzy with excitement. This was a day we had long anticipated!

After the Moscow conference, we were back in Silicon Valley, preparing for our annual March Gala. Following that, we would have a four-month sojourn in Paris, where we would be expanding our Parisian location to become our European head office. During this time, Lorraine was to engage in extensive hormonal and surgical procedures with Dr. Laplace in an attempt at in-vitro fertilization.

As a result of our activities at the Gala, we finally hired a young swinger couple to travel with us in Europe and attend social and business functions as well as swing parties. There was one glitch, however. Within a few weeks of being hired, the woman was offered a lucrative film contract. I released her, leaving us with just half a couple! The writer gentleman we hired, Mr. Zillary Zahn (ZZ), was anxious to travel with us to expand his collection of interviews and stories of international swingers that would make him the international authority on swinging.

But now we needed to find a partner for him to escort to swing parties in Paris. Luckily, and also suspiciously, Miss Renee Clare, a young, redheaded American beauty of French upbringing, became available. She proved to be a very valuable asset, reining in possible business clients with her irresistible charm and sexuality and complementing ZZ perfectly.

In June, memory ball experimentation led to a new level of success. We gained the ability to distinguish sets of photos resulting from several different sexual encounters. But because of our summer commitments in Paris, Lorraine and I were not going to be readily available to travel to most of the data centers and tune the supercomputers to read this latest gooey memory ball. Lorraine and I were able to test this newest memory ball and make appropriate adjustments at the Paris, London, and West Berlin Centers, but not the other seven before September. For Keslyn, that was too late. We had the Yugoslavian Conference in October as well as others in the months that followed.

In response, Keslyn developed a plan with DIA personnel stationed in Paris whereby tuning, maintenance, and experimentation at the other seven centers could continue without requiring participation on our part. With successful sexual transference becoming a reality, Keslyn and others at the DIA were exuberant about its continued development.

Keslyn stated that Lorraine would not have to get involved at all. But once a week for seven weeks, I would have to inseminate memory-goo photos into a hired woman, who would then fly with her husband the next day to the selected data center. "Each woman will be fitted with the special diaphragm by Dr. Laplace," Keslyn stated. "You will fill it with memory-goo photos by having sex with her in the group room at Chaillot Gardens. That's all you have to do. We will take care of all the details.

"My staff will recruit couples from swing parties in Paris that cater to a younger, less-affluent clientele. Couples will be interviewed and hired one-by-one. This will be a business proposition. They are not to know about any other couples' participation, or any more about The Rose than their individual responsibilities. We want the insemination to take place in the group room for all to see. We don't want the woman to be able to make any false claims about your physical contact with her.

"We will tell the women that we have a rich client who wants his hormone-enhanced semen analyzed at the fertility clinic. We don't want her to be able to identify you. Therefore, you will approach her from behind and have sex with her by rear entry. You are not to lay a hand on her other than what will be necessary for you to accomplish insemination. Afterwards, without looking back at you, she will get up and leave the group room. She and her husband will then be escorted home.

"The next day she and her husband will fly to the designated city. At the hospital data center, she will go to a private ladies room, where she will carefully remove her diaphragm as instructed and leave it in the designated container. Shortly after the woman's departure, the American intelligence officer on site will process her diaphragm and perform any necessary adjustments to the reader and supercomputer.

"We will offer each couple an all-expense-paid, three-day

vacation. If they successfully complete their mission, they will receive a cash bonus upon their return.

"You and Lorraine can continue to service the London, Paris, and West Berlin centers. The hired couples will go to the other seven sites, the first of which will be Washington, D.C., where I can personally observe any problems with our procedures."

That was Keslyn's idea, and it all worked according to plan. On August 1, 1980, Keslyn announced that all data centers were functioning properly. Five hundred flashlight-cameras and toy flashlights had been manufactured, with each camera containing the most effective memory ball Lorraine and I could devise.

At the beginning of September, surprisingly, Renee became available for hire. We grabbed her up, offering her a very generous contract. ZZ and Renee had become a couple, completing our foursome. We finally found the stability we had been seeking, traveling with a young, attractive swinger couple whom we liked, trusted, and enjoyed.

Our first big conference as a foursome was the 1980 Eastern European Biotech Conference in Yugoslavia. Everything was clicking. The addition of a young couple to our delegation provided much-needed pizazz. They charmed everyone and were the center of most social gatherings. At many of the conferences we attended in the Communist Bloc countries, we were the only Americans many of the delegates had ever met. We were a curiosity and to add to our mystique, we had established a reputation as swingers!

Beginning with Yugoslavia, we created a standard procedure for all conferences at which I was invited to make a presentation.

1. I would present my talk as early in the conference as possible, providing some time for inspired delegates to experiment together.

2. I would briefly discuss digital photography during my presentation so everyone would be introduced to the concept.

3. During the question-and-answer session, we would pass out copies of my speech that contained references along with the story of the sex practices of ancient Asian noblemen.

4. Also during this time, Lorraine would pass out toy flashlights to all officials and peripheral delegates, while Renee would distribute flashlight-cameras to all engaged participants.

5. ZZ and Renee would usually be available throughout the conference, dressed to be subtly sexually attractive.

6. We would have a swing party near the end of the conference.

7. The day after the party, Lorraine would fly to her fertility appointment and diaphragm examination.

Any delegate who somehow made it known that he was interested in attending a swing party with us had first priority, after the organizer, on the guest list. If there were an overabundance of men wanting to attend, Lorraine would choose those who seemed to be most likely to have information to impart to her.

Renee's assignment was to engage the organizer for as long as he wanted. She was to give him her specialty: a fucking he would never forget. Lorraine would have sex with all scientists who were interested. A keen interest could mean he had a pearl to pass on to her.

Soon another Moscow conference was upon us. Because Renee had just been added to our delegation, she was not yet eligible to attend this conference. ZZ decided to stay in Paris to be with her. Regrettably, Lorraine and I had to do this exciting, important conference without our jazzy new couple.

Last year's Moscow conference was the first at which we had distributed the flashlight-cameras. This conference was the first at which delegates would have had a year to discover what their flashlights really were! I was certainly very curious to know how many of them, if any, had made that discovery. And if anyone did, what was his response? Was he motivated to communicate information to us? Did he share his discovery with friends or public officials? Had we been found out or were we free to operate?

The last question was put to rest when, as we did last year, Lorraine opened the new box of toy flashlights in front of several officials, giving a couple to each of them, pointing out the emboss-ment *1981 Moscow Tech Conference* on the leather strap. The officials cordially accepted their flashlights and gave us permission to distribute them among the delegates.

During my talk, most of the delegates were now receiving their second set of flashlight-cameras and a copy of my new talk. As Lorraine and I were gathering up our stuff so that the next talk could get started, one large, gruff guy, — older than me, I would say — came up to me and slammed his flashlight down on the table, saying, "No damn good. Give me another one."

Nothing subtle about it. He just didn't seem to like the one he got for some reason. Then I noticed the leather strap. It was exactly the same as the ones I handed out, except for one detail. His said "1980." It was from last year! I tucked it away. I knew it was a camera because I remembered him from last year. I didn't believe there were any photos on it, but, of course, we would check it out.

When Lorraine came by, I pointed to the 1980 flashlight. Her eyes widened. Her jaw dropped. For a few moments, her face was in a motionless, blank state. Then she composed herself and ex-claimed, "Oh! Mitchy!"

The rest of the conference was business as usual, but both of us were nervously excited after receiving that 1980 camera. Again, we had no swing party, but I felt sure we would have had a fantastic party if ZZ and Renee had been there.

After the conference Lorraine and I flew to Athens, where we had our scheduled fertility appointment with Dr. Papalexopoulos — Dr. Pap. All three of us were very anxious to read that 1980 memory ball. Was it garbage, or did it hold important photos?

To our shock there were seven pages of text to print out. We couldn't believe it! All our planning, experimenting, and distributing cameras had actually produced a contact on the other side. Regardless of the worthiness of the information we were about to receive, one thing was for sure: THE PROCESS WORKS!

Then we read the photos: Lists of scientific projects and their priorities. Names of the scientists working on various projects. Lists of scientists and others who wanted to defect. Economic reports and economic expectations; hard times in the forecast. Reports of social disillusionment and unrest; cronyism and rampant corruption. And much more.

The Rose had bloomed!

Time would tell of the accuracy and value of this communication. Perhaps they were mocking us, presenting us with false, tantalizing information, just like the documents I presented to them. But Keslyn and his superiors were already overjoyed. Keslyn stated, "The Rose has crossed the threshold from an experimental, fiscally draining-project to an information-gathering conduit from behind the Iron Curtain, well worth all the brainpower, manpower, and expenditure to produce it!"

It could be months before we would know if there was anything of value in the communication with the Soviets. But we made a connection, an important milestone in validating the process.

Once in Paris, we settled in: Lorraine and I back in our security tight Parisian apartment, ZZ and Renee now living together in his apartment.

Then one day in mid-February, I received some shocking news from Keslyn. Because of all the phony secret documents I had passed to the Soviets, the FBI had been on my back for years! The bureau actually has a special agent tailing me! I was shocked the FBI had no idea what I was doing. After all, Lorraine and I were operating under the auspices of the Department of Defense. "Can't you just tell them that?" I asked Keslyn.

"Yes, I have now informed the FBI director. But you have to understand that up until now, very few people in all of government knew about The Rose since it is a super-secret project. Besides, it involves very few field operatives: you, Mrs. Hesten, and several doctors. It's hardly a project that would garner much attention within the FBI.

"And the FBI is in the Department of Justice, not the Department of Defense. Normally, there is not much communication between them. We have our own turf. Generally, the FBI handles domestic investigations while the DIA an CIA operate internationally. Occasionally, there is an overlap where one agency is not aware of what the other is doing. This is such a case.

We feel that the best course of action would be for all information to go to the Coordination Committee, which consists of representatives from the FBI, CIA, DIA, DARPA, and other defense and state agencies. They will garner reports from all government operatives involved to get a total picture of what everyone is doing and what everyone knows in connection with The Rose."

In this regard, Philip Keslyn requested I write a brief account of the overall development of The Rose from my personal perspective. I have provided my report herein.

Respectfully submitted,
Mitchell Lawnton Hesten
February 26, 1981

NINETEEN

Success!

Mitchell Hesten's Follow-Up Report
Continuous Updates to the Coordination Committee
European Travels
February 27 – October 8, 1981

IN THE SPRING of 1981, Lorraine and I traveled around Europe with ZZ and Renee, attending non-Soviet bloc conferences and expanding company operations. During this time, the interplay among the four of us and our technique in conducting business with European associates, had developed into a smooth-running machine. It was perfect in all respects: we had become a superb team.

During two weeks in June we participated at small, two-day mini-conferences held in Budapest, Vienna, East Berlin, and Prague. Consecutive Wednesdays and Saturdays were travel days. At each of the four small presentations, Renee, dressed conservatively sexy, took it upon herself to personally hand out flashlight-cameras to each delegate during the talk and copies of my speech during the Q&A session. Most of these delegates were receiving their second set of cameras, having obtained their first at the Yugoslavian conference last October. The delegates had the past eight months to discover the camera aspect of their souvenirs, and, perhaps, how to use sexual transference. Now they had access to a second set of cameras to photograph prepared statements and return the information to us. And there were plenty of extra souvenir flashlight-cameras available for delegates to experiment with.

With such a small number of delegates present at each of these mini-conferences, those with information for us had to go to the next level: sexual transference of the memory ball.

To discover this next level, the scientist would need to exercise extreme dedication and ingenuity. Sometime in the past eight months, he would have had to experiment with his flashlight-cameras. He would need to endure the complete frustration of watching his memory ball melt into goo in his hand when it was removed from the camera. Not giving up, he would next have to determine where, within ten seconds, he would need to place a new memory ball, in order to transfer it to an American at a very small gathering.

If he successfully analyzed the situation and especially if he read the article about the pearl, he would realize that his best opportunity of transferring his photos would be to lightly insert the memory ball into his penis before a swing party and then have sex with one of the two American women.

A dedicated scientist would want to test this process as much as possible before the real opportunity arose. When the opportunity presented itself, he would want to be prepared to respond in the best possible way. He would have eight months to experiment, during which he can obtain additional flashlights if he needs to.

All this experimenting presents challenges and games that scientists usually like to play. And, if he so inclined, he is going to play this game. He is going to test the process based on the concept of sexually passing a pearl. So, sometime in this eight month period, the scientist will carefully remove the pearl-like memory-ball from the camera chamber and place it at the tip of his penis. He observes it melt into a goo, and feels an erotic sensation as the goo coalesces inside his penis. He is very pleased with himself.

But now the scientist wants to see how the goo comes out. ("It better come out!" he is thinking.) He could urinate and observe, but a scientist usually wants to test results under conditions which most closely resemble the "event" conditions. Most likely, therefore, the scientist will masturbate, feel the sensation the goo creates, and the erotic orgasm he can have all by himself.

"Very clever!" he thinks to himself. He likes this game! Now all he has to do is photograph his statements with a fresh camera. Then, just before leaving for the swing party, he urinates and inserts the memory-ball in his penis. Now, at the party, he has to have sex with one of the two American women at his earliest opportunity. He can't wait too long, for once he needs to urinate, the goo will be lost!

So, did any of our delegates from any of our four small swing parties actually play this game?

YES!

On the second Wednesday of the June mini-conferences, when Lorraine removed her diaphragm in Dr. Mann's office, she noticed it contained a lot of goo. Dr. Mann told Lorraine that her diaphragm was testing positive! There were going to be photos! A highly motivated and ingenious East German head scientist, Hans Schiller, had information he wanted to pass to us. He was so contemptuous of the secret police and their paid informers that he wanted us to know who they were. He presented various documents and statements naming those in the West German government that we should not trust. His information confirmed, in part, suspicions the DIA already had but could not rely on. Other statements and documents were also very helpful.

Lorraine and I were extremely gratified that our hard work and experimentation paid off. THE PROCESS WORKS! This swing party concept seemed so outrageous, so implausible, but it worked! Wait until Keslyn hears about this!

When Keslyn got word, he and the guys at the DIA celebrated. He told me the committee members were genuinely impressed. Previously, they had expressed extreme pessimism that "ridiculous ideas" about sexual transference could possibly lead to anything productive. Now the committee had to admit we had the capability to obtain secret information that few, if any, other agents would be able to obtain. And as long as this was the case, we would have their full support. But, Keslyn cautioned, some of the committee members, speaking on behalf of the agencies they represented, found the concept of sex parties morally abhorrent and something the government should not be involved in. As long as we got information that was not otherwise obtainable, they were willing to look the other way, But they were unanimous that if the existence of the parties ever leaked out, they would have to denounce us as individual adventurers in no way connected to the government.

Now into July, Lorraine and I felt so positive about the value ZZ and Renee were bringing to the company that we extended their contracts with a hefty raise for another year. But more importantly, we felt they should have full knowledge of The Rose, providing they were willing to sign an oath of secrecy to the US government. They should know and experience the excitement and pride in what we were doing and accomplishing. Also, as the mission extended in time, the level of danger increases with the possibility of being discovered. We cannot lead Renee and ZZ into serious danger without their knowledge and consent.

Lorraine and I made a proposal to the DIA and the committee. If acceptable to the government, ZZ and Renee would be given the opportunity to permanently become part of The Rose, thereby making a second woman available to receive secret information at swing parties.

Keslyn got back to Lorraine and me, stating that the couple had been thoroughly investigated and would constitute a prize acquisition for the project. Keslyn recommended bringing them to one of our fertility appointments with Dr. Mann, Dr. Papalexopoulos, or Dr. Laplace. As intelligence officers, any of the three could administer an oath of secrecy and fully inform them about The Rose.

But Lorraine and I procrastinated. Our fear was that Renee and ZZ might want to leave the project altogether once they knew they were participating in dangerous international espionage activities. They were both great sports when it was all fun and games about obtaining information for ZZ's book and earning money. But how would they feel when they found out what we were really doing? They might find it very shocking, dangerous, and not something they would want to actively participate in.

Our ambivalent feelings in this regard became a moot point, at least temporarily, when, at the end of July, Renee suffered a tragic personal loss. Her ex-fiancé, whose family had ties to her family, inexplicably died. This wounded Renee to the very core. Returning to Paris after two weeks in California, she was morose and despondent. ZZ, who deeply loves her, nursed her back to mental health over the course of the next several weeks. In early September, they joyfully announced their engagement.

Now seemed to be a perfect time to acquaint Renee and ZZ with The Rose and get them fully involved. But with several conferences upon us, apprehension set in again. We needed them to be in top form and participate exactly as they had throughout the year. We didn't want to risk any disruption to our "well-oiled machine". Perhaps they would be accepting, but noticeably nervous. Perhaps they might even want to quit!

We decided to play it safe through the upcoming conferences. We took no action.

In late September, the Hamburg conference went well in all respects. The day after the swing party, the four of us flew to West Berlin, where Lorraine and I had an appointment with Dr. Mann. The first order of business was to check Lorraine's diaphragm to see if it contained any memory-ball goo. Upon removing her diaphragm, Lorraine didn't think so. Examination by the center's reader confirmed that it did not. No photos.

We moved on to the fertility aspect of our visit. Dr. Mann examined Lorraine head-to-toe, inside and out, asking her many questions about her physical condition.

"It's too early to say for sure," Dr. Mann declared, "but many signs point to the possibility that you may be about three weeks pregnant!"

For the next few days Lorraine and I experienced contained excitement. Was she pregnant or not? Do we celebrate or not? We didn't want to get our hopes up too high, but we both felt she was pregnant!

With each passing day, Lorraine became more and more convinced of her pregnancy. She was feeling all the body changes she felt years ago when she was pregnant with each of her daughters.

By the time the Prague conference began, ten days after our appointment with Dr. Mann, Lorraine felt absolutely certain about her pregnancy. The conference itself went according to plan, with each involved delegate receiving several flashlight-cameras. The conference was well-attended and very international. The four of us were perfectly social, getting to know many new delegates and renewing acquaintances with returning delegates. This latter group would be better prepared to secretly communicate with us.

As I write this report on October 8th, Thursday night of the conference, no flashlight-cameras have been returned to us. But Lorraine saw a lot of action at last night's swing party, and, according to plan, flew to West Berlin this morning to see Dr. Mann. I certainly would have liked to have gone with her, but Lorraine insisted I remain at the conference, continuing my participation at the various seminars, presentations, and panel discussions.

"I'm sure Dr. Mann is going to confirm my pregnancy," she said, "so mainly I need to get my diaphragm read. I'll give you a full report."

That seemed fine, since I would be attending Saturday's appointment with her. That appointment was set up in great anticipation of receiving additional photos from Schiller at tomorrow night's swing party in East Berlin.

When Lorraine returned to our hotel room earlier this evening, she walked in looking radiant and exceptionally beautiful. "We did it!" she declared glowingly. "I am five weeks pregnant!"

We went right into joyful and passionate hugs and kisses. But as I started to undress her, she stopped me, exclaiming "Wait! There's more! My diaphragm was pregnant, too! It had twins!"

We had received two sets of photos from the Prague swing party. Lorraine, not wanting to miss any possible sets of photos, felt compelled to have sex with all five of the visiting scientists attending the party: the Hungarian, Pole, Czech, Bulgarian, and Romanian. Renee was with the two organizers. Had Renee been knowledgeable about The Rose at this point, she could have shared the load.

This was the first party for the Hungarian, Pole, and Czech, so we were not expecting any communication from them. Yet, one never knows; they could have figured out the procedure. They could have been assisted by the Bulgarian and Romanian, who were now attending their third party, and had both left sets of photos. They seem to have become friends, palling around together at these conferences. Very possibly, they have been experimenting together, discovering what they need to do to pass on information at a swing party.

The Romanian wrote eloquently about suppression and suffering under the Ceausescu regime. "Secret police and informers are everywhere. Everyone lives in constant fear. It is against the law to even say anything negative about anyone in the government!" He appealed for American help, sending along pages of very important documents.

The Bulgarian wrote about the small, fragile, venerable liberal faction in the government. He pleaded for American support, urging American agents to help the liberal wing and bring down the suppressors. Pages of key documents named important figures of both factions.

Now we have two items left on our immediate agenda. First is our meeting tomorrow, Friday, in East Berlin. Lorraine and I hope to repeat our four-couple swing party. We are counting on Schiller passing on more extremely valuable information to Lorraine.

On Saturday, we hope to bring ZZ and Renee to Dr. Mann's office, where they will have the opportunity to learn about The Rose. We are counting on their acceptance and their eager participation.

This concludes this installment of Mitchell Hesten's report to the Coordination Committee.

TWENTY

Conclusion

Renee Clare's Follow-Up Report to the Coordination Committee
West Berlin
Saturday, October 10 – Sunday, October 11, 1981

"**W**E ACCEPT! We accept!" we cried in unison from Dr. Mann's adjoining room. For the past hour or so, ZZ and I had been reading and discussing Mitchell's reports on The Rose. We came out, running into the welcoming arms of the Mitch, Lorraine, and Dr. Mann.

We all engaged in massive hugs and produced some tears of joy.

ZZ declared, "We are both so excited by this opportunity! We are already experiencing the thrill of participation!"

I added, "We both feel so proud and so very honored to have this extraordinary opportunity."

"Excellent!" exclaimed Dr. Mann. "We are as excited about this as you are!"

Mitchell expressed that he and Lorraine were relieved. They had been fretting over this moment for months and fearing we might want to leave the project once we knew what it was really all about.

Dr. Mann continued, "Before we adjourn for today, I know you will want to see the results of Renee's interaction last night with Schiller. He sent very important information that I acted upon in the past hour while you two read up on The Rose. Judging from his previous documents, I fully expect that what he has to say is trustworthy. It confirms our suspicions.

"I have printed out a short version of the urgent section of his documents, deleting all names since those are details you have no need to know. All four of you can take great pride in the hard work you have been doing for your country.

"This morning when I was removing Renee's diaphragm, bringing forth Schiller's documents into the world, she expressed how the procedure emotionally felt like she had just given birth. How right she was! Here is a section of Renee's beautiful child!"

I am a proud German; a patriotic German. It sickens me to see one part of Germany at odds with another. I cannot sit idly by and watch Germans fighting Germans. It is not right. We Germans need to stand together, unified against all those of ill will.

It is in this spirit that I must tell you, with great urgency, that three of our East German government administrators have come under suspicion of being traitors to the Communist cause and are suspected of being spies for the West. Whether they are indeed spies or not, the suspicions alone will be enough for them to be killed.

You must act fast and arrange for a diplomatic exchange. I can tell you that there are four very high-ranking West German officials who are spying for the Communists.

You must arrange to exchange our three accused officials for the four spies in your government. Make diplomatic
overtures immediately to secure everyone's safety.

The names of the three East German officials who are
suspected of spying for the West are:

....

....

....

The names of the four West German officials who are
spying for the Communists are:

....

....

....

....

Wow!

In less than 24 hours after receiving Schiller's text and documents, I got to read the urgent message section. THRILLING! What
an experience! So exciting, so extraordinary. The thought that I had
carried those photos within me last night from East Berlin to West
Berlin was mind-boggling.

At last night's swing party, I had sensed something special was
about to happen. Koch asked to have sex with Lorraine instead
of me. Lorraine was slightly taken back, but quickly agreed. Then
Schiller looked slightly confused and mistook my casual remark
as reassurance that the messaging could proceed. Their confusion
alerted me.

Then, engulfed in Schiller's arms, I made a connection. The
shiny white ball in the camera resembled a small, shiny pearl. At

conference after conference, the reference to transferring a pearl from a man to a woman during sex appeared alongside information about digital photography. Since discovering it last year, I always thought the story had found its way into the pile of high-tech references by mistake. But now I made the connection: those were instructions for sexual transference.

Was Schiller about to pass secret information into me via a small white pearl or its goo? I was sure he was! I swooned at the thought of it and became physically wild with excitement.

My mind went into freefall. I flashed on the fertility appointment Lorraine had set for the next day. Then I remembered that she always had a fertility appointment the day after a swing party. Why?

I am sure Schiller thought I was really taken with him; he could see my excitement. That's all right, he can think that. All the better for the next time!

When Lorraine told me immediately after my encounter with Schiller that she would need my participation at her fertility appointment and not to take out my diaphragm, I knew my assessment was correct. I was convinced I had within me a secret communication from behind the Iron Curtain to the free world. Excited as I was, I had to pull myself together and calm down. We were in enemy territory! I held onto ZZ's hand and clammed up.

This was the first time I ever felt I was in mortal danger. I was carrying information the enemy would not want produced. If my assessment of the situation was correct, now I was the spy! I was the one who had to get away. I was the one who would be hunted. I realized that for the first time on the job, I was a bit scared. During the ride from East Berlin to West Berlin, I wanted desperately to relay some of this to ZZ. But it just wasn't feasible.

Last night at our hotel after making a morning appointment with Lorraine and Mitch to go to Dr. Mann's office, I just didn't know what or how much I could tell ZZ. As it turned out, he was as exhausted from the whole day as I was. I just told him the logistics and basics for today.

This morning at Dr. Mann's office, I wanted ZZ to observe him extract the pearl from within me, along with the semen from Schiller. After the doctor removed my diaphragm, he showed it to me and to the others. It contained a mound of gooey stuff.

Was that the pearl, I wondered? I was beginning to have doubts about my pearl discovery. All nuances seemed to be about fertility. And frankly, when ZZ and I were asked to sign a secrecy oath, I was beginning to think that this must be an international fertility enterprise, perhaps under the auspices of NATO.

Of course I would sign; I thought ZZ would, too. But I wanted him to make the commitment. When we received our oaths, I could see at first glance it was to the United States government. My initial theory was correct.

So Mitch and Lorraine were good guys after all. The FBI had it backwards. Mitch and Lorraine were not passing secrets. They were receiving them! Didn't the FBI know that? I guess not. I guess that's why I have been writing these reports to the committee. By now it should be clear that all of us have been working toward the same goal.

Having read Mitchell's reports on the history of The Rose, I think he and Lorraine deserve the Medal of Freedom. I consider Lorraine to be a true American heroine, flying to a data center to have her diaphragm read after every conference swing party this entire year, all the while attempting to become pregnant by her husband. I am honored to know her and work with her.

And, of course, similar accolades go to Mitch for his daring and resourcefulness to pursue this course of action, inventing and perfecting instruments uniquely required to fulfill this mission.

All four of us were supremely gratified to read Schiller's message of urgency confirming that the swing parties were actually lines of communication with the West. Our partying had been an avenue to obtain secret information in an effort to win the Cold War.

That night, when ZZ and I were alone after our big day at Dr. Mann's office, we both felt liberated to speak freely about ourselves. That night I revealed to ZZ what I had never revealed to anyone. I told him how I became a civil rights attorney, and then trained to became an undercover agent for the FBI. I explained how my assignment was to learn all about Mitchell Hesten because the FBI suspected him of passing government secrets to the Soviet Union. But during my assignment, I found myself hopelessly in love with the Hestens' traveling companion. This caused me to agonize for months on end about my lover being indicted along with Mitch and Lorraine. And then I find out that he and I, together as a couple, had been selected by our government to participate in an extremely important, highly secret government project! "I guess this is it!" I said. "The Rose!"

ZZ was astonished, of course, to hear all this, but he was extremely happy for me and for us. I had not been wasting my time and talents in the past months, and now I was with him on a new assignment. We talked about many more things that night; we completed our knowledge about each other, which enormously enhanced our love and respect for one another. In ZZ, I realized, I truly had a life partner.

But we did more than just talk that night. We engaged in a wild, sexually animalistic frenzy, sometimes gnawing and biting each other with great physical passion to psychically fuse our bodies and become one. I now felt totally, absolutely in love with no reservations. In ZZ, I had a partner in my life's aspirations. It was a time of love, passion, and total commitment. Being in love is truly ecstatic!

The next morning, we discussed wedding plans. We decided to get married in my hometown of Santa Clara the weekend after Christmas. We expected that all my family and ZZ's family would be able to attend. I would ask Monique to be my maid of honor and Lorraine to be matron of honor. ZZ would ask Mitch to be his best man.

When we met with Mitch and Lorraine later in the day, ZZ and I announced our engagement.

To our astonishment and delight, Lorraine announced that she was five weeks pregnant!

The four of us were hugging and celebrating and enjoying the moment. After we all settled down, I said I had something serious to disclose. I proceeded to explain what I had told ZZ the previous night. I explained my work as a civil rights attorney at the Department of Justice and how I was trained to become an undercover agent for the FBI.

Mitch and Lorraine looked on in astonishment.

"After becoming an agent, I was assigned to observe and learn all I could about a Silicon Valley entrepreneur who was suspected of passing government secrets to the Soviets. And here I am!"

Mitch and Lorraine were stunned!

After several moments of deafening silence, Mitch expressed his utter shock. He didn't see it coming, he confessed. Mitchell questioned why the FBI would be interested in him. After all, he reported to the Department of Defense.

I emphasized that the FBI was in the Department of Justice. "That is why you and I have been communicating with the Committee, which operates across the various departments; they want to sort everything out. Eight months ago when Keslyn discovered I was an agent for the FBI, he alerted the bureau about my involvement with The Rose."

After my surprising disclosure set in, Mitch and Lorraine expressed their wonder of how I could have deduced so much of an elaborate scheme like The Rose.

I explained how I had the huge benefit of the FBI confirming my discovery that the flashlights were cameras. That is a big step for someone to realize on their own. Then I had the benefit of hearing about digital photography at conference after conference. I was also referred repeatedly to the very strange story about ancient Asian noblemen. With the memory ball resembling a small pearl and melting into a semen-like substance, it became clear what a delegate needed to do to transfer his photos to Lorraine or me at a swing party. So when I met a momentarily confused and slightly nervous Mr. Schiller at the East Berlin swing party, it became clear what was going to happen."

"Renee, you are absolutely incredible!" exclaimed Lorraine. "It's such a relief to know that you and ZZ are going to continue working with us. Just as you have agonized over ZZ, we have agonized over both of you not wanting to continue once you realized what we were really doing.

"It's just wonderful that you are going to stay with us. But we need you both to understand the dangers you will face as we proceed with party after party. Right now, we are welcomed guests in most Communist countries. I am reasonably sure we are not suspected of doing anything against the regimes. But as time goes on and more and more people know what we are doing, word will get out. Our risk of being discovered by the authorities will always be increasing. Should Soviet bloc authorities catch on to us while we are there, you can be sure they will not let us leave.

"They could detain us indefinitely. Right now there are American citizens rotting away in foreign jails for drug trafficking or spying against the regime. Or we could all become victims of a mysterious accident: a collapsing bridge killing us and all those nearby; a deadly fire in our wing of the hotel; a fatal head-on collision in high traffic.

"This is why you two had to be fully informed of our operation before we proceeded any further. We didn't want to place you in highly-dangerous situations you had no knowledge about.

"You two are in a different position in life than we are. You are young, getting married, perhaps planning to start a family soon. We want you to be careful. We want you to live. Mitch and I can afford to take more chances. We stand to personally enrich ourselves by obtaining future business contracts. We can afford to do this more than you can. If you feel that attending a particular conference is unwise, don't go. And when the day comes that you feel you just can't do this anymore, we will understand."

Then Mitch had a request. "Thirty or forty years from now, if our reports are no longer secret and if the time is right, TELL OUR STORY. Take our reports, along with our personal stories, and slap them together. Change our names and identities; yours too, of course. It's not who we are that is important. It's what we have accomplished, and what we will accomplish in the next few years. That is what is important. The American people should know our story. TELL IT!"

ZZ and I were so thrilled! We realized that the four of us had a superb operation going. We were probably the only people in the world ideally set up to receive the information we hoped to obtain. Each of us has a specific role to play. We knew we needed to continue our roles exactly as we have done in the past.

Ahead of us is an extremely important conference. It's perhaps the most important conference for all of us so far, located in a city where neither ZZ nor I have ever been: Moscow, the very heart of the Soviet Union.

ZZ and I will have to be psychologically prepared. Last year's delegates received their second set of cameras. Very possibly, there will be delegates at the coming conference who will want to communicate with us and have learned how to do it. This is what all the years of planning have been about! We will have to be at our very best. Questions abound: Will everything go according to plan? Will we be in grave danger? Will anyone try to contact us? Will we have a swing party? Might I receive a pearl?

Now I more fully understand that all the hard work Mitch and Lorraine did up to this point was mainly preparation for the flow of information that we are now prepared to receive. Flashlight-cameras have been distributed at nearly all key Soviet conferences. At every conference swing party I go to, I could receive a pearl! This is truly just the beginning!

We have so many more places to go, so many more parties to attend, so much more information to obtain.

Here's to us! And to our future. May it be bright and productive!

* * * * *

Last note from ZZ: In accordance with Mitch and Lorraine's request, I hereby publish OUR STORY.

Acknowledgments and Appreciation

FIRST OF ALL, I want to thank the swing community of the 1970s and '80s for being so gracious and accepting of others, and for providing a loving and supportive environment. Their stories comprise most of this book.

In particular, I want to thank the main participants in this tale for taking me into their confidence, sharing their notes and files, and joining me on this journey. It is to them that I dedicate this book, and in particular to the memory of the most senior member of our group. He confided in me extensively, asking me to promise that I would tell our story when the time was right and our files were no longer classified. With publication of this book, it is with great satisfaction that I feel I have fulfilled that vow.

Secrets took me five years to write using notes I and my colleagues had written at the time. A dear friend who has known me since the early 1980s supported my vision, managed the project, and worked with me the entire five years to make this book possible. I deeply appreciate her assistance and especially her lifelong friendship.

Because of the ongoing classification of some aspects of this story by the U.S. government, all names in this book have been changed. However the names of those who have brought this book to fruition are very real and I want you to know who they are.

Polly Letofsky and her team at My Word Publishing made it possible for me to share this story with you, my readers. I want to especially thank Susie Schaefer, Publishing Consultant, for guiding the process to a successful completion that you can hold in your hands or view on a screen.

My writing was greatly enhanced by the expertise of Micah Pilkington's editing, and I appreciate her keen eye and facility with the complexities of the English language.

Andrea Costantine deftly designed the book's interior, adding my changes to the text with lightning speed and alacrity, as well as converting the text to ebook format.

The artistic skill of Jackie McShannon is beautifully illustrated in the cover image of the couple, and she creatively developed the drawing until it perfectly aligned with what I imagined.

My gratitude also goes to Victoria Wolf of Red Wolf Marketing, who designed the layout of the front and back covers and brought everything together in visual congruity.

The colorful website, www.RonasaurusPublishing.com, was created by a multi-talented digital maven, Jody Colvard at FMG Network. Our site offers a free chapter as well as a link to order the book.

Most of all, I want to thank my wife for encouraging me to write this book, patiently proofing all the revisions, and never once saying, "When are you *ever* going to finish this thing?" Her open-mindedness and appreciation of my past adventures places her in the center of my heart.

And to all of you, my faithful readers, I'd be delighted if you would visit www.RonasaurusPublishing.com or write to me at ZZ@RonasaurusPublishing.com with your comments about the book, and I'll do my best to answer every email.

Zillary Zahn

www.ingramcontent.com/pod-product-compliance
Lightning Source LLC
Chambersburg PA
CBHW032102280326
41933CB00009B/732